BACKYARD BLACKOUT

BACKYARD BLACKOUT

THE ESSENTIAL PREPPER'S GUIDE TO BUILDING THE PERFECT BACKYARD HOMESTEAD AND THRIVING IN A WORLD WITHOUT POWER (2-IN-1 COLLECTION)

SELF-SUFFICIENT LIVING
BOOK 3

ANTHONY BENNETT

Copyright © 2024 by Anthony Bennett

All rights reserved. No part of this book may be reproduced, stored in a retrieval system, or transmitted in any form or by any means, electronic, mechanical, photocopying, recording, or otherwise, without the prior written permission of the publisher, Book Bound Studios.

The information contained in this book is based on the author's personal experiences and research. While every effort has been made to ensure the accuracy of the information presented, the author and publisher cannot be held responsible for any errors or omissions.

This book is intended for general informational purposes only and is not a substitute for professional medical, legal, or financial advice. If you have specific questions about any medical, legal, or financial matters, you should consult with a qualified healthcare professional, attorney, or financial advisor.

Book Bound Studios is not affiliated with any product or vendor mentioned in this book. The views expressed in this book are those of the author and do not necessarily reflect the views of Book Bound Studios.

For the resilient spirits seeking harmony with the earth and the strength to forge their own path, may this book light your way.

In the middle of difficulty lies opportunity.

— ALBERT EINSTEIN

CONTENTS

HOW TO BUILD THE PERFECT BACKYARD HOMESTEAD

Introduction to Backyard Homesteading	3
1. SOIL AND COMPOSTING	15
The Basics of Soil Health	15
Creating and Maintaining a Compost System	17
Natural Fertilizers and Amendments	19
Cover Crops and Crop Rotation	21
Testing and Understanding Your Soil	23
Mulching Techniques	25
Chapter Summary	27
2. GARDENING	29
Planning Your Garden	29
Choosing the Right Plants	31
Seed Starting and Transplanting	33
Watering and Irrigation	35
Pest and Disease Management	36
Harvesting and Storing Your Produce	38
Chapter Summary	39
3. RAISING CHICKENS	41
Choosing the Right Breeds	41
Housing and Coop Design	43
Feeding and Nutrition	44
Health and Wellness	46
Egg Production	47
Dealing with Predators	50
Chapter Summary	51
4. BEEKEEPING	53
Understanding Bee Behavior	53
Setting Up Your Hive	55
Maintenance and Hive Health	57

Harvesting Honey	58
Common Problems and Solutions	60
The Importance of Bees in Your Garden	62
Chapter Summary	64

5. PRESERVING THE HARVEST — 67
- Canning Basics — 67
- Freezing and Drying — 69
- Fermenting and Pickling — 71
- Making Jams and Jellies — 73
- Storing Vegetables and Fruits — 75
- Creating a Root Cellar — 77
- Chapter Summary — 79

6. RENEWABLE ENERGY ON THE HOMESTEAD — 81
- Solar Power Basics — 81
- Wind Energy Fundamentals — 83
- Rainwater Harvesting — 85
- Geothermal Options — 87
- Energy Conservation Techniques — 89
- Chapter Summary — 91

7. WATER MANAGEMENT — 93
- Irrigation Systems for the Homestead — 93
- Greywater and Its Uses — 95
- Creating Ponds and Water Features — 97
- Water Purification and Filtration — 99
- Managing Water Runoff — 101
- Conserving Water in the Garden — 102
- Chapter Summary — 104

8. LIVESTOCK MANAGEMENT — 107
- Selecting Livestock for Your Homestead — 107
- Feeding and Nutrition — 109
- Health Care and Wellness — 111
- Breeding and Population Management — 113
- Fencing and Housing — 114
- Managing Manure — 116
- Chapter Summary — 118

9. HOMESTEAD CARPENTRY 121
    Basic Carpentry Skills 121
    Building Coops and Pens 123
    Constructing Raised Beds and Trellises 125
    Repair and Maintenance 126
    DIY Homestead Projects 128
    Safety and Tools 130
    Chapter Summary 133

10. NATURAL MEDICINE AND HOMESTEAD
    HEALTH 135
    Growing Medicinal Herbs 135
    Creating Herbal Remedies 137
    Natural First Aid 138
    Preventative Health Practices 140
    Integrating Natural Medicine into Daily Life 142
    Homestead Hygiene Practices 144
    Chapter Summary 146

11. SUSTAINABLE LIVING 149
    Reducing Waste 149
    Eco-Friendly Homestead Products 151
    Conservation Efforts 153
    Community Involvement and Education 155
    Living Off the Grid 157
    Chapter Summary 158

12. HOMESTEAD PLANNING AND
    MANAGEMENT 161
    Year-Round Planning 161
    Budgeting and Expenses 163
    Time Management and Efficiency 165
    Record Keeping and Documentation 167
    Scaling Up Your Homestead 169
    Dealing with Setbacks 171
    Chapter Summary 172

    The Future of Backyard Homesteading 175

HOW TO SURVIVE WHEN THE GRID GOES DOWN

Introduction to Grid Down Survival — 189

1. WATER PROCUREMENT AND PURIFICATION — 197
   - Finding Water Sources — 197
   - Methods of Water Purification — 199
   - Storing and Conserving Water — 201
   - Recognizing and Avoiding Contaminated Water — 203
   - Rainwater Collection Techniques — 204
   - Chapter Summary — 206

2. FOOD ACQUISITION AND STORAGE — 209
   - Hunting and Trapping for Food — 209
   - Foraging for Edible Plants — 211
   - Preserving Food Without Electricity — 212
   - Creating a Survival Garden — 214
   - Livestock and Animal Husbandry Basics — 215
   - Chapter Summary — 217

3. SHELTER AND SECURITY — 219
   - Choosing a Safe Location — 219
   - Building Temporary Shelters — 221
   - Constructing Long-Term Habitats — 222
   - Home Fortification Techniques — 224
   - Security Measures and Perimeter Defense — 226
   - Fire Safety and Management — 228
   - Chapter Summary — 230

4. HEALTH AND FIRST AID — 231
   - Basic First Aid Skills — 231
   - Handling Common Injuries and Illnesses — 233
   - Natural Remedies and Alternative Medicines — 235
   - Maintaining Hygiene and Sanitation — 236
   - Preventing and Treating Waterborne Diseases — 238
   - Mental Health and Coping Mechanisms — 239
   - Chapter Summary — 241

5. ENERGY AND POWER ALTERNATIVES 243
Solar Power Basics 243
Wind Energy Fundamentals 245
Hydro Power Options 246
Manual Power Generation Techniques 248
Battery Storage and Management 249
Creating a Renewable Energy Plan 251
Chapter Summary 253

6. COMMUNICATION AND NAVIGATION 257
Basic Signaling Techniques 257
Using Radios for Communication 258
Navigating Without GPS 260
Map Reading and Land Navigation 262
Creating and Using Codes 264
Maintaining Operational Security 265
Chapter Summary 267

7. SURVIVAL GEAR AND TOOLS 269
Essential Survival Gear 269
Choosing and Maintaining Tools 271
DIY Survival Tools 273
Multi-Use Items for Survival 275
Packaging and Transporting Gear 276
Innovative Uses for Common Items 278
Chapter Summary 280

8. SELF-DEFENSE AND TACTICAL TRAINING 283
Basic Self-Defense Techniques 283
Firearms Training and Safety 285
Improvised Weapons and Tools 287
Tactical Movement and Camouflage 287
Situational Awareness and Threat Assessment 289
Building a Survival Team 291
Chapter Summary 293

9. PSYCHOLOGICAL PREPAREDNESS AND
LEADERSHIP 295
Mental Resilience in Survival Situations 295
Effective Leadership and Team Dynamics 297
Conflict Resolution and Negotiation 299

Stress Management Techniques	300
Building Morale and Maintaining Hope	302
Training and Preparing Your Mind for Survival	304
Chapter Summary	306

10. COMMUNITY BUILDING AND NETWORKING — 309
- Forming and Strengthening Community Ties — 309
- Bartering and Trade Skills — 311
- Collaborative Survival Strategies — 313
- Creating Mutual Aid Networks — 315
- Legal and Ethical Considerations — 317
- Chapter Summary — 319

11. LONG-TERM SUSTAINABILITY AND SELF-SUFFICIENCY — 321
- Sustainable Agriculture and Permaculture — 321
- Waste Management and Recycling — 323
- Building and Maintaining Infrastructure — 325
- Education and Skill Sharing for Self-Sufficiency — 327
- Chapter Summary — 329

12. ADAPTING TO A NEW WORLD — 331
- Embracing Change and Overcoming Challenges — 331
- Innovative Problem Solving — 333
- The Role of Technology in a Post-Grid World — 335
- Preserving Knowledge and Culture — 337
- Environmental Stewardship — 338
- Chapter Summary — 340

The Path Forward — 343

Your Feedback Matters — 355
About the Author — 357

HOW TO BUILD THE PERFECT BACKYARD HOMESTEAD

A COMPREHENSIVE GUIDE TO SELF-SUFFICIENCY WITH GARDENING, RAISING CHICKENS, BEEKEEPING, FOOD PRESERVATION, BASIC CARPENTRY, AND MORE

INTRODUCTION TO BACKYARD HOMESTEADING

A lush garden with a wooden shed.

The Philosophy of Homesteading

Embarking on the journey of backyard homesteading is not just about transforming your outdoor space; it's about embracing a philosophy that intertwines self-sufficiency, sustainability, and a deep connection with the natural world.

Introduction to Backyard Homesteading

This philosophy is rooted in the belief that even the smallest plot of land can be a powerful source of food, joy, and life. It's about seeing potential where others see limitation, about nurturing the earth and, in return, being nurtured by it.

At the heart of homesteading is the desire to reduce one's carbon footprint and live less dependent on the systems that, while convenient, often distance us from the natural cycles of life. It's about learning to work with these cycles, understand the seasons' rhythm, and respect the resources we so often take for granted. This approach to living doesn't just benefit the individual or the immediate family; it extends its positive impact on the community and the environment.

The philosophy of homesteading encourages a mindset of growth, resilience, and creativity. It's about problem-solving, whether finding ways to maximize a small space for vegetable growing, devising water-saving techniques, or repurposing materials for garden structures. It teaches patience and persistence, as not every endeavor will be successful on the first try, but every failure is a lesson learned and an opportunity for growth.

Moreover, homesteading is about community. It fosters a sense of connection to the land and those around us. Sharing harvests, exchanging seeds, and passing on knowledge are all integral aspects of the homesteading philosophy. It's a way of living that encourages cooperation over competition, creating a network of support that benefits everyone involved.

In embracing the homesteading philosophy, one also embraces a learning life. There is always a new skill to master, a new plant to grow, or a new sustainability practice to implement. This continuous journey of discovery keeps the

Introduction to Backyard Homesteading

homesteader engaged and connected to their environment meaningfully. As we delve deeper into the practical aspects of what you can achieve in your backyard, remember that this philosophy is the foundation of all these endeavors. It's not just about the tangible outcomes but the values, principles, and connections these activities embody. Whether you're planting your first vegetable garden, setting up a rainwater collection system, or building a chicken coop, you're participating in a way of life that is both ancient and increasingly relevant in our modern world.

Backyard homesteading opens up a world of possibilities right at your doorstep. This section aims to illuminate your backyard's vast potential, transforming it from a mere outdoor space to a thriving homestead. Whether you have a sprawling lawn or a modest patch of green, the essence of homesteading is about making the most of what you have. Let's explore what you can achieve with dedication, creativity, and elbow grease.

One of the most rewarding aspects of backyard homesteading is the ability to grow your food. This is wider than sprawling vegetable gardens, although they are a fantastic start. To maximize space, you can cultivate various fruits and vegetables in raised beds, containers, or even vertical gardens. Herbs, too, can flourish in small pots on windowsills, adding fresh flavors to your meals. With some planning, you can enjoy fresh produce, reduce your grocery bill, and increase your self-sufficiency.

While the idea of livestock might conjure images of vast farmlands, certain animals are well-suited for smaller spaces. Chickens, for instance, can provide a steady supply of fresh

Introduction to Backyard Homesteading

eggs while contributing to pest control and composting. Rabbits and bees are other livestock that can be accommodated in a backyard, offering meat, wool, and honey. It's important to check local regulations and consider your capacity to care for these animals before diving in.

Homesteading is not just about food production; it's about creating a sustainable ecosystem in your backyard. Composting kitchen scraps and yard waste can produce rich soil for your garden, reducing waste and the need for chemical fertilizers. Rainwater harvesting systems can supplement your water supply, conserving this precious resource. Even incorporating native plants and creating habitats can attract beneficial wildlife, promote biodiversity, and aid in pest control.

For the more ambitious homesteader, exploring renewable energy options can reduce reliance on external power sources. Solar panels, for instance, can be a viable option for generating electricity or heating water. While the initial investment might be significant, the long-term benefits and potential savings are considerable. Though less common, wind turbines can also be an option depending on your location and property size.

Backyard homesteading also opens up opportunities for crafting and DIY projects. There are many projects to embark on, from building chicken coops and raised garden beds to creating homemade soaps and preserves. These activities provide practical benefits and allow for creative expression and the satisfaction of building something with your hands. Regardless of size, your backyard can be transformed into a productive and sustainable homestead. It's about leveraging your resources to create a self-sufficient space that meets your needs and reflects your values. As we move forward, planning will be crucial to effectively utilize your space and resources, turning your homesteading dreams into reality.

Planning Your Homestead Layout

Backyard homesteading is an exciting venture that promises a bounty of fresh produce and possibly livestock and a fulfilling connection to the earth and the food we consume. However, before diving into the practical aspects of planting and animal care, meticulously planning your homestead layout is crucial for laying a solid foundation. This step is vital for maximizing efficiency, ensuring sustainability, and, ultimately, enjoying the fruits of your labor.

First and foremost, assess the space available in your backyard. Every square foot counts, and understanding the dimensions of your land will help you make informed decisions about what you can realistically achieve. When evaluating your space, consider factors such as sunlight exposure, soil quality, and access to water. These elements are critical in determining which areas are best suited for gardening, which spots are ideal for composting, and where you could house small livestock.

Next, think about the kind of homestead you envision. Are you leaning more toward vegetable gardening, or are you interested in raising chickens for eggs? You may combine both with other ventures like beekeeping or growing medicinal herbs. Your interests and goals will significantly influence your layout plan. For instance, a vegetable garden requires well-draining soil and at least six hours of direct

Introduction to Backyard Homesteading

sunlight daily, while chickens need a secure coop and a fenced area to roam.

Once you have a clear idea of what you want to include in your homestead, it's time to sketch a layout. This doesn't have to be a professional blueprint; a simple drawing that outlines where each element will go is sufficient. Make sure to allocate space for pathways and consider the ease of access to each area. Efficient movement around your homestead will save you time and energy in the long run.

Incorporating companion planting and crop rotation into your layout can significantly benefit your garden's health and yield. Companion planting involves placing plants together that can help each other grow, deter pests, or enhance flavor. Crop rotation, on the other hand, prevents soil depletion and reduces the risk of disease. Planning these strategies from the outset can lead to a more resilient and productive homestead.

Lastly, remember that flexibility is critical. Your initial layout might need adjustments as you learn and grow in your homesteading journey. You may discover that a particular crop thrives in your soil, prompting you to allocate more space next season. Or you'll expand your chicken coop as you become more experienced in poultry care. Embrace these changes as they are a natural part of homesteading.

In conclusion, planning your homestead layout is a crucial step that sets the stage for a successful and rewarding backyard homesteading experience. By assessing your space, defining your goals, and sketching a thoughtful layout, you'll be well on your way to creating a sustainable and productive homestead that brings joy and abundance for years.

Essential Tools and Equipment

You'll need more than enthusiasm to transform your backyard into a thriving homestead. The right tools and equipment are essential to your success, acting as extensions of your hands and embodying your intentions. This section will guide you through the essential tools and equipment every backyard homesteader should have, ensuring you're well-equipped to turn your vision into reality.

Quality gardening tools are non-negotiable. A sturdy, sharp spade or shovel is indispensable for breaking ground, turning soil, and planting. Look for one with a comfortable handle and a durable blade. A good set of hand tools, including a trowel, pruning shears, and a garden fork, will also be invaluable for day-to-day tasks such as planting, weeding, and harvesting.

Watering equipment is another critical component. Depending on the size of your homestead, this might range from a simple watering can for small plots to a more sophisticated drip irrigation system for larger areas. The goal is to ensure your plants receive the hydration they need with minimal waste and effort.

For those planning to incorporate livestock into their homestead, the proper housing and fencing are crucial. Chickens require a secure coop to protect them from predators, while larger animals like goats or pigs will need sturdy fencing to contain them. Additionally, consider your animals' feeding and watering systems to ensure they have constant access to fresh water and food.

Composting is a key aspect of sustainable homesteading. It turns kitchen scraps and yard waste into rich soil. Investing

Introduction to Backyard Homesteading

in a compost bin or setting up a compost pile will help you manage organic waste and improve your soil's health over time.

Lastly, protective gear should not be overlooked. Gardening gloves, sturdy boots, and a wide-brimmed hat can make your work more comfortable and prevent injuries. Remember, your safety and well-being are just as important as the tools you use.

As you gather these essential tools and equipment, remember that quality matters more than quantity. Choose items that are durable, comfortable to use, and suited to your specific needs. With the right tools, you'll be well on your way to creating a productive and sustainable backyard homestead.

Understanding Your Land and Climate

Backyard homesteading requires a deep understanding of your land and climate, as these factors are pivotal in shaping your homestead's success. This section delves into the essentials of getting to know your backyard's unique characteristics and how they influence the planning and execution of your homesteading projects.

Assessing the soil quality of your land is crucial. Soil types can vary dramatically, even within the same property, and understanding your soil's texture, pH, and fertility will guide you in selecting suitable crops and determining if amendments are necessary. Simple soil tests can be conducted using kits available at local gardening centers or through cooperative extension services, providing valuable insights into your soil's condition.

Introduction to Backyard Homesteading

Next, consider the topography of your land. Your backyard's layout and elevation changes can influence water drainage, sunlight exposure, and wind patterns. Areas with southern exposure typically receive more sunlight, making them ideal for most vegetable and fruit crops. Conversely, low-lying areas might be prone to flooding or frost pockets and better suited for plants that thrive in wet conditions or for installing water management systems like rain gardens.

Climate plays a significant role in determining what you can grow and raise on your homestead. Understanding your region's hardiness zone will help you select plant varieties that thrive in your local conditions. Additionally, being aware of your area's average rainfall, temperature ranges, and seasonal changes will aid in planning your planting and harvesting schedules and preparing for extreme weather conditions.

Water availability is another critical aspect to consider. Whether relying on municipal water, a well, or rainwater collection systems, ensuring a reliable and sustainable water source is essential for irrigation, livestock, and household use. Assessing your water resources and planning for efficient water use can significantly impact your homestead's sustainability and productivity.

Lastly, observing your land's biodiversity can offer insights into creating a balanced and healthy ecosystem. Note the native plants and wildlife in your area, as they can indicate the health of your land and help you design your homestead to support local biodiversity. Encouraging beneficial insects, birds, and other wildlife can aid in pest control and pollination, enhancing your homestead's resilience and productivity.

By thoroughly understanding your land and climate, you

Introduction to Backyard Homesteading

can make informed decisions that align with the natural characteristics of your backyard, leading to a more productive and sustainable homestead. This foundational knowledge sets the stage for setting realistic goals and planning your homesteading projects confidently and clearly.

Setting Realistic Goals

After understanding your land and climate, the next step in establishing a thriving backyard homestead is to set realistic goals. This process is crucial, as it lays the foundation for what you aim to achieve with your space, resources, and time. It's about balancing dreams with practicality, ensuring that your homesteading efforts are both rewarding and sustainable.

First, assess your motivations for starting a backyard homestead. Are you looking to produce most of your own food, or are you more interested in the educational aspect of gardening and animal care for yourself or your family? Perhaps your goal is to reduce your carbon footprint or to create a more resilient lifestyle. Understanding your primary motivations will help guide your decisions moving forward.

Next, consider the resources you have available. This includes your physical space and climate, which you've already begun to understand, and your time, skills, and financial resources. Be honest about how much time you can dedicate to homesteading activities daily or weekly. Tasks like watering, weeding, feeding animals, and harvesting can become time-consuming, especially during peak seasons.

Financial resources are another critical factor. Start-up costs for a backyard homestead can vary widely depending on your goals. Simple gardening might require only seeds, soil,

Introduction to Backyard Homesteading

and essential tools, while more ambitious projects like keeping livestock or installing greenhouses can become quite costly. Plan a budget that reflects your goals and leaves room for unexpected expenses.

Skill level is another important consideration. If you're new to gardening, animal husbandry, or other homesteading activities, you may need to invest time in learning before you dive in. Fortunately, abundant resources are available, from books and online courses to local workshops and community gardens. Set goals that allow for a learning curve, starting with more straightforward projects and gradually working on more complex ones.

Finally, set specific, measurable, achievable, relevant, and time-bound (SMART) goals. Instead of a vague goal like "grow a garden," aim for something more concrete, such as "grow three types of vegetables to harvest by the end of the season." This approach will help you plan more effectively and track your progress, making necessary adjustments.

Remember, backyard homesteading is a journey, not a race. It's about learning and growing along with your garden and livestock. Setting realistic goals lays the groundwork for a fulfilling and sustainable homesteading experience that aligns with your lifestyle, resources, and aspirations. As you move forward, keep these goals in mind, but also be flexible and open to adjusting them based on what you learn and experience. The world of backyard homesteading is rich with opportunities for growth, discovery, and connection to the land.

1

SOIL AND COMPOSTING

A vibrant garden bathed in sunlight.

The Basics of Soil Health

Understanding the basics of soil health is crucial for any backyard homesteader. Soil isn't just dirt; it's a living, breathing entity that sustains your garden. Healthy soil is teeming with microorganisms, insects, and organic matter that work together to nourish the plants you grow. This section will guide you through the foundational knowledge needed to cultivate and maintain fertile soil in your homestead.

Soil health hinges on its structure and composition. Soil comprises minerals, organic matter, water, and air. The balance of these components determines the soil's texture and ability to retain water and nutrients. For instance, clay soils are nutrient-rich but often suffer from poor drainage, while sandy soils drain well but can struggle to hold onto nutrients and moisture.

To assess your soil's health, start with a simple texture test. Take a handful of moist soil and try to form it into a ball, then a ribbon. This tactile test can help you gauge whether your soil leans more towards clay, sand, or loam, which is the ideal balance of sand, silt, and clay. Loamy soil is the gold standard for gardeners, offering a perfect drainage and nutrient retention mix.

The pH level of your soil also plays a pivotal role in plant health. Most vegetables and fruits thrive in slightly acidic to neutral soil (pH 6.0-7.0). You can easily test your soil's pH with a kit from your local garden center. If your soil is too acidic or alkaline, it can be amended with lime or sulfur to bring it into the optimal range for your crops.

Organic matter is the lifeblood of healthy soil. It improves soil structure, aids in moisture retention, and provides a slow-release source of nutrients as it decomposes. Incorporating compost, aged manure, or leaf mold into your soil boosts its organic matter content and fosters a vibrant ecosystem below the surface.

Finally, understanding the importance of a living soil ecosystem is critical. A diverse microbial population aids in breaking down organic matter, making nutrients available to plants, and protecting against pests and diseases. Practices such as minimal tillage, cover cropping, and crop rotation support this underground community, enhancing soil health and fertility over time.

By grasping these basics of soil health, you lay the groundwork for a thriving backyard homestead. Healthy soil leads to robust plants, reduced pest and disease issues, and bountiful harvests. With this foundation, we can now focus on creating and maintaining a compost system, an essential practice for enriching your soil and closing the loop on your homestead's organic waste.

Creating and Maintaining a Compost System

Understanding the intricacies of creating and maintaining a compost system is a pivotal step in the journey toward a sustainable backyard homestead. Composting, the process of recycling organic matter into a rich soil amendment, is not just about waste reduction; it's about nurturing the soil that feeds us. This section delves into the practicalities of establishing a thriving compost system, offering a guide to transforming kitchen scraps and yard waste into black gold for your garden.

To begin with, select a suitable location for your compost pile or bin. It should be easily accessible but not too close to your living spaces to avoid potential odors. Consider the convenience of adding materials and turning the compost. A partially shaded spot is ideal, as it prevents the compost from drying out too quickly in the sun and keeps it warm enough to decompose in cooler weather.

There are various composting methods, depending on your space and needs. A simple heap in a garden corner works for some, while others may prefer a compost bin to keep things tidy. Tumbler bins are excellent for those with limited space, as they facilitate easy turning and aerate the compost well. Whichever method you choose, ensure good air circulation and drainage to prevent the compost from becoming too wet or compacted.

The key to successful composting lies in the balance of 'greens' and 'browns'—the nitrogen-rich and carbon-rich materials, respectively. Greens include kitchen scraps like vegetable peels, coffee grounds, and fresh plant material, while browns comprise dried leaves, straw, and shredded paper. A general rule of thumb is maintaining a ratio of about 2:1, browns to greens, to ensure a healthy decomposition process without attracting pests or creating unpleasant odors.

Regular maintenance of your compost pile is crucial. Turning the compost every few weeks introduces oxygen, essential for the aerobic bacteria responsible for breaking down the materials. This also helps to distribute moisture and heat evenly throughout the pile, speeding up the decomposition process. If the compost seems too dry, adding water can help, but be cautious not to overwater.

Monitoring the temperature of your compost pile can provide valuable insights into its health. A well-functioning compost will heat up as the materials break down, often reaching temperatures between 130°F to 160°F. This heat is beneficial as it kills weed seeds and harmful pathogens. If the pile isn't heating up, it may need more greens, water, or aeration.

Finally, knowing when your compost is ready to use is

essential. Mature compost is dark, crumbly, and has an earthy smell. It should no longer resemble the original materials but look like rich soil. This process can take several months to a year, depending on the conditions and materials used.

Incorporating compost into your garden beds enhances soil structure, moisture retention, and nutrient content, promoting healthy plant growth. It's a testament to the cycle of life in your backyard homestead, turning what was once considered waste into a valuable resource. As we move forward, understanding how to further enrich this compost with natural fertilizers and amendments will ensure your garden thrives in harmony with nature.

Natural Fertilizers and Amendments

Building on the foundation of a well-maintained compost system, it's essential to delve into the world of natural fertilizers and amendments to enrich your backyard homestead's soil further. These natural inputs are pivotal in creating a thriving, sustainable garden ecosystem. Unlike synthetic fertilizers, natural options feed your plants, improve soil structure, enhance microbial life, and reduce environmental impact.

One of the most straightforward and beneficial natural fertilizers is compost tea. Made by steeping finished compost in water, this nutrient-rich liquid can be applied directly to the soil or used as a foliar spray. It's an excellent way to give your plants a quick nutrient boost while introducing beneficial microorganisms to the soil.

Another valuable amendment is worm castings. Worms are nature's tillers and nutrient providers. Their castings are incredibly rich in essential plant nutrients, and incorporating them into your soil can significantly enhance plant growth and soil health. You can produce your worm castings by using kitchen scraps and garden waste by setting up a simple vermicomposting system.

Green manures, or cover crops, are also integral to natural soil fertility. Although they will be discussed in more detail in the following section, it's worth noting here that incorporating green manures into your garden rotation can significantly improve soil structure, fertility, and organic matter content. They are particularly beneficial for fixing nitrogen in the soil, a crucial nutrient for plant growth.

There are several natural options for those looking to add specific nutrients to their soil. Bone meal is an excellent source of phosphorus and vital for root development, while blood meal is a high-nitrogen amendment perfect for leafy growth. Wood ash can be lightly applied to the soil for potassium, which supports overall plant health and disease resistance. However, using these amendments judiciously is essential, as over-application can disrupt soil balance.

Seaweed, fresh, dried, or in a liquid extract form, is another fantastic soil amendment. It's a rich source of micronutrients and contains growth hormones and stimulants that can enhance plant health and productivity. Seaweed also increases plant stress tolerance, making your garden more resilient to drought, disease, and pests.

Lastly, rock dust is an often-overlooked amendment that can add a broad spectrum of minerals to the soil. Derived from finely ground rocks, it slowly releases essential minerals that plants need for growth. This is particularly beneficial for replenishing soils depleted over years of gardening.

Incorporating these natural fertilizers and amendments into your soil management practices can significantly enhance the health and productivity of your backyard homestead. By doing so, you provide your plants with the nutrients they need and contribute to a more sustainable and environmentally friendly gardening approach. As we move forward, understanding the role of cover crops and crop rotation will complement these practices, creating a holistic approach to soil health and fertility.

Cover Crops and Crop Rotation

Understanding the symbiotic relationship between cover crops and crop rotation is paramount to transforming your backyard into a thriving homestead. This section delves into how these practices nourish and protect your soil and set the stage for a bountiful harvest.

Cover crops, often called "green manure," are planted not for consumption but to cover the soil. They play a crucial role in enhancing soil health through various means:

- They prevent soil erosion by shielding the soil from the direct impact of raindrops.
- They suppress weeds by outcompeting them for sunlight and nutrients, reducing the need for chemical herbicides.
- Cover crops enhance soil fertility by fixing atmospheric nitrogen, mainly when using leguminous plants like clover or vetch.

When these crops are cut down and left on the surface,

they decompose, adding organic matter and nutrients to the soil, thus improving its structure and water retention capacity.

Crop rotation, on the other hand, is the practice of growing different types of crops in the same area across a sequence of growing seasons. It reduces the reliance on chemical fertilizers and pesticides by naturally breaking cycles of pests and diseases. Each crop type absorbs specific nutrients from the soil, and by rotating them, you help prevent nutrient depletion. For instance, following a nitrogen-fixing legume crop with a nitrogen-loving leafy vegetable can optimize the nutrient use efficiency. Crop rotation also diversifies the soil microbiome, which is essential for a healthy ecosystem.

Integrating cover crops into your crop rotation plan can magnify these benefits. After harvesting your main crop, planting a cover crop before the next crop in the rotation takes over can keep the soil covered and active. This prevents nutrient leaching during off-seasons and ensures that the soil is revitalized and ready for the next planting cycle. For example, you might plant a winter cover crop like rye after harvesting tomatoes to protect and enrich the soil before planting spring vegetables.

To implement these practices effectively, start by assessing your soil's current condition and the specific needs of your homestead. Consider climate, soil type, and the crops you wish to grow. Plan your crop rotation schedule by grouping plants with similar nutrient needs or pest issues, and decide on the appropriate cover crops to plant between these groups. Remember, the goal is to maintain a continuous cycle of growth, rest, and rejuvenation in your soil, mimicking natural ecosystems.

In conclusion, integrating cover crops and crop rotation into your backyard homestead is a testament to the power of working with nature rather than against it. These practices are not only beneficial for your soil and crops but also contribute to a larger ecological balance. By adopting these methods, you're taking significant steps towards sustainability and resilience in your homesteading journey.

Testing and Understanding Your Soil

Understanding the soil in your backyard is akin to getting to know a close friend. It requires patience, observation, and a bit of science to comprehend its needs, strengths, and weaknesses truly. This understanding is crucial for any homesteader cultivating a thriving garden or farm. Soil testing is the first step in this journey of acquaintance, providing a baseline from which to work and improve your soil's health.

Soil testing is more straightforward than it might seem. It involves collecting soil samples from various parts of your homestead and sending them to a local extension service or a private lab for analysis. These tests offer invaluable insights into your soil's pH level, nutrient content (such as nitrogen, phosphorus, and potassium), and the presence of organic matter. Understanding these components helps you make informed decisions about soil amendments and select the right plants for your garden.

The pH level is critical to soil health and influences plant nutrient availability. Most vegetables thrive in slightly acidic to neutral soil (pH 6.0-7.0). If your soil is too acidic or alkaline, it can be amended with lime or sulfur to bring it to an optimal pH range. However, it's essential to follow the recommendations from your soil test report to avoid over-amendment.

Nutrient levels are equally important. Nitrogen, phosphorus, and potassium are plants' primary nutrients for growing. If your soil test indicates a deficiency in any of these, you can address it by adding organic or synthetic fertilizers. Yet, the beauty of a backyard homestead lies in the potential to use compost, manure, and other organic matter to enrich the soil, thus reducing the need for synthetic inputs.

Organic matter content is another crucial piece of the puzzle. It improves soil structure, water retention, and nutrient availability. Composting is a homesteader's best friend in this regard, transforming kitchen scraps and yard waste into black gold that nourishes the soil and supports a vibrant ecosystem underground.

Once you've tested your soil and understood its characteristics, the next step is continuously improving its health. This doesn't happen overnight but is a gradual process involving regular amendments, crop rotation, and adding organic matter. Remember, healthy soil is the foundation of a productive homestead. By nurturing the soil, you're not just growing plants but cultivating a sustainable future.

In summary, testing and understanding your soil is fundamental to backyard homesteading. It informs your decisions, guides your gardening practices, and ultimately leads to a more fruitful and fulfilling homesteading experience. With patience and persistence, you'll see your efforts reflected in the health of your soil and the abundance of your harvests.

Mulching Techniques

Having explored the intricacies of testing and understanding your soil, it's time to delve into mulching techniques—a critical next step in nurturing and protecting your garden. Mulching is not just about making your garden look neat; it is crucial in maintaining soil health, conserving moisture, and suppressing weeds. Let's explore how you can effectively implement mulching in your backyard homestead.

Mulching involves covering the soil surface around your plants with a material layer—organic or inorganic. This practice offers numerous benefits, including temperature regulation, moisture retention, and the reduction of soil erosion. Moreover, organic mulches contribute to soil fertility as they decompose, enriching the soil with essential nutrients.

Organic mulches are derived from natural materials that decompose over time. Some popular options include straw, grass clippings, leaves, wood chips, and compost. Each type has its unique benefits and considerations:

- **Straw and Grass Clippings:** These are readily available and excellent for vegetable gardens. They decompose quickly, adding organic matter to the soil. However, ensure that the grass isn't treated with herbicides, which could harm your plants.
- **Leaves:** An abundant resource in the fall, shredded leaves can be spread around your plants to provide insulation and gradually enrich the soil as they break down.
- **Wood Chips:** Ideal for perennial beds and pathways, wood chips last longer than most

organic mulches but decompose slowly, adding less organic matter to the soil in the short term.
- **Compost:** Using compost as mulch not only suppresses weeds but also adds significant nutrients to the soil. It's particularly beneficial for improving soil structure and fertility.

Inorganic mulches include materials like plastic, landscape fabric, and gravel. While they don't improve soil fertility, they are effective in weed suppression and moisture conservation.

- **Plastic Mulch:** Commonly used in vegetable gardens, plastic mulch warms the soil and is excellent for heat-loving crops. However, it prevents water and air from reaching the soil and can be challenging to manage.
- **Landscape Fabric:** This porous material allows water and air to reach the soil while suppressing weeds. It's often used under gravel or other inorganic mulches to prevent them from sinking into the soil.
- **Gravel and Stones:** These materials are suitable for pathways and decorative purposes. They offer excellent weed control but can make the soil beneath them hotter.

When applying mulch, a few practical tips can ensure its effectiveness:

- **Depth:** Organic mulches should be layered 2-4 inches deep. Too much can suffocate plants, while too little may not effectively suppress weeds or retain moisture.
- **Timing:** Early spring is a great time to apply mulch after the soil has warmed up. Mulching too early can delay soil warming and plant growth.
- **Maintenance:** Refresh organic mulches to maintain the desired depth as they decompose. Keep inorganic mulches clean and free from debris to prevent soil compaction.

Incorporating mulching into your gardening practices is a straightforward yet impactful way to enhance the health and productivity of your backyard homestead. Choosing the right mulch and applying it thoughtfully can create a more resilient and vibrant garden ecosystem.

Chapter Summary

- Soil health is fundamental for backyard homesteading, requiring a balance of minerals, organic matter, water, and air.
- Soil texture and pH level are critical; loamy soil and a slightly acidic to neutral pH (6.0-7.0) are ideal for most plants.
- Organic matter, like compost and aged manure, is vital for improving soil structure and fertility.
- A diverse microbial population in the soil supports plant health by breaking down organic matter and

protecting against pests.
- Composting kitchen scraps and yard waste enriches soil and reduces waste, and a balance of greens and browns is necessary for successful decomposition.
- Natural fertilizers and amendments, such as compost tea, worm castings, and green manures, enhance soil without the environmental impact of synthetic options.
- Cover crops and crop rotation improve soil health by preventing erosion, suppressing weeds, fixing atmospheric nitrogen, and breaking pest cycles.
- Mulching with organic or inorganic materials conserves moisture, suppresses weeds, and can improve soil fertility as organic mulches decompose.

2
GARDENING

A person in a wide-brimmed hat tending to a garden.

Planning Your Garden

Planning your garden is akin to painting a canvas, where the soil is your medium, and the plants are your palette. The key to a successful garden, especially in the context of a backyard homestead, lies in meticulous planning and a deep understanding of the space you have at your disposal. This section will guide you through the essential steps to plan your garden efficiently, ensuring a bountiful harvest and a vibrant oasis in your backyard.

First and foremost, assess the space available to you. Not all homesteads are blessed with expansive yards, but even the smallest spaces can be transformed into productive gardens with the right approach. Observe the patterns of sunlight and shade throughout the day, as this will significantly influence what you can grow and where. To thrive, most vegetables and fruits require at least six hours of sunlight daily, so plot your garden accordingly.

Next, consider the soil quality in your chosen garden area. Soil health is paramount in organic gardening, and a backyard homestead relies heavily on the sustainability of its resources. Conduct a soil test to understand its composition, pH level, and nutrient profile. This information will guide you in amending your soil, ensuring it provides the perfect plant foundation. Composting is a fantastic way to enrich your soil naturally, turning kitchen scraps and yard waste into gold for your garden.

Water access is another critical factor in garden planning. Efficient water use conserves this precious resource and promotes healthier plants. Explore options like rainwater harvesting or setting up a drip irrigation system to provide a consistent and measured amount of water to your plants directly at their roots, where it's most needed.

Now that you understand your space, soil, and water setup, it's time to think about your garden's layout. Raised beds, container gardening, and traditional in-ground plots each have advantages and can be mixed to suit your needs and preferences. Raised beds, for example, offer excellent drainage and can help deter some pests, while container gardening allows for greater flexibility in managing sunlight exposure.

As you sketch out your garden plan, consider the importance of crop rotation and companion planting. These practices not only maximize space and yield but also contribute to the health of your garden by preventing soil depletion and reducing pest and disease issues. Integrate flowers and herbs to attract pollinators and beneficial insects, further enhancing the ecosystem of your backyard homestead.

In planning your garden, remember that flexibility and observation are your allies. Nature often reminds us of its unpredictability, so be prepared to adapt your plans as needed. Keep a garden journal to record what works and what doesn't, setting the stage for continuous learning and improvement in your gardening journey.

By following these steps, you're not just planning a garden; you're laying the groundwork for a sustainable, productive, and beautiful extension of your home. The effort you put into planning today will pay dividends in the coming seasons, providing nourishment and joy for your household.

Choosing the Right Plants

After carefully planning your garden, considering the layout, sunlight, and soil conditions, the crucial next step in your backyard homesteading journey involves selecting the right plants for your space. This decision is vital for a thriving garden and requires a thoughtful approach to match your garden's conditions with the plants' needs.

First, it's essential to understand your climate zone, as this knowledge will guide you in choosing plants well-suited to your area's weather patterns and temperature ranges. Each plant has specific climate preferences; selecting those adapted to your zone increases the likelihood of success.

Reflect on the sunlight and soil assessment you conducted during the planning phase. Different plants have varying requirements for sunlight, ranging from full sun to partial shade, and soil type and pH level can significantly affect plant growth. Choose plants that will thrive in the conditions you have to offer. Decide on the types of plants you want to grow, whether aiming for a vegetable garden, an herb garden, or a mix of both. To enhance your homestead's aesthetics, you may also be interested in fruit trees or ornamental flowers, each with considerations such as the space and care needed.

Think about the growing seasons of the plants you're considering. Some plants are perennials, returning year after year, while others are annuals or biennials, requiring replanting. Planning for a mix can ensure your garden remains productive and vibrant across different seasons. Evaluate the space requirements and growth habits of potential plants. Some plants, like squash, need much room to sprawl, while others, such as tomatoes, grow upwards and can be supported with stakes or cages. Understanding these habits will help you maximize your garden space and avoid overcrowding.

Consider the benefits of companion planting, where some plants, when grown together, can improve each other's health and yields. For example, marigolds repel certain pests and can be a great companion for many vegetable plants. Researching companion planting combinations can lead to a more harmonious and productive garden. Finally, think about your personal preferences and goals. Choose plants you and your family enjoy eating or that fulfill your desired purpose, whether cooking, herbal remedies, or creating a beautiful space.

Your garden should reflect your interests and needs, making the experience enjoyable and rewarding. By carefully selecting the right plants for your garden, you're setting the stage for a successful and fulfilling gardening season, looking forward to a bountiful harvest and the many joys of backyard homesteading.

Seed Starting and Transplanting

Cultivating a thriving backyard homestead garden begins with the pivotal steps of seed-starting and transplanting. These steps not only allow for a deeper connection with your plants but also provide the opportunity to kickstart your garden with a variety of species that may not be readily available as seedlings in your local area.

The adventure starts indoors, where seeds are given a controlled environment to sprout and grow into healthy seedlings. It's essential to select high-quality seeds and suitable containers with adequate drainage, such as recycled containers, peat pots, or commercially available seed trays, and fill them with a sterile, seed-starting mix to prevent disease. Maintaining moisture and warmth, around 65-75°F (18-24°C), is crucial for encouraging germination, and a plastic cover or dome can help retain humidity. However, it should be removed once seeds sprout to prevent mold growth.

Once seeds have germinated, ensuring they receive at least 16 hours of light daily is vital to prevent them from becoming leggy and weak. As seedlings grow, it's important to harden them off by gradually exposing them to outdoor conditions over a week to reduce transplant shock and acclimate them to their new environment.

When it's time to transplant, choosing a cool, overcast day can ease the transition for young plants. The garden soil should be well-prepared, enriched with compost, and moist. Seedlings should be carefully removed from their containers, handled by the leaves to avoid stem damage, and placed in a hole big enough to accommodate the root ball. The soil should be gently firmed around them to eliminate air pockets. Watering thoroughly after planting is crucial for root establishment.

Spacing is critical to prevent overcrowding and ensure each plant has enough room to grow and access nutrients. Specific spacing recommendations are usually found on the seed packet or plant tag. After transplanting, it's important to keep a close eye on the seedlings, especially during the first few weeks, to ensure they adapt well to their new environment and provide support structures for climbing plants early on to avoid disturbing the roots later.

In conclusion, seed starting and transplanting are rewarding steps in the gardening process that pave the way for a bountiful harvest, and by nurturing your plants with patience and care, you'll cultivate a vibrant garden and a deeper appreciation for the cycle of growth and renewal in your backyard homestead.

Watering and Irrigation

Watering and irrigation are the lifelines of a thriving garden. After successfully starting your seeds and transplanting them into the garden, the next critical step is ensuring they receive the right amount of water. This section will guide you through the essentials of watering and irrigation, providing your plants with the best chance for growth, health, and productivity.

Understanding your plants' needs is the first step in effective watering. Different plants have varying water requirements, and even the time of day you water can significantly impact their health. Early morning is generally the best time to water your garden. It allows the water to reach deep into the soil, encouraging deep root growth while minimizing evaporation and the risk of fungal diseases that can occur with evening watering.

There are several methods of watering, each with its own set of benefits. Hand watering with a hose or watering can is the most straightforward method, allowing for direct control over the amount of water each plant receives. However, it can be time-consuming and is not always the most efficient method for larger gardens.

Drip irrigation systems are a more efficient alternative, delivering water directly to the base of each plant. This method reduces water waste and helps keep the leaves dry, crucial in preventing many common plant diseases. Setting up a drip irrigation system might require an initial investment of time and resources, but the long-term benefits of water conservation and healthier plants are well worth it.

For those looking for a more automated solution, soaker hoses and sprinkler systems can cover larger areas with minimal effort. Like drip irrigation, soaker hoses allow water to seep slowly along their length, providing a steady supply of moisture to the plant roots. Sprinkler systems, on the other hand, can water a large area from above, simulating rainfall. While sprinklers are less targeted than drip or soaker systems, they can effectively water lawns or large garden areas.

No matter your chosen method, monitoring your garden's moisture levels is crucial. Over-watering can be as harmful as under-watering, leading to root rot and other issues. A simple way to check soil moisture is to insert a finger into the soil near your plants; if the soil feels dry at a depth of about an inch, it's time to water.

Incorporating mulch around your plants can also aid in moisture retention, reducing the frequency of watering needed. Mulch acts as a barrier, slowing evaporation and contributing to soil health as it breaks down over time.

As we progress in our gardening journey, understanding the balance and techniques of watering and irrigation sets the stage for a healthy, productive garden. This knowledge conserves water and ensures that our plants have the resources they need to thrive. With our watering strategies in place, we can turn our attention to the next critical aspect of gardening: managing pests and diseases to protect our hard-earned harvests.

Pest and Disease Management

A flourishing garden is a source of pride and sustenance in backyard homesteading. However, this green paradise can quickly become a battleground where pests and diseases threaten to overrun your hard work. Effective management of these unwelcome visitors is crucial to ensure the health and productivity of your garden. This section delves into practical strategies for keeping pests and diseases at bay, ensuring your garden remains a thriving part of your homestead.

Understanding the enemy is the first step in effective pest and disease management. Common garden pests include aphids, caterpillars, slugs, and beetles, each with their preferred plants and attack methods. On the other hand, diseases can be fungal, bacterial, or viral, with symptoms ranging from mildew to leaf spots and wilting. Regularly monitoring your garden will help you identify problems early, which is key to controlling outbreaks.

Prevention is always better than cure. Maintaining healthy soil through composting and crop rotation supports strong plant growth and is less susceptible to pests and diseases. Choosing disease-resistant plant varieties can also significantly reduce the risk of outbreaks. Additionally, encouraging natural predators into your garden, such as ladybugs, birds, and frogs, helps keep pest populations in check.

When intervention is necessary, opting for organic and natural remedies is advisable to maintain the balance of your backyard ecosystem. Neem oil, diatomaceous earth, and insecticidal soaps are effective against many pests without harming beneficial insects. Similarly, baking soda, copper fungicides, and sulfur can organically treat many common plant diseases.

Sometimes, despite all efforts, pests or diseases may establish a foothold in your garden. In such cases, removing and destroying infected plants or parts of plants can prevent the spread of disease. For severe pest infestations, manual removal or the use of pheromone traps may be necessary.

Remember, pest and disease management aims not to create a sterile environment but to maintain a healthy balance that allows your garden to thrive. By adopting a proactive and mindful approach, you can protect your garden from pests and diseases, ensuring it remains a vibrant and productive part of your backyard homestead.

Harvesting and Storing Your Produce

Diligently managing pests and diseases in your garden leads to the rewarding phase of harvesting and storing your produce, which is crucial for maximizing the fruits of your labor, ensuring that nothing goes to waste, and enjoying your garden's bounty long after the growing season.

The key to successful harvesting is timing, as most vegetables and fruits have a prime period when their flavor and nutritional content peak. For instance, leafy greens are best harvested in the morning when their moisture content is highest, while root vegetables like carrots and beets should be picked when they reach a desirable size.

Tomatoes, on the other hand, are ripe for picking when brightly colored and slightly firm. Using the right tools and techniques is essential to avoid damaging the plant or produce, with a sharp knife or gardening shears for clean cuts and gentle handling to prevent bruising.

Once harvested, proper storage is essential to preserve the freshness and flavor of your produce. Different fruits and vegetables have varying storage needs.

Root vegetables like potatoes and onions prefer cool, dark,

and dry places and can last for months under the right conditions, typically in a cellar or cool pantry. Leafy greens, however, need refrigeration and a moisture-retaining bag to stay fresh.

Fruits like apples and pears can be stored in a cool, humid environment for an extended period. Still, it's essential to be mindful of ethylene-producing fruits like apples, which can hasten the ripening and spoiling of other produce if stored too closely together.

For those with a surplus of produce, preserving methods such as canning, freezing, or drying can extend the life of your harvest and provide you with homegrown flavors even in the off-season.

Canning tomatoes, making jams from berries, freezing vegetables like beans, peas, and corn, and drying herbs and some fruits are excellent ways to preserve the nutritional value and taste of your garden's bounty.

Harvesting and storing produce is a way to extend its shelf life while maintaining its nutritional value and taste. This allows you to enjoy the fruits of your labor throughout the year and makes your backyard homestead a truly rewarding endeavor.

Chapter Summary

- Planning a garden involves assessing space, understanding soil quality, and ensuring water access for a successful harvest.
- The garden layout, including raised beds and container gardening, should consider sunlight

exposure and incorporate crop rotation and companion planting.
- Choosing the right plants for your garden requires understanding your climate zone, assessing sunlight and soil, and considering plant types and their seasonal growth.
- Seed starting indoors involves selecting quality seeds, providing moisture and warmth, and ensuring adequate light. Then, with proper spacing and care, the seeds are transplanted into the garden.
- Effective watering and irrigation methods, like drip systems or soaker hoses, are crucial for plant health, with early morning watering being optimal.
- Pest and disease management includes regular monitoring, using organic remedies, and encouraging natural predators to maintain a healthy garden ecosystem.
- Harvesting produce at the right time maximizes flavor and nutritional content, with proper storage methods extending freshness and usability.
- Preserving surplus produce through canning, freezing, or drying ensures a year-round supply of homegrown fruits, vegetables, and herbs.

3

RAISING CHICKENS

A chicken coop standing in a vast field.

Choosing the Right Breeds

Raising chickens in your backyard homestead brings the exciting task of choosing the right breeds to suit your needs and environment. This decision is crucial, as the breeds you select will directly impact your homesteading experience, from the quantity and quality of eggs produced to the temperament and adaptability of the chickens to your specific climate.

Firstly, consider what your primary goal is in raising chickens. Are you looking for prolific egg layers or are you more interested in meat production? You may be seeking dual-purpose breeds that are capable of providing both. For those focused on egg production, breeds like the Leghorn or Rhode Island Red are renowned for their high yield of eggs. On the other hand, if meat production is your goal, breeds such as the Cornish Cross grow quickly and provide a substantial amount of meat. For homesteaders looking for versatility, the Plymouth Rock and Sussex breeds balance egg production and meat quality.

Another important factor to consider is the climate of your homestead. Some chicken breeds are more resilient to cold weather, such as the Buff Orpington and the Barred Rock, known for their thick feathering that provides insulation during colder months. Conversely, if you live in a warmer climate, breeds like the Australorp or the Welsummer, which are more tolerant of heat, might be more suitable.

Temperament is another critical consideration. If you're raising chickens in a family setting, you might prefer breeds known for their docile and friendly nature, such as the Silkie or the Cochin. These breeds are less likely to be aggressive and can become affectionate pets.

Lastly, think about the space you have available. Some breeds, like the Bantam varieties, are smaller and require less space, making them ideal for smaller backyards. Meanwhile, larger breeds will need more room to roam and forage.

In choosing the suitable breeds for your backyard

homestead, it's essential to do thorough research and consider all these factors. By aligning your choices with your goals, climate, space, and lifestyle, you'll ensure a rewarding and sustainable chicken-raising experience. Remember, each breed has unique characteristics and needs, so take the time to understand what each can bring to your homestead. With careful selection, your chickens will thrive and become a cherished part of your homesteading journey.

Housing and Coop Design

After selecting the breeds that best suit your backyard homestead, it's essential to focus on their future home. A well-designed chicken coop is crucial for the shelter, health, and happiness of your chickens.

The space inside the coop should be at least 3-4 square feet per chicken, with about 10 square feet in the outdoor run to prevent overcrowding, stress, pecking, and the spread of diseases. For a flock of 6 chickens, a coop of at least 18-24 square feet with an attached run of 60 square feet is recommended.

Proper ventilation in the coop is necessary to remove moisture and ammonia fumes, keeping the air fresh and reducing the risk of respiratory issues. However, the coop also needs to be insulated enough to keep the chickens warm in colder climates while allowing air circulation. This can be achieved with strategically placed vents or windows.

The coop must also be secure against predators, using durable hardware cloth for enclosures and burying it at least 12 inches underground to deter digging predators. Lockable doors and windows will enhance security.

Nesting boxes should be provided for hens to lay their eggs, with one box for every three to four hens, placed in a quiet, darker part of the coop. Roosting bars, positioned higher than the nesting boxes, should accommodate all chickens comfortably, aligning with their instinct to roost in high places.

The coop design should also facilitate easy cleaning to maintain health, including removable trays and hose-down floors. Accessibility is important for egg collection, refilling feeders and waterers, and performing cleaning and maintenance tasks, so ensure the door is large enough for comfortable entry.

A well-thought-out coop design is vital for the well-being of your chickens, leading to a more productive and rewarding backyard homestead experience. With the coop set up, attention can then turn to feeding and nourishing your flock to keep them in peak condition.

Feeding and Nutrition

Transitioning from the essentials of housing and coop design, we delve into the equally critical aspect of raising chickens: **feeding** and **nutrition**. This section equips you with the knowledge to nourish your flock effectively, ensuring they are healthy, happy, and productive.

Chickens require a balanced diet consisting of carbohydrates, proteins, fats, vitamins, and minerals, usually formulated by commercial poultry feed to meet these needs. It's crucial to understand the components of their feed and any additional supplements they might need for their overall well-being.

Different feed types exist for different stages of a chicken's life. Starter feed, high in protein, is essential for chicks up to 6 weeks old to support their rapid growth. With slightly less protein, grower feed is for chickens from 6 weeks until they begin laying eggs. Layer feed, rich in calcium, is necessary once hens start laying eggs to ensure strong eggshells and maintain their health. Scratch grains, a mix of grains, can be offered sparingly as a treat to encourage natural foraging behavior.

While commercial feeds are formulated to meet all nutritional requirements, offering supplements like oyster shells for additional calcium or grit to aid digestion can address specific needs or deficiencies. Treats can include fruits, vegetables, and grains but should be given in moderation to avoid nutritional imbalances and obesity. Ensuring chickens access fresh, clean water is vital for their digestion and overall health.

Feeding practices, such as feeding chickens at the same time each day, help establish a routine, reduce stress, and promote health. Monitoring feed intake to adjust portions as necessary and cleaning feeders regularly to prevent mold and contamination is essential for preventing health issues. Seasonal changes may affect chickens' nutritional needs, requiring more feed during colder months to stay warm and ensuring access to cool, clean water in summer to prevent dehydration.

Proper feeding and nutrition are foundational to raising a healthy, productive flock. By understanding and meeting your chickens' dietary needs, you ensure their well-being and the success of your backyard homestead. As we move on from feeding and nutrition, we'll explore health and wellness, ensuring your chickens remain in peak condition year-round.

Health and Wellness

Maintaining the health and wellness of your backyard chickens is not just a responsibility; it's necessary to ensure a thriving homestead. This section delves into practical strategies and insights to keep your feathered friends in peak condition, focusing on preventive care, recognizing signs of illness, and addressing common health issues.

Preventive care is the cornerstone of chicken health and wellness. Regularly scheduled check-ups are crucial, even for backyard flocks. These check-ups should include examining your chickens for signs of distress, injury, or illness. Vaccinations play a vital role in preventing diseases that can devastate unvaccinated flocks. Consult with a veterinarian with poultry experience to establish a vaccination schedule tailored to your specific needs and local disease risks.

Parasite control is another critical aspect of preventive care. External parasites like mites and lice can cause discomfort and health issues in chickens, while internal parasites like worms can lead to more severe health problems. Regular inspection and treatment for parasites are necessary to keep your chickens healthy. Various treatments are available, including natural remedies and chemical treatments, but choosing the method that best suits your homestead's philosophy and your chickens' needs is essential.

Recognizing the signs of illness early can be the difference between life and death for your chickens. Symptoms such as lethargy, reduced appetite, abnormal droppings, and changes in egg production can indicate health issues. Respiratory problems, often characterized by sneezing, coughing, or discharge from the nostrils, require immediate attention. Isolating sick birds from the rest of the flock is crucial to prevent the spread of disease.

Common health issues in backyard chickens include respiratory infections, digestive problems, and reproductive disorders. Many of these conditions are manageable with prompt and appropriate care. For instance, providing a clean, dry, and well-ventilated living environment can prevent many respiratory and digestive problems. Additionally, ensuring your chickens have a balanced diet of essential nutrients can help prevent nutritional deficiencies that lead to health issues.

Consulting with a poultry veterinarian is always the best course of action in cases of illness. They can provide accurate diagnoses and treatment options. Sometimes, despite our best efforts, chickens will fall ill. Knowing when to seek professional help is vital to responsible chicken care.

In conclusion, the health and wellness of your backyard chickens depend on a combination of preventive care, early detection of illnesses, and appropriate treatment. By staying informed and vigilant, you can ensure your chickens lead healthy, productive lives, paving the way for a successful transition into discussions about egg production and beyond. Remember, healthy chickens are happy chickens, and happy chickens are the heart of a thriving backyard homestead.

Egg Production

In backyard homesteading, egg production from your flock of chickens can be both a rewarding and practical aspect of self-sufficiency. After ensuring the health and wellness of your chickens, the next logical step is to optimize their environment and care for maximum egg production. This section will guide you toward a plentiful and consistent egg yield from your backyard flock.

First and foremost, the breed of chicken you choose plays a significant role in your egg production efforts. Some breeds, like the Leghorn, Australorp, and Rhode Island Red, are known for their prolific egg-laying abilities. When selecting your flock, consider the climate of your area and the breed's adaptability to ensure their comfort and productivity.

Nutrition is the cornerstone of healthy, productive chickens. A balanced diet is crucial for egg production. Layers require a diet rich in calcium, protein, and essential vitamins. Providing a quality layer feed is the most straightforward way to meet these nutritional needs. Additionally, supplementing their diet with kitchen scraps, garden waste, and a constant fresh water supply can boost their overall health and egg output.

Light exposure significantly influences a chicken's laying cycle. Chickens need about 14-16 hours of daylight to maintain optimal egg production. During shorter winter days, consider using a light in the coop to extend the amount of perceived daylight. However, balancing this with periods of natural darkness is essential to ensure the chickens' health and well-being.

The living conditions of your chickens also affect their ability to lay consistently. Ensure the coop is clean, well-ventilated, and protected from extreme weather conditions. Each chicken requires enough space to move freely, roost, and lay eggs without stress. Nesting boxes should be cozy, dark, and soft bedding to encourage laying. Typically, one nesting box for every three to four hens is sufficient.

Stress reduction is another critical factor in maximizing egg production. Chickens are sensitive to changes and can be stressed by loud noises, predators, and overcrowding. Maintaining a calm, safe environment and handling your chickens gently can help keep stress levels low and egg production high.

Regular health checks are vital to prevent diseases and parasites, which can significantly impact egg production. Implementing preventative health measures and addressing any issues promptly will keep your flock healthy and productive.

In conclusion, optimizing egg production in your backyard homestead involves:

- A combination of selecting the suitable breeds.
- Providing a balanced diet.
- Managing light exposure.
- Ensuring comfortable living conditions.
- Reducing stress.
- Maintaining good health practices.

By focusing on these areas, you can enjoy a steady supply of fresh, nutritious eggs from your backyard flock, contributing significantly to your homestead's self-sufficiency and sustainability.

Dealing with Predators

Discussing the intricacies of egg production naturally leads to a more challenging aspect of raising chickens: dealing with predators. This part of the guide is designed to equip you with the knowledge and strategies necessary to protect your flock from common threats and ensure their safety and well-being.

Predators can vary widely depending on location, but foxes, raccoons, hawks, and neighborhood dogs are among the most common. Each predator has its method of attack, necessitating specific defensive strategies.

Understanding the behavior of potential predators is crucial to protecting your chickens effectively. For example, raccoons can open latches and climb over fences due to their dexterity, while hawks target free-ranging chickens from the sky. Tailoring your defenses to the specific threats posed by local predators is essential.

The first line of defense is a well-constructed coop and run. Ensuring your chicken coop is sturdy, with no gaps or weak points, is essential. Hardware cloth is recommended over the chicken wire for its durability and difficulty in tearing. Burying the wire at least a foot deep around the perimeter can deter digging predators like foxes.

Consider covering the run with a solid roof or securely attached netting for aerial threats, which protects chickens from hawks and owls without blocking sunlight.

Various deterrents can also help protect your flock. Motion-activated lights, sprinklers, and noise deterrents like radios left on at night can scare away nocturnal predators. Guard animals, such as dogs, geese, or llamas, can effectively deter predators, provided they coexist peacefully with your chickens.

Vigilance in protecting your chickens from predators involves regularly inspecting your coop and run for signs of attempted entry or damage and addressing any vulnerabilities immediately. Keeping the area around the coop clean and free of attractants, such as spilled feed, can reduce the likelihood of predators being drawn to your backyard.

By understanding local predator threats and implementing a combination of physical barriers, deterrents, and vigilant monitoring, you can create a safe environment for your chickens. Protecting your flock is an ongoing effort, but with the right strategies, you can minimize risks and enjoy the rewards of raising chickens in your backyard homestead.

Chapter Summary

- Choosing the right breed involves selecting chicken breeds for your backyard homestead by considering goals such as egg production, meat, or both, along with climate adaptability, temperament, and space requirements.
- Housing and coop design requires creating a healthy and safe environment for chickens with adequate space, ventilation, insulation, predator protection, nesting boxes, roosting bars, ease of cleaning, and accessibility.
- Feeding and nutrition involve providing a balanced diet with commercial poultry feed, supplements for specific needs, and clean water, adjusting feeding

practices, and considering seasonal changes to maintain health and productivity.
- Health and wellness focuses on keeping chickens healthy through preventive care, recognizing signs of illness, managing parasites, consulting with a veterinarian, and promptly addressing common health issues.
- Egg production can be optimized by selecting the right breed, ensuring proper nutrition, light exposure, living conditions, stress reduction, and health practices to maximize egg yield and contribute to homestead sustainability.
- Dealing with predators includes understanding predator behavior, fortifying the coop and run, implementing deterrents, and maintaining vigilance to protect chickens from common threats.
- The overall strategy for raising chickens emphasizes the importance of thorough planning and consideration in breed selection, coop design, nutrition, health management, egg production optimization, and predator protection for a successful backyard homestead.
- Sustainable homesteading highlights that raising chickens is a rewarding aspect of self-sufficiency that requires careful selection, proper care, and protection to ensure the well-being and productivity of the flock.

4
BEEKEEPING

A beekeeper in protective gear holding a box of honey.

Understanding Bee Behavior

Diving into the world of beekeeping, starting with a foundational understanding of bee behavior, is crucial. This knowledge enriches the beekeeping experience and ensures the safety and productivity of your beekeeping endeavors.

Bees, fascinating creatures that they are, exhibit complex and highly organized behaviors, reflecting their roles within the hive and their interaction with the environment.

At the heart of bee behavior is the hive's social structure, which is dominated by the queen bee, whose primary role is reproduction. Worker bees, which are female, perform various tasks, including foraging for nectar and pollen, feeding the queen and larvae, and maintaining the hive's cleanliness and temperature. Drones, or male bees, solely aim to mate with a new queen. Understanding these roles is crucial for managing your hive effectively.

Communication among bees is another fascinating aspect. They use a combination of pheromones, or chemical signals, and the famous "waggle dance" to convey information about food sources, hive health, and other critical factors. Observing these communication methods can provide insights into the hive's needs and challenges.

Bees also exhibit defensive behaviors to protect the hive. They may sting when they perceive a threat to their hive or queen. To minimize stress on the bees and the beekeeper, it's essential to approach beekeeping with respect for these natural behaviors, using protective gear and learning how to interact with bees.

Understanding seasonal behaviors is equally important. Bees are active in warmer months, focusing on foraging and building up the hive's resources. In winter, they cluster around the queen, keeping her warm and focusing on survival. This seasonal cycle affects how you care for your bees, from feeding in the winter to managing the hive's growth in the summer.

Lastly, bees face various challenges, from diseases and

pests to environmental stressors. Being attuned to your hive's signs of distress or disease can help you promptly address these issues.

A deep understanding of bee behavior is not just about becoming a successful beekeeper; it's about fostering a harmonious relationship with these incredible insects and contributing to their preservation. As we move forward, we'll delve into the practical steps of setting up your hive, building on the foundation of understanding we've established here.

Setting Up Your Hive

After gaining a foundational understanding of bee behavior, the next logical step is to set up your hive - a task that requires careful planning, respect for the bees, and a bit of elbow grease.

First and foremost, selecting the right location for your hive is paramount. Bees thrive in environments that provide ample sunlight, protection from strong winds, and easy access to water and foraging materials. An ideal spot is a south-facing spot that catches the morning sun yet is shaded during the hottest part of the day. Use a sturdy stand or concrete blocks to ensure the hive is elevated from the ground to protect it from moisture and predators.

Several types of hives exist when choosing your hive, including the traditional Langstroth hive, the top-bar hive, or the more recent Warre hive. Each has advantages and is designed to cater to different beekeeping philosophies and practices. The Langstroth, for instance, is widely used due to its practicality and ease of honey extraction. However, the choice ultimately depends on your preference, the amount of time you can dedicate to beekeeping, and the goals you wish to achieve with your hive.

Assembling your hive requires attention to detail. Whether starting with a pre-assembled kit or building from scratch, ensure all components fit snugly together to prevent drafts and protect your bees from the elements. The hive should consist of a bottom board, the hive boxes or supers where the bees will live and store honey, frames to build their comb, a queen excluder to keep the queen in the brood chamber, and a cover to seal the top.

Before introducing your bees to their new home, take the time to familiarize yourself with the tools of the trade. A bee suit, gloves, a smoker, and a hive tool are essential for handling your bees safely and effectively. The smoker calms the bees, making them easier to work with during hive inspections and maintenance.

Introducing bees to your hive is a thrilling moment. The process requires gentleness and patience, whether starting with a nucleus colony, a package of bees, or capturing a swarm. Open the hive and carefully place the frames inside, ensuring the queen is securely introduced. Once the bees are in, close the hive and give them time to acclimate to their new surroundings, resisting the urge to check on them too frequently in the first few days.

Setting up your hive is just the beginning of a fascinating journey into beekeeping. As your bees settle in, the focus shifts to maintaining the health and productivity of the hive, ensuring both your bees and your backyard homestead thrive in harmony. With dedication and care, your beekeeping endeavors will yield sweet rewards and contribute to the well-being of the local ecosystem, making your homestead a beacon of sustainability and biodiversity.

Maintenance and Hive Health

Once your hive is established, the ongoing journey of maintenance and ensuring hive health begins. This critical phase in beekeeping is about keeping your bees alive and helping them thrive. A healthy hive is a productive hive, and as a backyard beekeeper, your role shifts to that of a caretaker, closely monitoring and managing the well-being of your buzzing inhabitants.

Regular inspections are the cornerstone of hive maintenance. Aim to check your hive every two weeks during the active season. These inspections are vital for spotting early signs of disease, assessing the queen's health and productivity, and ensuring the hive has enough space to grow. When inspecting, look for a pattern of healthy brood (eggs, larvae, and pupae), which indicates a strong, laying queen. Also, watch for pests such as varroa mites or hive beetles, which can quickly bring down a healthy colony.

Varroa mites are among the most common and destructive pests beekeepers face. These tiny parasites attach themselves to bees and larvae, weakening and spreading diseases within the colony. Integrated pest management strategies, such as regular mite counts and natural miticides, can help keep these pests at bay. Remember, a proactive approach is always better than a reactive one regarding pest management.

Another aspect of hive health is ensuring bees access diverse and abundant food sources. Planting a bee-friendly garden or ensuring your bees can forage in a pesticide-free environment can significantly impact their health and productivity. Water is also essential, especially in hot weather, so providing a clean, accessible water source near the hive is crucial.

Swarming is a natural part of bee behavior, especially in strong, growing colonies. However, it can significantly reduce your hive's population and productivity. To manage swarming, consider splitting strong colonies or providing additional space and resources to accommodate your hive's growth.

Finally, preparing your bees for winter is an essential part of maintenance. This includes ensuring they have enough honey stores to last through the cold months, reducing the hive's entrance to protect against intruders, and providing insulation to help maintain a stable temperature within the hive.

By staying vigilant and responsive to your hive's needs, you can foster a thriving bee community in your backyard. Remember, beekeeping is a journey of learning and adaptation. Each hive has its unique challenges and rewards, and with patience and care, you'll be well on your way to a successful harvest.

Harvesting Honey

Harvesting honey is one of the most rewarding aspects of beekeeping, offering a sweet payoff for the care and effort you've invested in your hives. While enjoyable, this process requires careful timing and technique to ensure the health of your bee colony and the quality of the honey collected. Let's delve into the practical steps and considerations for a successful honey harvest.

Firstly, timing is crucial. Honey should be harvested at the end of the blooming period when bees have had ample time to gather nectar and convert it into honey. This typically occurs in late summer or early fall, depending on your local climate and flora. The honey must be fully mature, which bees indicate by capping the honey cells with wax. Harvesting too early can lead to honey that's too high in moisture and prone to fermentation.

Before you begin, ensure you have the right tools on hand. A bee suit, gloves, and a smoker are essential to protect yourself from stings and to calm the bees. You'll also need a hive tool to open the hive and separate the frames, a bee brush to remove any bees from the frames gently, and an extractor to spin the honey out of the comb.

The process starts with gently smoking the hive to calm the bees and reduce aggression. Carefully remove the lid and the inner cover, then gradually pull out the frames, inspecting them to ensure they're capped and ready for extraction. Working calmly and steadily is essential to minimize disturbance to the bees.

Once you've selected the frames to harvest, use the bee brush to sweep any remaining bees off the frames gently. It's crucial to do this gently to avoid harming the bees. Then, transport the frames to your extraction area, which should be set up in a clean, bee-proof space to avoid attracting bees or other insects.

The next step involves uncapping the wax seals on the honeycomb, either with a heated knife or a special uncapping fork. This exposes the honey, making it ready for extraction. Place the uncapped frames in the extractor, a centrifuge that forcefully spins the honey out of the comb. After extraction, the honey can be filtered to remove wax particles and stored in clean, airtight containers.

It's essential to leave enough honey in the hive to sustain the bee colony through the winter. A common rule of thumb is to leave at least 60 pounds (27 kilograms) of honey in the hive, though this can vary based on your local climate and the size of your bee colony.

After the harvest, return any wet frames to the hive. The bees will clean up the remaining honey and repair the comb, preparing it for the next season. This not only minimizes waste but also helps the bees maintain their hive.

In conclusion, harvesting honey is a delicate balance between taking what we need and ensuring the health and sustainability of the bee colony. With the right timing, tools, and techniques, you can enjoy the fruits of your labor while contributing to the well-being of these essential pollinators.

Common Problems and Solutions

Beekeeping on your backyard homestead can be a rewarding endeavor, offering the sweet reward of honey and the satisfaction of contributing to the health of the environment. However, like any agricultural pursuit, it comes with challenges. Understanding common problems and their solutions is crucial for maintaining a healthy bee colony and ensuring a successful harvest.

One of the most frequent issues beekeepers face is the Varroa mite infestation. These tiny parasites can wreak havoc on bee colonies by attaching themselves to bees and sucking their hemolymph, weakening and eventually killing the host bee. To combat Varroa mites, regular monitoring of the bee population is essential. This can be done through methods such as the powdered sugar roll or alcohol wash to estimate mite loads. If mite levels are high, treatments such as organic acids (formic or oxalic acid), essential oils (thymol-based products), or synthetic acaricides may be used, following the manufacturer's instructions closely to avoid harming the bee colony.

Another common problem is hive beetles, which thrive in a hive's warm, humid environment and can quickly become a nuisance by laying eggs in the comb and spoiling the honey. Maintaining hive hygiene is critical to controlling hive beetles. Regularly removing weak or dead colonies that attract beetles and using beetle traps can help keep their numbers in check.

Swarming is a natural part of bee behavior but can become problematic if not managed properly. It typically occurs when the colony grows too large for the hive, and a new queen is produced, leading half of the colony to leave in search of a new home. This can significantly reduce your hive's productivity. To prevent swarming, ensure your bees have enough space by adding new boxes or frames, particularly in the spring when the colony grows rapidly. Regularly checking for and removing queen cells can also discourage swarming.

Diseases such as American Foulbrood (AFB) and European Foulbrood (EFB) pose significant risks to bee colonies. These bacterial infections can spread quickly and are often fatal. The best defense against foulbrood is prevention through good apiary management practices. This includes purchasing bees from reputable sources, regularly inspecting colonies for signs of disease, and maintaining cleanliness in and around hives. If a colony is infected with AFB, it is often recommended to destroy the hive to prevent the spread of the disease, as AFB spores are highly resistant to disinfectants.

Lastly, pesticide exposure can severely impact bee health, leading to weakened or dead colonies. Advocating for responsible pesticide use in your community and planting bee-friendly flora can help mitigate these risks. Additionally, placing hives away from treated fields and notifying neighbors of your beekeeping can help protect your bees from accidental exposure.

By staying vigilant and proactive in managing these common problems, you can ensure the health and productivity of your bee colonies. Remember, successful beekeeping is about addressing issues as they arise and preventing them through sound management practices. This benefits your backyard homestead and supports the broader ecosystem by contributing to the health and diversity of local bee populations.

The Importance of Bees in Your Garden

Bees play a pivotal role in the health and productivity of your garden, acting as the linchpin in the pollination process vital for many plants' reproduction.

Pollination, the transfer of pollen from the male parts of a flower to the female parts, is necessary for fertilization and, subsequently, the production of fruits and seeds. Bees are among the most effective pollinators, not by chance but by nature. As they move from flower to flower in search of nectar, they inadvertently transfer pollen, facilitating the growth of many of the foods and flowers we enjoy.

The importance of bees in your garden extends beyond the mere act of pollination. Their activity helps increase the quality and quantity of your crops. Well-pollinated plants tend to produce larger, more uniform fruits and vegetables, which is a boon for any homesteader looking to maximize their garden's yield. Moreover, a diverse bee population encourages plant diversity, which can help make your garden more resilient to pests and diseases.

Incorporating beekeeping into your backyard homestead also contributes to the broader ecosystem. Like many other pollinators, bees are threatened by various environmental pressures, including habitat loss, pesticides, and climate change. By providing a haven for bees, you're enhancing your garden's productivity and contributing to the conservation of these essential creatures.

To make your garden inviting to bees, consider planting various flowering plants that bloom at different times throughout the year. This ensures a continuous food source for the bees, encouraging their presence in your garden. Additionally, providing water sources, avoiding pesticides, and allowing for natural areas within your garden can create a hospitable environment for bees.

Embracing beekeeping and understanding the symbiotic relationship between bees and gardens can transform your backyard homestead. It's a step towards sustainability, promoting a healthier ecosystem while reaping the tangible benefits of higher crop yields and a more vibrant garden. As we move forward, we'll explore how to get started with beekeeping, ensuring you have the knowledge and tools to integrate these vital pollinators into your homesteading journey successfully.

Chapter Summary

- Beekeeping begins with understanding bee behavior, which is crucial for safety and productivity. This focuses on the complex and organized nature of bees, including their social structure, roles, and communication methods.
- The queen bee's primary role is reproduction; worker bees perform tasks like foraging and maintaining the hive, and drones exist solely for mating.
- Bees communicate through pheromones and the "waggle dance" to share information about food sources and hive health.
- Defensive behaviors in bees include stinging to protect the hive, and beekeepers must approach with respect, using protective gear and proper handling techniques.
- Seasonal behaviors affect beekeeping practices, with bees being active in warmer months and focusing on survival in winter, influencing hive care across seasons.
- Challenges such as diseases, pests, and environmental stressors require beekeepers to be vigilant and responsive to maintain hive health.
- Setting up a hive involves selecting a location, choosing the type of hive, assembling it with care, and gently introducing bees, emphasizing creating a sustainable environment for the bees.

- Regular hive maintenance, understanding and addressing common problems like Varroa mites and hive beetles, and preparing for winter are essential for a healthy bee colony. These activities lead to successful honey harvesting and contribute to the ecosystem.

5

PRESERVING THE HARVEST

A rustic farmer's shack with an abundance of fresh fruits and vegetables in baskets.

Canning Basics

Canning is a time-honored method of preserving food from your backyard homestead, allowing you to enjoy the fruits of your labor throughout the year. This section will guide you through the basics of canning, ensuring you have the knowledge to safely and effectively preserve your harvest.

Understanding the two primary canning methods is crucial: water bath canning and pressure canning. Water bath canning suits high-acid foods such as fruits, tomatoes (with added acid), pickles, jellies, and jams. The acidity in these foods prevents the growth of bacteria, making the water bath method sufficient. On the other hand, low-acid foods like vegetables, meats, and poultry require pressure canning to reach the higher temperatures necessary to eliminate the risk of botulism.

Before you begin, it is essential to assemble the right equipment. You'll need a large pot with a lid and a rack for water bath canning to keep the jars off the bottom. Pressure canning requires a specialized pressure canner designed to reach higher temperatures than a regular pot. Regardless of the method, you'll also need canning jars with new lids and rings, a jar lifter, a funnel, and a bubble remover/headspace tool.

Preparing your produce is the next step. Start with fresh, high-quality fruits or vegetables. Wash them thoroughly and prepare them according to your recipe, whether peeling, chopping, or crushing. Pay close attention to the recipe's instructions on preparing and adding additional ingredients, such as sugar, salt, or vinegar, which can be crucial for preservation.

Filling your jars correctly is critical to successful canning. Use a funnel to pack your prepared food into the jars, leaving the appropriate headspace as indicated by your recipe. This space is necessary for the expansion of food as it heats and creates a vacuum seal as it cools. After filling, use a bubble remover tool to release any trapped air bubbles, then wipe the rims clean before placing the lids and screwing on the bands until they are fingertip tight.

Processing your jars is the final step. Place them in your canner with enough water to cover them completely, then bring the water to a boil for water bath canning or follow your pressure canner's instructions for that method. Processing times vary depending on the food and your elevation, so consult a reliable source for accurate times. Once processed, carefully remove the jars and let them cool undisturbed for 12 to 24 hours. You'll know your jars are sealed properly when the lids are concave and do not flex when pressed.

The last step in the process is labeling and storing your canned goods. Write the contents and the date on each jar, then store them in a cool, dark place. Properly canned foods can last up to a year, sometimes longer, though quality may diminish over time.

Canning is a rewarding way to preserve your harvest, providing homegrown goodness long after the growing season. You'll find it a valuable addition to your homesteading skills with a bit of practice.

Freezing and Drying

Mastering the arts of freezing and drying is akin to unlocking new levels of self-sufficiency and culinary creativity in the journey of transforming your backyard bounty into a pantry full of provisions. These preservation methods extend the shelf life of your harvest and ensure that summer flavors can be savored long after the season has passed.

Freezing is perhaps one of the most straightforward and

accessible methods of food preservation. It works by slowing down the activity of enzymes and preventing the growth of bacteria, yeasts, and molds that cause food spoilage and decay. Almost every home has a freezer, making this method particularly convenient.

To begin, select fresh, ripe produce at its peak quality. Wash and prepare the fruits or vegetables by peeling, chopping, or blanching as required. Blanching – briefly boiling and then plunging the produce into ice water – is critical for most vegetables. It halts enzyme activity that can cause flavor, color, and texture loss, even in frozen storage.

After preparing your produce:

1. Pack it into freezer-safe containers or bags, removing as much air as possible to prevent freezer burn.
2. Label each package with the date and contents.
3. Remember, while freezing preserves texture, flavor, and nutritional value, it's best to use frozen fruits and vegetables within 8 to 12 months for optimal quality.

Drying, one of the oldest food preservation techniques involves removing moisture from food to inhibit the growth of microorganisms and enzymes. When done correctly, dried foods are lightweight, space-saving, and can last for months or years.

There are several methods to dry foods: air drying, oven drying, and using a food dehydrator. Each method has its advantages and is suited to different types of food. Herbs and leafy greens, for instance, dry well in the gentle breeze of an airy, shaded spot. However, fruits, vegetables, and meats often require the consistent heat of an oven or dehydrator to remove moisture effectively.

Before drying, prepare your produce by washing, slicing, and sometimes pretreating to preserve color and nutritional content. Pretreatment can include blanching or dipping in solutions like ascorbic acid. Spread the prepared items in a single layer on drying racks or trays, ensuring good air circulation around each piece.

Once dried, store your foods in airtight containers in a cool, dark place. Check periodically for moisture or mold growth, which can occur if foods are not sufficiently dried.

Both freezing and drying preserve the fruits of your labor and provide a canvas for culinary experimentation. From smoothies and soups made from frozen produce to the complex flavors of dried fruits and vegetables rehydrated in innovative dishes, these methods allow the backyard homesteader to enjoy the harvest in many ways throughout the year.

As we continue to explore the spectrum of preservation techniques, the journey from garden to table evolves, revealing not just the practicality of these methods but the profound satisfaction of sustaining oneself from the yield of one's backyard.

Fermenting and Pickling

Fermenting and pickling are ancient methods that have preserved the bounty of gardens long before refrigerators and freezers became household staples. These techniques extend the shelf life of your harvest, enhance nutritional value, and introduce a delightful array of flavors to your table.

Fermentation is a metabolic process that produces chemical changes in organic substrates through the action of enzymes. In simpler terms, it's the transformation of your cucumbers into crunchy pickles or cabbage into tangy sauerkraut. This magic is primarily performed by lactobacilli, beneficial bacteria that thrive in an anaerobic (oxygen-free) environment. They feed on the natural sugars in food, producing lactic acid as a natural preservative. The beauty of fermentation lies in its simplicity and the minimal equipment required. With just a clean jar, some salt, water, and fresh produce, you can start fermenting. The key is to ensure that your vegetables are fully submerged under the brine to prevent mold growth, keeping the anaerobic process intact.

While similar to fermenting, pickling takes a slightly different route. It involves immersing fruits or vegetables in a solution of vinegar or brine. This acidic environment kills bacteria, preventing spoilage. Pickling can be quick, needing only a few hours, or a longer fermentation-like process. The variety of spices and herbs you can add to your pickling solution is vast, allowing for endless creativity. From classic dill pickles to exotic spiced peaches, the flavors you can achieve are limited only by your imagination.

Both fermenting and pickling do more than preserve food; they transform it. Fermented foods are known for their probiotic qualities, contributing to a healthy gut microbiome. Meanwhile, pickled foods acquire a unique taste that can elevate a meal from good to gourmet.

Remember to start small as you embark on your fermenting and pickling journey. Experiment with different recipes and quantities until you find what works best for you and your family. Whether it's the tangy crunch of sauerkraut on a homemade burger or the zesty zing of pickled radishes in a salad, these preserved delights are sure to add a new dimension to your meals.

By mastering these age-old techniques, you'll preserve your harvest, embrace a sustainable lifestyle, reduce food waste, and ensure that your pantry is stocked with nutritious, flavorful options year-round. So, let's roll up our sleeves and transform the fruits of our labor into fermented and pickled masterpieces that our ancestors would be proud of.

Making Jams and Jellies

Transforming your garden's bounty into delicious jams and jellies is a rewarding endeavor and a delightful way to preserve the season's flavors. This guide will help you through the process of making jams and jellies, ensuring you can enjoy the fruits of your labor long after the harvest has ended.

Making jams and jellies might seem daunting initially, but it's pretty straightforward once you grasp the basics. Jams are made from crushed or chopped fruits cooked with sugar, while jellies are made from the fruit's juice, sugar, and often pectin, resulting in a clear, firm product. Achieving the perfect set and flavor requires a balance of fruit, sugar, and acid.

The journey to delicious jam or jelly starts with high-quality fruit. Ideally, you should use ripe fruit from your garden, ensuring it has the perfect combination of natural sugars and pectin. Pectin is essential for helping your jam or jelly set, and while some fruits naturally have high levels of pectin, such as apples and citrus fruits, others may need the addition of commercial pectin.

For jams, wash your fruit thoroughly, remove any stems or pits, and chop it into small pieces. For jellies, you'll need to extract the juice by chopping the fruit, cooking it until soft with a bit of water, and then straining it through a jelly bag or cheesecloth.

Next, combine your prepared fruit or juice with sugar in a large, heavy-bottomed pot. The sugar sweetens your preserve and helps it set by drawing out water from the fruit. Add lemon juice or another acid to balance the sweetness and aid the setting process. If using commercial pectin, follow the packet instructions for when to add it to your mixture.

Bring your mixture to a boil over medium-high heat, stirring frequently to prevent sticking. Once it reaches a rolling boil and starts to thicken, test if your jam or jelly is ready using the "wrinkle test" by placing a small amount on a chilled plate. If it wrinkles when you push it with your finger, it's done.

To preserve your jam or jelly:

1. Process it in sterilized jars.
2. Fill your jars, leaving a quarter-inch headspace, then wipe the rims clean and seal them with lids and bands.
3. Process the jars in a boiling water bath for the recommended time based on your altitude and jar size.
4. Once processed, remove the jars and let them cool undisturbed for 12-24 hours. The lids should be

concave and not flex when pressed, indicating a proper seal.

Homemade jams and jellies make for a treat for your family and thoughtful gifts. Label your jars with the contents and the date, and store them in a cool, dark place. Properly canned, they can last for up to a year. Once opened, keep them refrigerated and enjoy them within a few weeks. By mastering the art of making jams and jellies, you'll preserve the flavors of your garden and create lasting memories and traditions. Whether spread on fresh bread or served as a sweet accompaniment to a cheese platter, your homemade preserves will surely delight.

Storing Vegetables and Fruits

After mastering the art of making jams and jellies, it's time to turn our attention to another crucial aspect of preserving the bounty of your backyard homestead: storing vegetables and fruits. This process ensures that your produce's freshness and nutritional value are maintained for as long as possible, allowing you to enjoy the fruits of your labor throughout the year.

The key to successful storage is understanding the specific needs of each type of produce. Different vegetables and fruits have varying temperature, humidity, and light exposure requirements. You can significantly extend your shelf life by creating the right environment for each type of produce.

A cool, dark, and moderately humid environment is ideal for most root vegetables, such as carrots, beets, and potatoes. These conditions mimic the natural underground habitat where these vegetables thrive. Storing them in a cellar, basement, or even a cool, dark cabinet can help preserve their freshness for several months. Removing any soil clinging to the vegetables is important, but avoid washing them until you're ready to use them, as moisture can promote decay.

Leafy greens, on the other hand, require a slightly different approach. These vegetables tend to wilt quickly if not stored properly. Wrapping them loosely in a damp cloth or paper towel and placing them in a plastic bag in the refrigerator can help maintain their moisture and crispness for a week or more.

Fruits generally prefer a cooler environment than vegetables. Apples, pears, and other tree fruits can be stored in a cool basement or garage where temperatures remain just above freezing. However, be mindful of ethylene gas, which many fruits emit as they ripen. This gas can accelerate the ripening process of nearby produce, so it's wise to store ethylene-producing fruits separately from those sensitive to the gas.

Berries and soft fruits present a unique challenge due to their delicate nature. These fruits are best consumed soon after harvest but can be stored in the refrigerator for a few days if necessary. To extend their shelf life, consider spreading them on a tray to avoid crushing and storing them in a single layer in a container.

In addition to these specific storage techniques, general principles apply to all produce. Always inspect your fruits and vegetables before storing them and remove any damaged or decaying items to prevent the spread of rot. Proper ventilation is also crucial to prevent the buildup of ethylene gas and moisture, which can lead to spoilage.

By employing these storage methods, you can enjoy the vibrant flavors and nutritional benefits of your garden's produce beyond the harvest season. Whether you're storing root vegetables in a cool basement, wrapping leafy greens in damp cloths, or carefully managing the storage of fruits, each technique plays a vital role in extending the life of your harvest.

Creating a Root Cellar

One of the most rewarding endeavors in backyard homesteading is the ability to preserve your harvest for the colder months. After exploring the various methods of storing vegetables and fruits, it becomes clear that creating a root cellar is an indispensable step for any serious gardener or homesteader. This traditional storage method not only extends the shelf life of your produce but also maintains its nutritional value, making it a cornerstone of self-sufficiency.

A root cellar is a natural underground storage area that leverages the earth's constant temperature to store fruits and vegetables. Its beauty lies in its simplicity and the minimal energy it requires to function. Unlike modern refrigeration, a root cellar uses the earth's natural coolness and humidity to preserve produce. This method is eco-friendly and cost-effective, making it an ideal choice for the environmentally conscious homesteader.

To create your root cellar, start by selecting an appropriate location. Ideally, this should be a spot where the ground naturally slopes away from the cellar entrance to prevent water from pooling around or entering the storage area. It's also crucial to consider the water table in your area; you want to ensure that your cellar is not prone to flooding during heavy rains.

The size of your root cellar will depend on your storage needs and the space available on your property. A small cellar might suffice for a family looking to store a modest harvest, while larger operations may require a more spacious design. Regardless of size, insulation is critical. Straw bales, earth mounds, or modern insulation materials can be used to maintain the cellar's temperature and humidity levels.

Ventilation is another critical aspect of root cellar design. Proper airflow prevents the buildup of ethylene gas, which can cause produce to spoil prematurely. A simple ventilation system with an intake and exhaust vent can help maintain the optimal environment for your stored goods.

When outfitting your root cellar's interior, simplicity and functionality should guide your choices. Shelves and bins made from wood or wire mesh materials allow for organized storage and adequate air circulation around the produce. It's also beneficial to group fruits and vegetables by their storage requirements; some produce emits more ethylene gas than others, and separating these can minimize spoilage.

Incorporating a root cellar into your backyard homestead is not only a nod to traditional food preservation methods but also a practical solution for extending your garden's bounty. With some planning and effort, you can create a sustainable storage space that keeps your harvest fresh and nutritious throughout the year. This endeavor enhances your self-sufficiency and deepens your connection to the land and the cycles of nature.

Chapter Summary

- Canning is a method to preserve food, with water bath canning for high-acid foods and pressure canning for low-acid foods.
- Essential canning equipment includes jars, lids, a canner, and tools like a jar lifter and funnel.
- Preparing produce involves washing and possibly adding ingredients like sugar or vinegar for preservation.
- Proper jar filling and sealing are crucial, with headspace for expansion and airtight sealing to prevent spoilage.
- Process jars in a canner, with processing times varying by food type and elevation.
- Label and store canned goods in a cool, dark place for up to a year.
- Freezing and drying are other preservation methods, with freezing halting enzyme activity and drying removing moisture to prevent microorganism growth.
- Fermenting and pickling transform food, extending shelf life and enhancing flavor. Fermenting relies on bacteria, and pickling uses vinegar or brine.

6

RENEWABLE ENERGY ON THE HOMESTEAD

Vibrant sunset colors over a farm with wind turbines.

Solar Power Basics

Harnessing the sun's power has become an increasingly popular and practical way to generate electricity, especially for those looking to reduce their carbon footprint and achieve a more sustainable lifestyle on their backyard homestead.

Solar power, with its promise of clean, renewable energy, offers a beacon of hope and independence for homesteaders. In this section, we'll delve into the basics of solar power, covering how it works, the types of solar systems available, and some considerations for installation and maintenance.

At its core, solar power converts sunlight into electricity using photovoltaic (PV) panels. These panels are made of semiconductor materials, such as silicon, which absorb sunlight and release electrons, generating an electric current. This process, known as the photovoltaic effect, is the foundation of solar power technology.

Two primary types of solar power systems for the backyard homestead are grid-tied and off-grid. Grid-tied systems are connected to the local utility grid, allowing homeowners to feed excess electricity back into the grid through net metering. This can offset electricity costs and generate income. On the other hand, off-grid systems are entirely independent of the utility grid, relying on batteries to store the electricity generated by the solar panels for use when the sun isn't shining. Off-grid systems are ideal for remote locations where connecting to the grid is impractical or too expensive.

When considering solar power for your homestead, assessing your energy needs is essential. This involves calculating your household's average energy consumption and determining the size and number of solar panels required to meet this demand. Factors such as the orientation and angle of your roof, local climate conditions, and potential shading from trees or buildings can all impact the efficiency of your solar power system.

Solar panel installation typically requires professional

help, although DIY kits are available for those with the necessary skills and confidence. Ensuring your installation complies with local building codes and regulations, including obtaining permits and having the system inspected upon completion, is crucial.

Maintenance of solar power systems is relatively minimal. It primarily involves keeping the panels clean and free of debris to ensure maximum efficiency. Regular checks to ensure all components are functioning correctly can help extend the life of your system.

Incorporating solar power into your backyard homestead can provide numerous benefits, including reducing your reliance on fossil fuels, lowering your electricity bills, and contributing to a healthier planet. With technological advancements and increasing affordability, solar power has become an accessible and viable option for homesteaders embracing renewable energy.

Wind Energy Fundamentals

Harnessing the power of the wind is an ancient practice, refined over centuries into a sophisticated method of generating renewable energy. For the modern backyard homesteader, wind energy presents an invaluable opportunity to complement solar power, ensuring a more consistent and diversified approach to self-sufficiency in energy production.

Wind energy operates on a simple principle: converting kinetic energy from wind into mechanical power or electricity. This is achieved through a wind turbine, which captures the wind's force using blades connected to a rotor. The rotor then spins a generator to create electricity. For homesteaders, small-scale wind turbines offer a feasible and efficient method to generate power, especially in favorable wind conditions.

Before considering installing a wind turbine, it's essential to understand the fundamentals of wind energy, including assessing your local wind resources. Wind speed and consistency vary greatly by location, influenced by local topography and obstacles such as buildings or trees. An ideal site for a wind turbine is typically an open, exposed area with high average wind speeds. Tools and resources are available to help homesteaders evaluate their wind resource potential, including wind maps and anemometers for measuring local wind speeds.

The size and type of wind turbine suitable for a homestead depend on the energy needs and the wind resource assessment. Small wind turbines can range from under 100 watts, suitable for charging batteries and powering small appliances, to systems capable of generating several kilowatts, enough to power an entire home. The height of the turbine's tower also plays a critical role in performance, as wind speeds increase with elevation above ground level.

Installing a wind turbine requires careful planning and consideration of local zoning laws, permits, and potential impacts on neighbors and the environment. It's also important to consider integrating wind energy with other renewable energy sources, such as solar panels, to create a hybrid system that can provide more consistent power under varying weather conditions.

Maintenance is another critical aspect of wind energy on the homestead. While modern wind turbines are designed for durability and long-term use, regular inspections and maintenance are necessary to ensure optimal performance and prevent potential failures. This includes checking the turbine's blades, bearings, and electrical connections for wear and damage.

In conclusion, wind energy offers a promising avenue for backyard homesteaders to achieve energy independence and sustainability. By understanding the fundamentals of wind energy, assessing local wind resources, and carefully planning the installation and maintenance of a wind turbine, homesteaders can harness the power of the wind to complement their renewable energy portfolio. This approach contributes to a more resilient and self-sufficient homestead and supports broader environmental sustainability goals by reducing reliance on fossil fuels and lowering carbon emissions.

Rainwater Harvesting

The sky above us is an invaluable resource that often goes overlooked. Not for solar power, which certainly has its place, but for the life-giving rain it provides. Rainwater harvesting is not just an ancient practice rekindled for modern times; it's a practical, sustainable solution for water needs that aligns perfectly with the ethos of renewable energy.

Rainwater harvesting involves collecting and storing rainwater from rooftops, greenhouses, or other surfaces to be used later for irrigation, livestock, or even household needs after proper treatment. This method is a cornerstone of self-sufficiency on the homestead, reducing dependence on municipal water supplies and minimizing the ecological footprint of your homestead.

The beauty of rainwater harvesting lies in its simplicity

and the variety of methods available for implementation, ranging from basic rain barrels to more sophisticated systems with cisterns, filters, and pumps. The system choice depends on your water needs, the space available, and your budget.

Starting with the basics, a rain barrel can be easily connected to a downspout from your roof, capturing water that would otherwise be lost to runoff. This water can then be used to water your garden, reducing your water bill and providing your plants with chlorine-free water that they will thrive on. For those looking to take a step further, incorporating first-flush diverters and filters can improve the quality of the water collected, making it suitable for a broader range of uses.

Installing a large cistern can provide a substantial water reserve for the more ambitious. These systems can be designed to supply water for all your irrigation needs and, with proper filtration and purification, can even provide potable water for your household. The initial investment may be higher, but the long-term savings and resilience it adds to your homestead are invaluable.

Beyond the practical benefits, rainwater harvesting contributes to managing stormwater runoff, reducing erosion and the burden on local water treatment facilities. It's a way to directly engage with the natural water cycle, fostering a deeper connection with the environment and promoting sustainable living practices.

Implementing a rainwater harvesting system on your homestead is not just about saving money or being eco-friendly; it's a step towards self-reliance and resilience. It complements other renewable energy initiatives, such as wind and solar power, creating a holistic approach to sustainable living. With careful planning and consideration of local regulations, rainwater harvesting can be a rewarding addition to your backyard homestead, ensuring you make the most of every drop of rain falling from the sky.

Geothermal Options

Harnessing the Earth's natural heat through geothermal options presents an intriguing and increasingly accessible avenue for energy self-sufficiency on the backyard homestead. Geothermal energy, derived from the Earth's internal heat, offers a stable and continuous power source, distinguishing it from other renewable resources that may fluctuate with weather conditions.

At the core of geothermal energy utilization for the homesteader is the geothermal heat pump system, which exploits the ground's constant temperature beneath our feet. Even just a few feet below the surface, the Earth maintains a nearly constant temperature, ranging from 45°F (7°C) to 75°F (24°C), depending on the location. This consistency can be leveraged to both heat and cool homes and outbuildings in an incredibly efficient manner.

The basic mechanism involves circulating a fluid, typically water or a water-antifreeze mix, through a loop of underground pipes. During the winter, this fluid absorbs the Earth's natural warmth and carries it into the home, where a heat pump extracts and distributes the heat. In the summer, the process reverses, extracting heat from the building and dispersing it into the ground, thus cooling the interior.

Implementing a geothermal system on a homestead requires an initial investment and some land for the underground loop system. However, the long-term benefits can be substantial. These systems are known for their longevity, low maintenance, and the ability to reduce heating and cooling costs by up to 70%. Moreover, they significantly decrease a homestead's carbon footprint, aligning well with the principles of sustainable living.

For those considering geothermal options, conducting a thorough site assessment is essential. Factors such as soil composition, land area, and local climate will influence the system's design and efficiency. Professional installation is recommended, as the setup requires specialized knowledge and equipment. Additionally, some regions offer incentives or rebates for geothermal systems, making it a financially viable option for many.

In embracing geothermal energy, homesteaders tap into a renewable and efficient power source and contribute to a more sustainable and resilient energy system. This approach aligns seamlessly with the broader goals of homesteading, which emphasize harmony with nature, self-sufficiency, and reduced reliance on external resources.

As we transition from exploring the potential of geothermal energy, it becomes clear that the journey towards a sustainable homestead continues with the adoption of renewable energy sources. The next step involves a holistic approach to energy use, focusing on conservation techniques that ensure the efficient utilization of these renewable resources, thereby maximizing the benefits and minimizing the environmental impact.

Energy Conservation Techniques

Understanding and implementing energy conservation techniques is as crucial as harnessing renewable energy sources in the journey toward a sustainable and self-sufficient homestead. This section delves into practical strategies to significantly reduce energy consumption, lower utility bills, and minimize environmental impact. By adopting these methods, homesteaders can ensure a more efficient use of the renewable energy systems they have in place, such as those discussed in the context of geothermal options.

One of the foundational steps in energy conservation is conducting an energy audit of your homestead. This process involves assessing where and how energy is used and identifying areas where improvements can be made. Simple changes, such as sealing leaks around doors and windows, adding insulation, and upgrading to energy-efficient appliances, can profoundly impact reducing energy waste.

Lighting is another area where significant savings can be achieved. Switching to LED bulbs, which use at least 75% less energy and last 25 times longer than incandescent lighting, can dramatically decrease energy consumption. Additionally, maximizing natural light during the day can reduce the need for artificial lighting, further conserving energy.

Water heating is a significant energy expense in many homes. To conserve energy, consider lowering the water heater's temperature setting, insulating the water heater tank and the first six feet of hot and cold water pipes, and using water-saving fixtures to reduce hot water usage. Solar water heaters can effectively reduce reliance on traditional energy sources for those looking to invest in renewable energy.

Appliances and electronics also contribute significantly to a household's energy footprint. Using energy-efficient appliances, unplugging devices when not in use, and employing smart power strips can help manage and reduce energy consumption. When purchasing new appliances, look for the Energy Star label, which indicates the product meets energy efficiency guidelines set by the U.S. Environmental Protection Agency.

Heating and cooling systems are among the largest energy consumers in a home. Regular maintenance of these systems and smart thermostat use can optimize their efficiency. Using fans instead of air conditioning can provide comfort at a fraction of the energy cost during warmer months. Strategies such as layering clothing, using thermal curtains, and ensuring proper insulation can keep the home warm without excessive heating in cooler months.

Lastly, embracing a lifestyle that prioritizes energy conservation can lead to innovative solutions and habits that further reduce energy use. Simple practices like cooking with a pressure cooker or solar oven, drying clothes on a line, and choosing manual tools over electric ones for gardening and yard work conserve energy and enhance the homesteading experience.

By integrating these energy conservation techniques, homesteaders can make significant strides toward achieving a more sustainable and energy-efficient lifestyle. These practices complement the existing renewable energy systems and pave the way for a more resilient and self-sufficient homestead.

Chapter Summary

- Solar power converts sunlight into electricity using photovoltaic (PV) panels, offering a clean, renewable energy source for homesteaders with grid-tied and off-grid options.
- Assessing energy needs, roof orientation, local climate, and potential shading is crucial for efficient solar power system installation, which may require professional help and adherence to local regulations.
- Wind energy, generated through small-scale turbines, complements solar power for a diversified renewable energy approach, requiring site assessment for wind resource potential.
- Rainwater harvesting, a sustainable method for water needs, involves collecting rain from surfaces for later use, with systems ranging from simple barrels to sophisticated cisterns.
- Geothermal energy, utilizing the Earth's constant underground temperature, provides efficient heating and cooling through a geothermal heat pump system. It requires an initial investment but offers long-term benefits.
- Energy conservation techniques, including conducting energy audits, using LED bulbs, and optimizing heating and cooling systems, enhance the efficiency of renewable energy systems and reduce environmental impact.

- Integrating renewable energy into the homestead involves careful planning. Starting with small projects and potentially expanding, consider solar panels, wind turbines, and micro-hydro power based on individual needs and site conditions.
- Community engagement and shared knowledge among homesteaders are valuable tools for navigating the complexities of renewable energy integration and offering support and innovative solutions for sustainable living.

7

WATER MANAGEMENT

A modern water tank nestled among lush greenery in a garden.

Irrigation Systems for the Homestead

In backyard homesteading, mastering the art of water management is akin to unlocking one of nature's most vital secrets. Implementing an efficient irrigation system is a cornerstone for sustainable agriculture among the myriad techniques at the homesteader's disposal. This section delves into the various irrigation systems that can be adapted to a homestead's unique needs and constraints, ensuring that every drop of water is utilized to its fullest potential.

At the heart of the homestead, irrigation delivers water that mimics the natural hydration plants receive in their native habitats. This involves considering the timing, quantity, and method of water delivery to optimize plant health and minimize waste. While effective for small gardens, traditional methods, such as hand watering with a hose or watering can, quickly become impractical as the homestead scale expands. This is where more sophisticated systems come into play.

Drip irrigation emerges as a frontrunner for its precision and efficiency. Delivering water directly to the base of each plant through a network of tubing, emitters, and connectors minimizes evaporation and runoff, making it ideal for arid climates and water-conservation areas. The system can be customized to suit the layout of any garden. A timer can automate the watering process, saving time and ensuring consistent moisture levels.

Another system worth considering is soaker hoses. These porous hoses allow water to seep slowly along their length, providing a gentle, even watering perfect for raised beds and row crops. They are simpler to install than drip systems and can be covered with mulch to reduce water loss through evaporation further.

Sprinkler systems might be the answer for homesteaders with larger plots or various crops. While water usage is less efficient than drip and soaker hose systems, they can cover large areas quickly and are adjustable to meet different watering needs. However, they are best used in the early morning or late evening to reduce water loss to evaporation during the day's heat.

Rainwater harvesting is another critical component of a homestead's irrigation strategy. By collecting runoff from roofs and storing it in barrels or tanks, homesteaders can create a sustainable water source that reduces dependence on municipal systems and wells. This harvested rainwater can then be integrated into the irrigation system, providing a free, eco-friendly solution to water the garden.

Lastly, creating swales or rain gardens can enhance the efficiency of any irrigation system. These landscape features are designed to capture and hold rainwater, allowing it to percolate slowly into the soil, recharging groundwater, and providing moisture to plants over time. This method conserves water, reduces erosion, and improves soil health.

In conclusion, selecting the right irrigation system for a homestead is a multifaceted decision that depends on the local climate, soil type, water availability, and the specific needs of the crops being grown. By combining one or more of these systems with sustainable practices like rainwater harvesting and creating water-conserving landscape features, homesteaders can ensure their gardens thrive while stewarding the precious water resource.

Greywater and Its Uses

One of the most innovative and sustainable practices in backyard homesteading is the utilization of greywater, which is gently used water from bathroom sinks, showers, tubs, and washing machines. This resource can be crucial in efficiently managing a homestead's water needs. Greywater, distinct from fresh water and black water (sewage), is less polluted than black water and can be reused for various purposes without extensive treatment. However, it's essential to handle greywater carefully due to its potential content of dirt, food, grease, hair, and household cleaning products to avoid health risks and environmental harm.

The benefits of reusing greywater are significant. It can drastically reduce the demand on the main water supply, conserving fresh water for drinking and cooking, and lead to substantial savings on water bills. Additionally, using greywater for irrigation can enhance soil fertility by adding nutrients and promoting plant growth.

Setting up a greywater system requires thoughtful planning and compliance with local regulations, which vary considerably. Simple systems might directly divert greywater to gardens or orchards using gravity, while more complex setups could include filters, pumps, and surge tanks for temporary storage. Regardless of the system's complexity, using biodegradable, non-toxic soaps and detergents is crucial to avoid harming plants and soil.

To safely use greywater, avoid contact with edible plant parts and focus on watering the roots. Rotating greywater use with fresh water helps prevent the soil's build-up of salts or potential contaminants. Regular monitoring of soil pH and salinity is also beneficial for adjusting greywater usage and maintaining soil health.

Incorporating greywater into a backyard homestead's water management strategy is an intelligent step toward sustainability. By understanding its uses, benefits, and necessary precautions, homesteaders can effectively leverage this resource, contributing to a more self-sufficient and environmentally friendly living space. Exploring additional water features and conservation methods will further enhance the ability to create resilient and productive homesteads.

Creating Ponds and Water Features

In backyard homesteading, the addition of ponds and water features not only enhances the aesthetic appeal of your space but also plays a crucial role in sustainable water management. This section delves into the practical steps and considerations for creating these water elements, ensuring they contribute positively to your homestead's ecosystem.

Creating a pond or water feature begins with careful planning. First, consider the location. If you plan to include aquatic plants, they should be placed in an area with adequate sunlight. However, too much direct sunlight can lead to excessive algae growth, so a balance is necessary. Additionally, think about the proximity to your home and garden. A pond near your garden can serve as a source of irrigation water, while one closer to your home can provide a tranquil view and attract wildlife.

The size and depth of your pond are also important considerations. A deeper pond can support a wider variety of aquatic life and is less prone to rapid temperature fluctuations, which can stress fish and plants. On the other hand, a shallow pond is easier to construct and maintain. The size depends mainly on your available space and the pond's purpose. Whether for keeping fish, attracting wildlife, or simply for the beauty of water lilies blooming, your goals will dictate the design.

When it comes to construction, there are several methods

to choose from. Preformed pond liners are popular for small to medium ponds, offering ease of installation and a predetermined shape. For larger or custom-designed ponds, flexible liners allow for more creativity in shape and depth but require more skill to install correctly. Regardless of the type, ensuring a secure and leak-proof liner is paramount to the success of your pond.

Water circulation is another critical aspect. A good filtration system and a pump will keep the water moving and oxygenated, creating a healthier environment for plants and fish. Additionally, incorporating a waterfall or fountain adds a captivating visual and auditory element and aids in aeration.

Finally, introducing plants and fish can transform your pond from a simple water feature into a thriving ecosystem. Aquatic plants play a vital role in oxygenating the water and providing habitat for wildlife. When selecting fish, consider species well-suited to your climate and the size of your pond. They can help control mosquito larvae and algae, contributing to the overall health of your pond.

In conclusion, creating ponds and water features in your backyard homestead requires thoughtful planning and execution. By considering location, size, construction method, water circulation, and the introduction of plants and fish, you can create a sustainable and beautiful water element that enhances your homestead's ecosystem. It will serve as a water source for irrigation and provide a habitat for wildlife, contribute to biodiversity, and offer a serene spot for relaxation and enjoyment.

Water Purification and Filtration

Eensuring the purity and quality of your water sources is as crucial as any other aspect of self-sufficiency. After exploring the creation of ponds and water features, it's natural to delve into the methods and importance of water purification and filtration. This process guarantees a healthier environment for your homestead and secures a sustainable water source for both household and agricultural needs.

Water purification and filtration can be approached through various methods, each tailored to your homestead's specific needs and resources. The simplest form of filtration is the construction of a biofilter, which utilizes natural materials such as gravel, sand, and charcoal to remove impurities from water. This method is particularly effective for smaller water features or as a preliminary step in a more complex purification system.

More advanced purification methods may be necessary for those relying on rainwater collection or natural water bodies as their primary water source. Boiling is the most straightforward technique to eliminate pathogens, but it's not always practical for large volumes of water. Solar water disinfection, or SODIS, offers a sustainable alternative, using the sun's ultraviolet rays to purify water in transparent containers over time. Though effective, this method requires ample sunlight and time, making it less reliable in certain climates or during emergencies.

Chemical purification, using chlorine or iodine, is another option for homesteaders. While effective in killing bacteria and viruses, these chemicals must be used cautiously, as they can pose health risks if not properly dosed. It's essential to follow guidelines carefully and consider using a secondary filtration method to remove residual chemicals before consumption.

For those seeking a more hands-off approach, commercially available water filters and purifiers offer convenience and efficiency. These systems range from simple pitcher filters to complex whole-house systems that meet various needs and budgets. When selecting a commercial system, consider factors such as the volume of water it can process, the specific contaminants it targets, and the maintenance it requires.

Regardless of the chosen method, regular water source testing is paramount. This ensures that your purification and filtration efforts are practical and that your water remains safe for consumption and use around the homestead. Water testing kits are readily available and provide a simple way to monitor the quality of your water over time.

In conclusion, integrating effective water purification and filtration systems into your backyard homestead is essential for maintaining a healthy, sustainable lifestyle. By understanding the options available and tailoring them to your specific needs, you can ensure a reliable supply of clean water for your family and your homestead's various needs. As we move forward, the principles of managing water runoff will further enhance our ability to sustainably manage our precious water resources, highlighting the interconnectedness of all water management aspects in backyard homesteading.

Managing Water Runoff

After exploring the intricacies of water purification and filtration, it's crucial to address another vital aspect of water stewardship: managing runoff. This section delves into practical strategies for controlling and utilizing runoff water, ensuring that every drop serves a purpose in your homestead.

Water runoff can lead to soil erosion, water wastage, and potential flooding if not appropriately managed. However, with thoughtful planning and implementation, runoff can be transformed from a potential problem into a valuable asset for your garden and homestead.

One effective method for managing water runoff is the creation of rain gardens. Rain gardens are strategically placed where runoff accumulates, acting as natural filtration systems. By planting native shrubs, perennials, and grasses, you can enhance your landscape's beauty while reducing runoff and improving water quality. These gardens absorb and filter runoff, preventing pollutants from reaching water bodies and recharging the groundwater.

Another technique involves the installation of rain barrels or cisterns to capture rainwater from rooftops. This collected water can later be used for irrigation, reducing your reliance on municipal water supplies and lowering your water bills. It's a simple yet effective way to harness runoff, turning a potential excess into a valuable resource for watering plants.

Swales and berms offer additional solutions for managing runoff. Swales, shallow trenches that follow the contour of the landscape, capture runoff and allow it to slowly infiltrate into the soil, hydrating plants along its path. Berms, raised soil areas, can be used with swales to direct water flow away from structures and toward more beneficial areas.

Another strategy to consider is incorporating permeable paving into walkways and driveways. Permeable materials allow water to seep through, reducing runoff and replenishing groundwater. This approach not only aids in water management but also enhances the aesthetic appeal of your homestead.

Finally, mulching plays a crucial role in managing water runoff. Applying a generous layer of organic mulch around plants and over garden beds helps retain soil moisture, reduces evaporation, and prevents soil erosion. Mulch acts as a sponge, absorbing water and slowly releasing it into the soil, making it available for plant roots.

By implementing these strategies, you can effectively manage water runoff on your homestead, turning potential challenges into opportunities for sustainability and resilience. As we transition to the next section, we'll explore how to further optimize water usage by conserving water in the garden, ensuring that our homesteading practices are as efficient and environmentally friendly as possible.

Conserving Water in the Garden

Conserving water in the garden is not just a practice but a necessity in the pursuit of a sustainable and efficient backyard homestead. With the growing awareness of water scarcity and the importance of resource management, gardeners are turning towards innovative and traditional methods to ensure their gardens thrive without wasting precious water. This section delves into practical strategies that can be seamlessly integrated into your gardening routine, ensuring your green space is both lush and environmentally conscious.

Mulching is a gardener's best friend when it comes to water conservation. By applying a generous layer of organic mulch around your plants, you suppress weeds and significantly reduce water evaporation from the soil. Mulch acts as an insulating layer, keeping the soil cool and moist and encouraging root growth and water retention. Organic mulches, such as straw, wood chips, or leaf litter, break down over time and enrich the soil with nutrients.

Another effective strategy is rainwater harvesting. By collecting rainwater from rooftops and storing it in barrels or tanks, you have a ready supply of water that can be used during dry spells. This reduces your reliance on municipal water supplies and ensures your plants benefit from chemical-free water. Simple systems can be set up to direct rainwater from downspouts into storage containers, making this a practical and eco-friendly solution for water conservation.

Choosing the right plants is crucial for a water-efficient garden. Opt for native or drought-tolerant species that are well-adapted to your local climate and soil conditions. These plants require less water and are more resistant to pests and diseases, reducing the need for frequent watering and chemical interventions. Creating a garden that harmonizes with the local ecosystem conserves water and supports biodiversity.

Drip irrigation systems represent a significant advancement in efficient water use. Drip irrigation minimizes waste and ensures that water goes precisely where it's needed by delivering water directly to the base of each plant. This method effectively reduces evaporation and runoff, making it ideal for vegetable gardens, flower beds, and even potted plants. With the addition of a timer, the system can be automated, saving time and further optimizing water use.

Finally, understanding your garden's watering needs can lead to significant water savings. Overwatering is a common issue that wastes water and harms plant health. By learning to recognize the signs of water stress in plants and adjusting your watering schedule accordingly, you can ensure your garden receives just the right amount of water. Early morning or late evening watering reduces evaporation, and using a rain gauge can help you keep track of natural precipitation, adjusting your watering practices accordingly.

Incorporating these water conservation strategies into your gardening practices contributes to a more sustainable homestead and fosters a deeper connection with the natural world. By being mindful of our water use, we can create thriving gardens that are resilient, productive, and in harmony with the environment.

Chapter Summary

- Efficient water management is crucial for backyard homesteading, emphasizing sustainability and self-sufficiency.
- Greywater, wastewater from baths, sinks, and washing machines (excluding toilet waste), can be repurposed for irrigation and other non-potable uses.
- Using biodegradable and plant-friendly detergents is essential for greywater recycling to protect the

homestead's ecosystem.
- Greywater systems can range from simple setups, like rerouting washing machine water to plants, to more complex systems involving filtration for broader use.
- Local regulations on greywater use vary, and it's important to ensure compliance and consider the suitability of plants for greywater irrigation.
- Creating ponds and water features enhances the aesthetic and sustainability of a homestead, supports a variety of aquatic life, and provides irrigation sources.
- Water purification and filtration methods, including biofilters, boiling, solar disinfection, and commercial systems, are vital for maintaining water quality for household and agricultural use.
- Managing water runoff through rain gardens, rain barrels, swales, berms, permeable paving, and mulching helps prevent soil erosion and water wastage and supports water conservation in gardening.

8

LIVESTOCK MANAGEMENT

A man standing in a field surrounded by sheep under a cloudy sky.

Selecting Livestock for Your Homestead

Selecting livestock for your backyard homestead is an exciting and pivotal decision. It marks the beginning of a closer relationship with your food sources and a step towards sustainable living. However, it's not a decision to be taken lightly. The right choice can lead to a rewarding homesteading experience, while the wrong one can cause unnecessary challenges.

Firstly, consider the size of your land. Space is a premium resource in backyard homesteading, and each animal you introduce requires a portion of it, not just for roaming but for shelter, feeding areas, and waste management. For instance, chickens need less space than goats or sheep, making them a popular choice for smaller homesteads. On the other hand, if you have more space, you might consider larger livestock like cows or pigs.

Next, think about the purpose of raising livestock. Are you looking for animals that will provide meat, milk, eggs, or a combination of these? Chickens can offer both meat and eggs, making them an efficient choice for many homesteaders. Goats and cows can provide milk, with the former requiring less space and potentially more manageable for beginners. If meat production is your primary goal, consider the types of meat you and your family prefer and select species and breeds accordingly.

Another critical factor is the care and time you can dedicate to your livestock. All animals require daily attention, but some need more than others. Chickens, for example, are relatively low maintenance, needing regular feeding, egg collection, and coop cleaning. In contrast, dairy animals like goats and cows demand a more significant time investment due to milking routines, which can be twice daily.

Your decision should also be influenced by the local

climate and the livestock's adaptability to your environment. Some animals fare better in colder climates, while others thrive in warmer conditions. Researching breeds that can comfortably adapt to your local weather patterns will ensure their health and productivity.

Lastly, consider the legalities and regulations in your area regarding keeping livestock. Zoning laws can vary significantly, with specific areas allowing a wide range of animals while others may have strict restrictions. It's essential to be informed and compliant to avoid any legal issues down the line.

Selecting suitable livestock is a foundational step in creating a thriving backyard homestead. By carefully considering your space, the purpose of raising animals, the time you can commit, the adaptability of different livestock to your climate, and local regulations, you can make informed decisions that align with your homesteading goals and lifestyle. With the right choices, the animals you bring into your homestead will contribute to your self-sufficiency and bring joy and fulfillment to your daily life.

As we move forward, our next focus will be understanding your chosen livestock's nutritional needs and feeding strategies, ensuring their health, productivity, and well-being in your care.

Feeding and Nutrition

After selecting the right livestock for your homestead, it is crucial to dive into the essentials of feeding and nutrition to ensure their health, productivity, and well-being. This section provides a comprehensive guide to understanding and implementing a balanced diet for your animals, tailored to their specific needs and the resources available on your homestead.

Firstly, it's essential to recognize that each type of livestock has unique dietary requirements. Chickens, for example, thrive on a diet rich in grains, vegetables, and protein, often found in commercial poultry feed supplemented with kitchen scraps and free-range insects. On the other hand, ruminants like goats and sheep require a diet high in fibrous plants like hay, with additional grains or commercial feed to meet their energy needs, especially during pregnancy or lactation.

Quality and quantity of feed play pivotal roles in the health and productivity of your animals. Overfeeding can lead to obesity and health issues while underfeeding can result in malnutrition and decreased productivity. Calculating the correct portions based on the animal's weight, age, and productivity level is essential, and adjusting as necessary to maintain optimal health.

Water, often overlooked, is a critical component of livestock nutrition. Clean, fresh water must always be available to prevent dehydration and support overall health. The amount of water needed can vary significantly depending on the species, the weather, and the animal's diet and stage of life.

Understanding the nutritional value of different forages is critical for those looking to sustain their livestock on pasture. Rotational grazing practices can help maintain the health of the pasture and ensure that animals have access to the most nutritious plants. Supplementing with hay, silage, or commercial feed may be necessary during winter or dry periods when pasture quality declines.

Homesteaders should also know the nutritional supplements and minerals their livestock requires. These can include salt blocks, calcium for laying hens, or mineral mixes for goats and sheep. Deficiencies in these areas can lead to health issues, so monitoring and supplementation according to the animals' needs are crucial.

Lastly, it's important to recognize signs of nutritional deficiencies or imbalances in your livestock, such as poor coat quality, weight loss, reduced productivity, or health issues. Regular observation and, if necessary, consultation with a veterinarian can help you adjust your feeding strategies to address any problems.

By understanding and implementing these feeding and nutrition principles, you can ensure the health and productivity of your livestock, contributing to the sustainability and success of your backyard homestead.

Health Care and Wellness

Ensuring the health and wellness of your livestock in backyard homesteading is as crucial as providing them with proper nutrition. This involves essential practices, preventive measures, and treatments that support effective livestock management, helping your animals survive and thrive.

Regular health assessments are vital in maintaining a healthy flock or herd, allowing you to catch potential health issues before they escalate. Observing your animals daily helps identify signs of distress, changes in eating habits, abnormal discharge, or sudden weight loss, with each species having specific health indicators.

Preventive care through vaccination and deworming is pivotal in livestock health. It protects against common diseases and prevents parasitic infestations that can lead to malnutrition, disease, and even death. Consulting with a local veterinarian to establish a vaccination schedule and adhering to a judicious deworming schedule are essential steps. It's also important to note that overusing dewormers can lead to resistance, emphasizing the need for veterinary advice.

The role of nutrition in health cannot be overstated, with nutritional deficiencies or imbalances leading to various health issues, from weakened immune systems to reproductive problems. Ensuring your livestock's diet meets their specific nutritional requirements is crucial.

Introducing new animals to your homestead poses a risk of introducing diseases to your existing livestock, making quarantine practices essential. A quarantine period of at least 30 days allows for observation of new animals for any signs of illness before integration.

Despite the best preventive measures, emergencies can happen, underlining the importance of having a first aid kit for your livestock and knowing the basics of animal first aid. This includes having items like wound disinfectant, bandages, and tools for hoof care and knowing when to seek veterinary help. Effective health management also includes meticulous record-keeping, tracking vaccinations, deworming, illnesses, treatments, and other health-related events, which aids in managing your livestock's current health and making future management decisions.

In conclusion, the well-being of your livestock reflects the care and attention you provide. By implementing routine health checks, adhering to a preventive care schedule, and being prepared for emergencies, you can ensure the health and wellness of your backyard homestead's animals. As you move forward, remember that healthy, well-cared-for animals are the foundation of a successful breeding program.

Breeding and Population Management

In backyard homesteading, the sustainability and productivity of your homestead significantly depend on how you manage the breeding and population of your livestock. This involves a deep understanding of breeding practices, genetic diversity, and population control to maintain a healthy and thriving livestock population. Each livestock species has its specific breeding cycle, which is crucial for homesteaders to grasp.

For example, chickens lay eggs almost daily that can be incubated to hatch new chicks, whereas goats and sheep typically breed in the fall, resulting in spring births. Recognizing these cycles is essential for planned breeding, ensuring you have the necessary resources and space for new additions.

Selective breeding is another critical aspect, allowing homesteaders to enhance the quality of their livestock by choosing animals with desirable traits such as good temperament, high productivity, and hardiness for breeding. However, it's vital to keep genetic diversity in mind to avoid inbreeding, which can lead to health issues and reduced vitality.

Managing the population effectively is also crucial. This involves decisions on which animals to keep, sell, or process for meat based on the homestead's capacity and the family's needs. This helps keep the population sustainable, ensuring adequate resources for each animal.

Accurate and detailed record-keeping plays an invaluable role in breeding and population management. Recording each animal's birth date, parentage, health history, breeding dates, and other relevant details is crucial for making informed decisions about breeding practices and managing the livestock's overall health and productivity.

Ethical considerations are central to breeding and population management, emphasizing the importance of treating all animals with respect and care. This includes providing proper nutrition, shelter, and medical care and making humane decisions about culling or processing animals for meat.

Effective breeding and population management form the backbone of a thriving backyard homestead. You can ensure a healthy, productive, and sustainable livestock population by understanding breeding cycles, engaging in selective breeding, managing population levels, maintaining detailed records, and adhering to ethical standards. This contributes to the self-sufficiency of your homestead and the welfare of the animals in your care.

Fencing and Housing

Ensuring the well-being and safety of your livestock is a multifaceted task that requires a deep understanding of their dietary and health needs, as well as providing them with appropriate fencing and housing. These aspects are critical for

How to Build the Perfect Backyard Homestead

their protection, comfort, and maintaining order and cleanliness within your homestead.

Fencing serves as the initial safety barrier, fulfilling several roles: it secures your animals within your property, shields them from predators, and manages their grazing patterns to avoid the overuse of any particular area. The fencing required varies with the type of livestock; for instance, poultry needs chicken wire or poultry netting, whereas larger animals like goats or sheep might require sturdier materials such as wood or metal.

Electric fencing is another versatile option that can deter predators and prevent escapes, though it's crucial to introduce your animals to it cautiously to prevent stress and injury. Regular maintenance to ensure the fence's functionality and to clear any vegetation that might short-circuit the current is also essential.

The primary aim of providing housing for your livestock is to offer a safe and comfortable shelter that protects them from the elements and predators while also playing a significant role in health management. Adequate ventilation is key to avoiding respiratory problems, and surfaces that are easy to clean help maintain hygiene and minimize disease risks. The design of your animal housing should cater to the specific needs of your livestock; for example, laying hens requires nesting boxes, whereas goats need a dry, draft-free space.

It's essential that the size of your housing can accommodate the growth of your herd or flock, ensuring ample space for all animals. Incorporating natural light can enhance the well-being of your animals and assist in regulating their biological cycles, with windows or skylights being beneficial, provided they are secure and predator-proof.

The integration of fencing and housing into your homestead should be seamless, not only meeting the needs of your animals but also fitting well with your property's overall design and functionality. The placement of animal housing should be considered for its impact on daily routines, such as feeding and cleaning, emphasizing accessibility and convenience. The choice of materials and the design should also align with your homestead's aesthetic, with sustainable and locally sourced materials offering an environmentally friendly boost to your setup.

In essence, careful planning and consideration in the fencing and housing of your livestock are pivotal to the success and sustainability of your backyard homestead. By focusing on your animals' safety, comfort, and health, you foster a harmonious environment that supports their well-being and your homesteading aspirations.

Managing Manure

After ensuring your livestock have a secure and comfortable environment, the next logical step in managing a backyard homestead involves addressing the inevitable byproduct of animal husbandry: manure. This section delves into the practicalities of managing manure in a way that benefits your homestead, keeps your animals healthy, and minimizes environmental impact.

Firstly, it's essential to understand the value of manure. Far from mere waste, manure is a potent organic resource, rich in nutrients that can significantly enhance soil fertility and structure. However, it must be managed correctly to unlock its potential without causing harm.

Establishing a regular cleaning routine is the cornerstone of effective manure management. Daily removal of manure from animal enclosures prevents the buildup of harmful gases, reduces the risk of disease, and keeps your animals clean and comfortable. Equip yourself with the necessary tools—shovels, forks, and wheelbarrows—to make this task as efficient as possible.

Once collected, decide on a manure management strategy that aligns with your homestead's size and gardening needs. Composting is a highly recommended approach, transforming manure into a nutrient-rich, soil-enhancing material. A well-maintained compost pile requires balancing carbon-rich materials, like straw or leaves, with the nitrogen found in manure. This balance encourages aerobic decomposition, minimizing odors and killing off pathogens. Turn your compost regularly to aerate it; within a few months, you'll have a valuable addition to your garden beds.

Creating a manure spreader system might be viable for those with more land. This method directly applies aged or composted manure to fields as a natural fertilizer. However, it's crucial to understand local regulations regarding manure application to prevent nutrient runoff into waterways, which can cause environmental harm.

Consider partnering with local gardeners or community gardens in smaller homesteads, where composting might not be feasible due to space constraints. Many are eager for organic matter to enrich their soils and may be willing to collect and compost their manure.

Lastly, managing manure is not just about disposal or

recycling; it's also about health and safety. Always wear protective gear when handling manure to avoid direct contact with pathogens. Ensure your storage or composting site is well away from water sources to prevent contamination.

By viewing manure management not as a chore but as an integral part of your homestead's ecosystem, you can create a sustainable cycle that benefits your soil, plants, and, ultimately, your table. With the right approach, what was once waste transforms into black gold, enriching your homestead and ensuring its productivity for years.

Chapter Summary

- Choosing suitable livestock involves considering land size, animal purpose, care needs, climate, and legalities for a successful homestead.
- Essential animal health and productivity hinge on tailored nutrition, including balanced diets, water, forage understanding, and mineral supplements.
- Livestock wellness relies on regular health checks, vaccinations, deworming, emergency plans, and quarantine for new arrivals.
- Sustainable homesteading demands knowledge of breeding cycles, selective breeding, population control, record-keeping, and ethical practices.
- Safety and comfort for livestock require proper fencing and well-designed shelters for protection and health management.
- Effective manure management, including regular cleaning, composting, and adherence to

regulations, benefits soil fertility and environmental health.
- Selecting livestock necessitates evaluating available space, animal raising goals, care time, climate adaptability, and legal compliance.
- Sustainability and productivity in homesteading are achieved through comprehensive livestock management, including feeding, healthcare, and breeding.

9
HOMESTEAD CARPENTRY

A woman in a workshop measuring and sawing wood for a project.

Basic Carpentry Skills

Mastering basic carpentry skills is a cornerstone of self-sufficiency that empowers you to create and maintain your structures in your homestead. Whether you're a novice with a hammer or someone with some experience looking to refine your skills, understanding carpentry fundamentals will be the foundation for all your homestead projects, including constructing coops and pens for your animals.

Safety is paramount. Always wear appropriate safety gear, including gloves and eye protection, and ensure that your workspace is clean and free of hazards. Familiarize yourself with your tools before starting any project and understand their proper use and maintenance.

Measuring and marking accurately are the bedrock of successful carpentry. Invest in a quality tape measure, a carpenter's square, and a level. Learning to measure twice and cut once will save you time, materials, and frustration. Practice marking your materials clearly and precisely, as accurate cuts depend on accurate markings.

Next, cutting materials is a skill that requires patience and practice. Whether using a handsaw or a power saw, the key is making smooth, controlled cuts. Start with straight cuts before moving on to more complex angles. Remember, the type of saw blade you use can significantly affect the quality of your cut, so choose accordingly based on the material you're working with.

Joining materials together is where your projects start to take shape. Nailing, screwing, and gluing are basic techniques you'll use regularly. Understanding when and how to use each method is crucial. For instance, screws provide more strength and are easier to remove than nails, making them ideal for structures that may need disassembly or adjustment. Glue can add extra stability to joints but requires clamping and drying time.

Finally, finishing your projects improves their appearance and protects them from the elements. Sanding, painting, or staining your creations will extend their life and enhance the aesthetic appeal of your homestead.

As you hone these basic carpentry skills, you'll be better equipped to tackle various projects, from simple repairs to more complex constructions like animal coops and pens. Each project will build your confidence and expand your capabilities, bringing you closer to the self-sufficient homestead of your dreams.

Building Coops and Pens

After mastering basic carpentry skills, you're poised to tackle one of the most satisfying backyard homestead projects: constructing coops and pens. These structures are vital for your poultry and livestock's safety, comfort, and productivity. This guide will walk you through the entire process, from initial planning to construction, ensuring that even novices can succeed.

The first step, before even touching any tools, is thorough planning. You need to consider the size of your flock or herd and their specific requirements. Chickens, for instance, need nesting boxes and roosting bars, whereas goats require robust fencing to prevent them from escaping. It's essential to research the needs of the animals you plan to keep and design your structure to meet those needs.

Choosing the right materials follows planning. Treated lumber is often the go-to choice for many coops and pens because of its durability and resistance to decay. However, it's crucial to ensure that any materials you use are safe for animals and do not release harmful chemicals. Corrugated metal or shingles can offer sufficient protection against the weather for roofing. The essential tools for this project include a saw, hammer, drill, screws, and nails.

When it comes to construction, several tips can help ensure success. A solid foundation prevents predators from burrowing into your coop or pen. A buried hardware cloth or a concrete base can offer additional security. Proper ventilation is crucial for animal health, yet it's essential to safeguard against drafts. Placing vents or windows strategically can achieve this balance.

Design your structure with maintenance in mind; doors should be wide enough to facilitate cleaning, and nesting boxes should be easy to access for egg collection. Security against predators is paramount, so cover all openings with hardware cloth and secure doors with predator-proof latches. Remember your animals' comfort; insulation can help with temperature control, and perches and hideaways offer security.

Adding a few finishing touches can significantly enhance your project once the structure is built. Painting or staining the wood not only extends its lifespan but also improves the aesthetics of your homestead. Personal touches like decorative trim or a weathervane can add character to your project.

Constructing coops and pens is a rewarding endeavor that boosts the functionality and self-sufficiency of your backyard homestead. With meticulous planning, the appropriate materials, and hard work, you can create a secure and comfortable home for your animals that will last years.

Constructing Raised Beds and Trellises

Transitioning from the foundational structures for your animals, we delve into the critical components that will bolster your plant life in your backyard homestead: the construction of raised beds and trellises. These elements are functional, enhancing the productivity and health of your garden and adding an aesthetic appeal to your homestead. With a few tools, some lumber, and some effort, you can create durable and efficient structures that will benefit your garden for years.

Raised beds are a vital feature of efficient backyard gardening, offering improved soil conditions, better drainage, and easier weed and pest control, alongside making gardening spaces more accessible. To construct a raised bed, you'll need untreated lumber like cedar or redwood, which is naturally rot-resistant, galvanized screws or nails, a drill or hammer, landscape fabric, and a mix of soil and compost.

Start by deciding the dimensions of your bed. A standard size is 4 feet by 8 feet, allowing easy access from either side. Cut your lumber to size, assemble a simple box frame, and, if building taller beds, reinforce the corners to prevent bowing. Place the frame in its desired location, line it with landscape fabric, and fill it with soil and compost.

Building trellises is essential for supporting climbing plants such as beans, peas, and cucumbers. They maximize vertical space and can improve yields and air circulation around plants. You'll need wooden stakes or metal poles, wire mesh or netting, strings or garden twine, a hammer or mallet, and staples or ties.

Decide the location and size of your trellis, drive the stakes or poles into the ground, and if using wooden stakes, connect the tops with a horizontal beam for stability. Attach your climbing material securely, ensuring it's tight and stable. For strings or twine, a grid pattern or vertical lines will support the plants as they grow.

Both raised beds and trellises are customizable to fit the size and style of your garden, improving its functionality and beauty. With these structures in place, your backyard homestead is well on its way to becoming a productive and sustainable oasis.

Remember, the longevity of these structures relies on regular maintenance and occasional repairs. This ensures they continue to effectively support your homesteading efforts and allow you to enjoy the fruits of your labor season after season.

Repair and Maintenance

In backyard homesteading, the ability to maintain and repair your carpentry projects is as crucial as constructing them. This section delves into the essential skills and knowledge every homesteader should possess to ensure their wooden structures remain sturdy, functional, and aesthetically pleasing over time.

Regular inspection is vital. Seasonal changes can cause wood to expand, contract, and sometimes warp. Periodically checking your raised beds, trellises, fences, and other wooden structures for signs of wear and tear can help you catch issues before they become significant problems. Look for loose screws or nails, cracks in the wood, or any signs of rot or pest infestation.

When it comes to repairs, having a basic toolkit is indispensable. This should include a hammer, screwdrivers, a saw, a drill, sandpaper, and a set of nails and screws. A wood filler can patch small holes or cracks for more specialized tasks. When larger sections of wood are damaged, they may need to be cut out and replaced entirely. This is where your saw and drill will come in handy, allowing you to remove the damaged section and secure a new piece.

Maintenance also involves protecting your wood from the elements. If your structures are made from something other than treated or naturally rot-resistant wood, consider applying a wood preservative. These products can significantly extend the life of your projects by protecting against decay, insects, and weathering. For an added layer of protection, especially for structures that come into direct contact with soil, a coat of paint or stain can beautify your project and seal the wood from moisture.

Another aspect of maintenance is ensuring the stability of your structures. Over time, the ground can shift, causing posts to lean or become unstable. Regularly check the alignment of posts and supports, and be prepared to reinforce them if necessary. This might involve digging around the base of a post to reset it to a more stable position or adding additional supports to a structure showing signs of strain.

Lastly, consider the lifecycle of your carpentry projects. Even with the best care, all wood eventually reaches the end of its useful life. Planning for this inevitability means designing your projects so they can be easily repaired, parts can be replaced, or the entire structure can be dismantled and repurposed or composted if made from untreated wood.

Incorporating these repair and maintenance practices into

your routine ensures that your backyard homestead remains a place of beauty, productivity, and sustainability. This will save you time and money in the long run and deepen your connection to the land and the structures you build upon it. As we move forward, we'll explore more DIY projects that can enhance your homesteading experience, each requiring a blend of creativity, skill, and a willingness to learn and adapt.

DIY Homestead Projects

Embarking on DIY homestead projects is not just a way to save money; it's a journey into self-reliance and creativity. Whether crafting a cozy chicken coop, building sturdy raised garden beds, or assembling a functional compost bin, each project you undertake adds value and versatility to your homestead. This section will guide you through several foundational projects, offering practical advice to ensure your carpentry endeavors are both successful and satisfying.

Building a Chicken Coop

A chicken coop is essential for keeping your poultry safe and comfortable. Consider size (allowing 2-3 square feet per chicken inside the coop), ventilation, insulation, and predator-proofing when planning your coop. Use durable materials to construct the frame and walls, and ensure the coop is elevated off the ground to prevent moisture and predators from getting in. Adding nesting boxes and a roosting area will make it a welcoming home for your chickens.

Constructing Raised Garden Beds

Raised garden beds improve drainage and soil quality and reduce back strain when tending to your plants. To build one, you'll need untreated lumber, screws, and a good-quality soil mix. Assemble the frame to your desired size, ensuring it's not too wide that you can't reach the center from the sides. Fill it with a mix of compost, topsoil, and other amendments to create a fertile growing environment for your plants.

Assembling a Compost Bin

A compost bin is a simple yet effective way to recycle kitchen scraps and yard waste into nutrient-rich compost for your garden. You can build a basic bin using pallets or wire mesh. The key is ensuring proper aeration and easy access to turn the compost. Consider a three-bin system for a continuous supply: one bin for fresh scraps, one for compost in progress, and one for finished compost.

Crafting a Rainwater Harvesting System

Collecting rainwater is an eco-friendly way to water your garden. A simple rainwater harvesting system can be constructed using gutters, downspouts, and a storage container. Ensure the container is covered to prevent debris and mosquitoes from getting in. Also, consider installing a first flush diverter to improve water quality by diverting the initial runoff, which may contain contaminants from the roof.

Creating a Tool Shed

A well-organized tool shed can significantly enhance your

efficiency and enjoyment of homestead projects. It doesn't have to be large; even a small space can be maximized with shelves, hooks, and bins. Use recycled materials where possible to keep costs down. Ensure your shed is weatherproof and secure to protect your tools from the elements and potential theft.

As you embark on these projects, remember that carpentry is as much about the process as it is about the outcome. Take your time, measure twice, cut once, and don't be afraid to make mistakes—they're often the best learning opportunities. With each project you complete, you'll improve your homestead and build a repertoire of skills that will serve you for years to come.

Safety and Tools

Transitioning from the realm of DIY homestead projects, where creativity and self-reliance are paramount, we now delve into the critical aspects of safety and the essential tools required for homestead carpentry. This section is designed to equip you with the knowledge and tools necessary to safely and effectively bring your carpentry projects to life, ensuring that your homestead not only thrives but does so with an unwavering commitment to safety.

Before we explore the tools that will transform raw materials into functional homestead assets, it's imperative to underscore the importance of safety. While carpentry is rewarding, it also comes with its share of risks, from minor cuts and bruises to more serious injuries. Therefore, adopting a safety-first mindset is non-negotiable.

- **Personal Protective Equipment (PPE):** Always wear appropriate PPE. This includes safety goggles to protect your eyes from flying debris, gloves to safeguard your hands from splinters and cuts, ear protection to shield your ears from the noise of power tools, and dust masks or respirators, especially when working with treated lumber or creating a lot of sawdust.
- **First-Aid Kit:** Keep a well-stocked first-aid kit readily accessible in your workshop. Accidents can happen, and being prepared to treat minor injuries immediately is crucial.
- **Workshop Cleanliness and Organization:** A cluttered workspace is a hazardous workspace. Regularly clean your workshop to remove sawdust, which can be a fire hazard and a health risk. Ensure tools are stored correctly and ample space to work without tripping or knocking something over.

With safety protocols in place, let's focus on the tools that are the backbone of any homestead carpentry project. Whether building a chicken coop, repairing a fence, or creating custom furniture, having the right tools is essential.

- **Measuring and Marking Tools:** Precision is key in carpentry. Tools such as tape measures, rulers, squares, and marking gauges will ensure your projects are aesthetically pleasing and structurally sound.

- **Saws:** Depending on the project, a variety of saws will be required. Hand saws, circular saws, and jigsaws each serve different purposes, from rough cuts to delicate, detailed work.
- **Hammers and Mallets:** From driving nails to fitting joints, hammers and mallets are indispensable. A good claw hammer can serve multiple purposes, while a rubber mallet can be used for more delicate tasks that require a softer touch.
- **Chisels and Planes:** Chisels and planes allow for precision shaping and smoothing of wood for fine woodworking projects. These tools require skill and practice but are essential for detailed work.
- **Power Drill and Bits:** A power drill, along with a variety of drill bits, is crucial for drilling holes for screws or dowels. It's also useful for pilot holes to prevent wood splitting.
- **Safety Equipment:** No tool is as important as your safety equipment. This includes items already discussed under the safety-first heading.
- **Maintenance:** Keeping your tools clean, sharp, and in good working order will make your projects more enjoyable and safer. Regular maintenance includes cleaning after each use, sharpening blades, and checking for wear or damage.

In conclusion, transitioning from planning and designing your DIY homestead projects to the actual building phase requires a shift in focus toward safety and tool mastery. By understanding and implementing safety protocols and equipping yourself with the essential tools of the trade, you're well on your way to successfully tackling a wide range of carpentry projects that will enhance your homestead's functionality and aesthetic appeal. Remember, each project completed safely and skillfully is a step towards a more self-sufficient and rewarding homestead life.

Chapter Summary

- Mastering basic carpentry skills is essential for backyard homesteading, enabling the construction of structures like animal coops and pens.
- Safety is paramount in carpentry; wear protective gear and ensure a clean workspace.
- Accurate measuring and marking are crucial for successful carpentry, as is practicing smooth, controlled cuts with appropriate tools.
- Joining materials through nailing, screwing, and gluing is fundamental, with each method serving different purposes in project construction.
- Finishing projects with sanding, painting, or staining protects them from elements and enhances their appearance.
- Building animal coops and pens requires planning, selecting safe materials, and constructing with security and comfort in mind.
- Constructing raised beds and trellises improves garden productivity and aesthetics, requiring basic

tools and materials like untreated lumber and landscape fabric.
- Regular maintenance and repair of carpentry projects ensure their longevity and functionality. This involves inspections, the use of protective finishes, and structural stability.

10

NATURAL MEDICINE AND HOMESTEAD HEALTH

Freshly picked herbs and flowers on a garden table.

Growing Medicinal Herbs

Growing medicinal herbs in your backyard can be a fulfilling and practical addition to your homestead. It offers a natural approach to health and wellness while enhancing your garden's biodiversity.

Starting with the selection of the right herbs is crucial. Opt for those known for their healing properties and suitability to your climate, such as lavender for relaxation, chamomile for digestive health, and echinacea for immune support. Tailor your choices to meet your household's health needs for a more personalized garden.

Before planting, it's essential to assess your garden's conditions. Medicinal herbs generally need well-drained soil and a minimum of six hours of sunlight daily. Be cautious with herbs like mint, which can spread aggressively; growing them in containers can help keep them in check. Testing and amending your soil will give your plants the best start.

The planting process involves spacing your herbs appropriately to avoid overcrowding and ensuring they receive enough water, particularly in their early growth stages and during dry periods. However, be mindful not to overwater, as many medicinal herbs prefer drier conditions. Mulching can help maintain soil moisture and control weeds.

Harvesting your herbs at the right time is critical to maximizing their medicinal properties. This is typically before they flower when their oils and flavors are most concentrated. Harvest in the early morning for the best results. Drying the herbs by hanging them in small bundles in a warm, airy spot away from direct sunlight is an effective preservation method. Store the dried herbs in airtight containers in a dark place to maintain their potency.

As your experience with medicinal herbs grows, seek further knowledge through books, workshops, and herb societies to deepen your understanding of their uses and benefits. This ongoing learning will enhance your ability to use your garden's bounty for health and wellness.

Incorporating medicinal herbs into your homestead adds to its beauty and diversity and moves you towards a more self-sufficient approach to healthcare. With dedication and proper care, your medicinal herb garden will thrive, offering you a natural remedy resource right in your backyard.

Creating Herbal Remedies

Creating herbal remedies combines the joy of gardening with the science of natural healing, allowing you to transform your garden's bounty into potent natural medicines. The process begins with harvesting your herbs at the optimal time, usually in the morning when the dew has evaporated but before the sun gets too intense. This ensures the plants are at their peak in terms of active compounds. Flowers and leaves should be picked when the plants are in full bloom, while roots are best harvested in the fall when the plant's energy is concentrated below ground.

After harvesting, most herbs need to be dried in a well-ventilated, dark, and dry room. They should be spread out in a single layer and turned regularly to ensure even drying. Once they crumble easily between your fingers, they're ready to be stored in airtight containers away from direct sunlight to maintain their potency.

One of the simplest remedies is an herbal infusion, which involves pouring boiling water over dried or fresh herbs, covering them, and letting them steep. The steeping time varies depending on the part of the plant you're using but generally ranges from 10 to 20 minutes. These infusions can serve various purposes, from soothing teas to bases for creams and ointments.

Tinctures are another way to harness the power of your herbs. They create concentrated extracts by soaking the herbs in alcohol or vinegar. This method pulls the active compounds out of the herbs, resulting in a potent remedy after four to six weeks of shaking the mixture daily and then straining it.

Salves are particularly useful for topical applications, such as treating skin conditions or muscle pain. They're made by infusing herbs in a carrier oil and mixing them with beeswax to create a spreadable salve that can be applied directly to the skin.

Engaging in the creation of herbal remedies enhances your self-sufficiency and deepens your connection to the natural world and its healing powers. The success of these remedies lies in the quality of the herbs, and the care put into crafting them, offering a satisfying way to take control of your healthcare and well-being.

Natural First Aid

Having a well-prepared natural first aid kit is essential in backyard homesteading, where self-sufficiency and natural living are paramount. This section delves into the essentials of creating and utilizing a natural first aid kit, ensuring you're prepared for minor injuries and ailments that might occur on your homestead.

A natural first aid kit is not just a collection of items; it's a testament to the homesteader's ability to harness nature's bounty for health and healing. It complements the knowledge you've gained from creating herbal remedies, extending the use of those remedies into immediate and practical applications.

Herbal Salves and Balms are indispensable for treating cuts, scrapes, and bruises. Calendula salve, for example, is renowned for its healing and antiseptic properties. A range of salves can address different types of skin issues, from soothing insect bites to healing minor wounds.

- **Essential Oils:** A select few essential oils can be incredibly versatile in a first aid setting. Lavender oil, known for its calming and antibacterial properties, can be applied to burns and stings. Tea tree oil is another powerhouse, effective against fungal infections and as a disinfectant for cuts and scrapes.
- **Bandages and Wraps:** While not directly from the garden, having a supply of natural fiber bandages and wraps can help secure dressings made from your herbal preparations. These are essential for managing wounds and preventing infection.
- **Activated Charcoal:** This a must-have for any natural first aid kit. It effectively treats poisonings and stings, absorbing toxins from the body. It can also be used to make a poultice to draw out infections.
- **Herbal Tinctures and Extracts:** These concentrated herbal preparations are potent and have a long shelf life. Tinctures such as echinacea can support the immune system in the event of a wound, while others like witch hazel are invaluable for their astringent properties and help treat hemorrhoids and varicose veins.

- **Aloe Vera:** A fresh aloe vera plant or a bottle of pure aloe vera gel is essential for treating burns, sunburns, and skin irritations. Its soothing and healing properties make it a go-to remedy for skin issues.

Having a natural first aid kit is one thing; knowing how to use it effectively is another. It's crucial to familiarize yourself with each component of your kit—understanding their uses and contraindications. Remember, while natural remedies are effective, they are not a substitute for professional medical treatment in severe cases. Always assess the situation carefully and seek medical help when necessary.

Moreover, consider taking a course in natural first aid to enhance your skills and knowledge. This can empower you to act confidently and correctly when using your natural first aid kit.

A natural first aid kit is a vital component of the backyard homestead, bridging the gap between everyday accidents and the healing power of nature. By carefully selecting and understanding the uses of various natural remedies, you can ensure the health and well-being of your family and yourself. This approach to first aid complements the homesteading lifestyle and reinforces the importance of living in harmony with nature, prepared for whatever challenges come your way.

Preventative Health Practices

Adopting preventative health practices is not just wise—it's essential. This approach to wellness emphasizes the importance of maintaining balance and harmony within our bodies and our environment, leveraging nature's bounty to foster health and prevent illness.

Cultivating a diverse and nutritious diet is at the heart of preventative health on the homestead. The food we grow and consume is pivotal in our overall health. By focusing on various fruits, vegetables, herbs, and medicinal plants, homesteaders can get a wide range of nutrients, antioxidants, and phytochemicals that support the body's natural defenses. For instance, incorporating leafy greens rich in vitamins A, C, and K can bolster the immune system, while herbs like garlic and ginger are renowned for their antimicrobial properties.

Water is another cornerstone of good health, and ensuring access to clean, safe water is a priority for any homesteader. Rainwater harvesting systems and well water testing are practical measures to secure an adequate supply of water for both consumption and cultivation purposes.

Physical activity, an inherent part of homesteading life, is crucial in preventative health. The daily tasks of planting, harvesting, and tending to animals provide a source of exercise and foster a deep connection to the land and a sense of accomplishment. This physical engagement is complemented by the mental and emotional benefits of being in nature, which include reduced stress and improved mood.

Rest and relaxation are equally important. Homesteading can be demanding, and allowing time for restorative practices such as meditation, yoga, or simply enjoying the tranquility of nature is vital for maintaining balance. Sleep, too, is a critical component of health, and establishing a routine that promotes restful sleep is beneficial for both mental and physical well-being.

Preventative health on the homestead also involves being

proactive about potential health risks. This includes natural pest control methods to reduce exposure to harmful chemicals, proper handling, food storage to prevent foodborne illnesses, and personal protective equipment when necessary to prevent injuries.

Incorporating natural remedies and traditional healing practices into daily life complements these preventative measures. Many homesteaders find value in learning about the medicinal properties of plants they can grow, using these natural remedies to treat minor ailments and support overall health.

By embracing these preventative health practices, homesteaders can create a living environment that nurtures well-being, resilience, and a deep connection to the natural world. This holistic approach to health benefits the individual and their family and contributes to the homestead's sustainability and vitality.

Integrating Natural Medicine into Daily Life

In the rhythm of homestead life, integrating natural medicine into daily routines emerges as a seamless and intuitive process. This integration not only enhances homesteaders' overall health and resilience but also deepens their connection to the land and its cycles.

At the heart of this approach is the cultivation of a medicinal garden, a dedicated space where herbs and plants known for their healing properties thrive. Each plant is selected for its specific benefits, from the calming chamomile and lavender to the immune-boosting echinacea and elderberry. Homesteaders learn to tend these gardens with care, understanding that the health of these plants directly influences the potency of their healing properties.

Homesteaders harvest these plants at their peak and transform them into various natural remedies. Tinctures, salves, teas, and poultices become part of the homestead's toolkit for addressing minor ailments and injuries. For instance, a calendula salve can soothe skin irritations, while a peppermint tea eases digestive discomfort. These remedies, rooted in generations of traditional knowledge, offer effective and gentle alternatives to over-the-counter medications.

Beyond the medicinal garden, integrating natural medicine into daily life involves a holistic approach to food. The homestead kitchen becomes a place of alchemy where every meal is an opportunity to nourish and heal. Foods rich in vitamins, minerals, and antioxidants support the body's natural defenses. Fermented foods, such as sauerkraut and kombucha, introduce beneficial probiotics that promote gut health. By choosing seasonal and locally sourced ingredients, homesteaders ensure their diet is nutritious and sustainable.

Mindfulness practices also play a crucial role in this integrated approach to health. Homesteaders recognize the importance of tuning into their bodies and the natural world. Walking barefoot in the garden, practicing yoga at sunrise, or sitting quietly under a tree become vital components of daily life. These moments of connection and reflection are restorative for the mind and spirit and reinforce the homestead's rhythms and cycles.

In embracing these practices, homesteaders find that natural medicine is not just about treating illness but about nurturing a way of life in harmony with nature. It's a path that requires patience, observation, and a willingness to learn from successes and setbacks. Yet, the rewards are manifold, offering a sense of empowerment, well-being, and a deepened respect for the natural world.

As we move forward, it becomes clear that maintaining health on the homestead extends beyond individual practices to encompass the environment in which we live. The principles of cleanliness and order, vital to preventing disease and promoting well-being, are reflected in our living spaces' thoughtful organization and care. This holistic view of health, where personal practices and environmental stewardship are intertwined, sets the stage for exploring the next crucial aspect of homestead health: hygiene practices.

Homestead Hygiene Practices

In backyard homesteading, maintaining a high standard of hygiene is not just a matter of personal health; it's a cornerstone for sustainable living and the well-being of both the homestead and its inhabitants. As we delve into the practices underpinning homestead hygiene, we must recognize that these routines are deeply intertwined with our environment's natural cycles and resources.

First and foremost, water plays a pivotal role in homestead hygiene. Access to safe drinking, cooking, and cleaning water is paramount. Rainwater harvesting systems can be a sustainable water source, but it's crucial to implement proper filtration and purification methods to make this water safe for use. Additionally, greywater systems can recycle water from baths, sinks, and washing machines for irrigation, reducing waste and conserving resources.

Personal hygiene on the homestead goes beyond regular

bathing and handwashing. Natural soaps and shampoos, which can be made from ingredients grown right in your backyard, such as herbs and essential oils, offer a sustainable alternative to store-bought products. These homemade products reduce exposure to synthetic chemicals and minimize plastic waste and the carbon footprint of purchasing and transporting commercial hygiene products.

When maintaining a clean living environment, natural cleaning solutions like vinegar, baking soda, and lemon juice are effective, eco-friendly alternatives to harsh chemical cleaners. These ingredients can tackle many cleaning tasks, from disinfecting surfaces to removing stains without introducing harmful substances into your home or the environment.

Composting is a fundamental practice for any homestead in managing waste. By composting organic waste, you reduce the amount of trash sent to landfills and create a valuable resource for enriching the soil in your garden. Composting systems can vary from simple backyard piles to more sophisticated composting toilets, which offer a solution for recycling human waste into safe, usable compost.

Pest control is another critical aspect of homestead hygiene. Natural and preventative measures, such as companion planting, natural predators, and physical barriers, can effectively manage pests without using chemical pesticides. These practices protect your garden and livestock from pests and preserve your homestead's biodiversity and ecological balance.

Lastly, animal husbandry practices must prioritize cleanliness and disease prevention. Regular cleaning of animal living spaces, proper disposal of manure, and ensuring access to clean water and healthy food are essential measures for preventing illness and maintaining the health of your livestock.

By adopting these homestead hygiene practices, you not only safeguard the health of your family and animals but also contribute to the sustainability and resilience of your homestead. These practices demonstrate a commitment to living harmoniously with nature, leveraging its cycles and resources to nurture our health and the environment.

Chapter Summary

- Growing medicinal herbs on your homestead can enhance biodiversity and offer a natural approach to health and wellness. You can select herbs based on their healing properties and climate suitability.
- Essential steps in cultivating a medicinal herb garden include understanding your growing conditions, proper planting and care, and techniques for harvesting and preserving herbs.
- Expanding knowledge of medicinal herbs through reputable sources can improve the effectiveness and safety of using these plants for health benefits.
- Creating herbal remedies involves harvesting herbs at the right time, drying and storing them properly, and crafting infusions, tinctures, and salves to support health and well-being.
- A well-prepared natural first aid kit, including herbal salves, essential oils, and other natural

remedies, is crucial for addressing minor injuries and ailments on the homestead.
- Adopting preventative health practices, such as a diverse diet, clean water, physical activity, and rest, along with natural pest control and hygiene practices, supports overall health and prevents illness.
- Integrating natural medicine into daily life through a medicinal garden, holistic food choices, mindfulness practices, and environmental stewardship enhances the health and resilience of homesteaders.
- Maintaining high hygiene standards on the homestead, including clean water access, natural personal care products, eco-friendly cleaning solutions, composting, pest control, and animal husbandry, is essential for sustainable living and well-being.

11

SUSTAINABLE LIVING

Sustainable urban landscape with rooftop solar panels.

Reducing Waste

Reducing waste is a pivotal chapter in the journey towards a more sustainable backyard homestead. It's not just about minimizing what we throw away but transforming our perspective on resources, seeing potential where we once saw refuse. This transformation begins with understanding the core principles of waste reduction: reduce, reuse, recycle, and rot (compost). These principles can be applied innovatively to support a thriving homestead while minimizing our environmental footprint.

Firstly, reducing waste means carefully considering our purchases and opting for items with minimal packaging or those made from sustainable materials. It's about making conscious choices, such as selecting bulk seeds or loose-leaf teas over individually packaged products. This mindset extends to every corner of the homestead, from the kitchen to the garden, encouraging us to question the necessity and longevity of each item we bring into our space.

Reusing is the next step in our waste reduction journey. It's a creative challenge that invites us to see the potential in items that might otherwise be discarded. Glass jars from kitchen staples can be repurposed for storing seeds, homemade jams, or as vessels for propagating plants. Old t-shirts become rags for cleaning or material for crochet projects. Even broken tools can offer parts for repair or new creations. This approach reduces waste and fosters a culture of resourcefulness and innovation.

Recycling is the most recognized aspect of waste management, yet it requires a thoughtful approach to be truly effective. Not all materials are equally recyclable, and understanding the specifics of local recycling programs is crucial. Homesteaders can prioritize easily recyclable materials and educate themselves on how to properly prepare items for recycling, ensuring they don't contaminate the stream. This awareness helps make recycling a more efficient and impactful practice.

Lastly, composting, or 'rot,' is a cornerstone of waste reduction on the homestead. We close the loop by transforming kitchen scraps, yard waste, and even certain paper products into rich compost, returning nutrients to the soil to support the next growth cycle. Composting reduces the amount of waste sent to landfills and enhances the health of our gardens, creating a direct link between our waste reduction efforts and our food production.

Each of these principles offers a pathway to reducing waste on the homestead, but they also represent a shift in mindset. It's about seeing the value in our resources and understanding the impact of our choices. By embracing these practices, we move towards a more sustainable homestead and contribute to a larger culture of conservation and respect for the natural world.

Eco-Friendly Homestead Products

Our choices about the products we use in our backyard homesteads play a pivotal role in the journey towards a more sustainable and self-sufficient lifestyle. Embracing eco-friendly homestead products is not just about reducing our environmental footprint; it's about nurturing a healthier ecosystem in our backyards and fostering a deeper connection with the natural world.

One of the first steps in this direction is to consider the tools and materials we use in our gardens and for animal care. Opting for tools made from sustainable materials, such as bamboo, wood, or recycled metal, can significantly reduce the demand for plastic products. These materials are not only more environmentally friendly but often offer a longer lifespan and a touch of natural beauty to your homestead.

Regarding pest control, natural and organic methods are at the heart of eco-friendly homesteading. Chemical pesticides, while effective, can harm beneficial insects, soil health, and even the water supply. Instead, consider introducing beneficial insects that naturally control pest populations, such as ladybugs and lacewings. Companion planting is another powerful technique, where certain plant combinations naturally repel pests or attract their natural predators.

In the realm of animal care, sustainable practices are equally important. Feeding your livestock and poultry with organic feed, free from genetically modified organisms (GMOs), not only supports their health but also ensures that your homestead remains a bastion of natural integrity. Moreover, consider implementing systems that allow your animals to contribute to the homestead's ecosystem, such as using chicken manure as a potent organic fertilizer.

Water conservation is another critical aspect of eco-friendly homesteading. Simple practices such as collecting rainwater in irrigation barrels can significantly reduce water usage. Drip irrigation systems, which deliver water directly to the base of plants, are an efficient way to minimize water waste in the garden.

Lastly, our cleaning and maintenance products around the homestead should be eco-friendly. Natural cleaning products, made from ingredients like vinegar, baking soda, and essential oils, are effective and safe for the environment and your family. For maintenance tasks, look for products with minimal packaging and those made from natural or recycled materials.

By integrating these eco-friendly products and practices

into our homesteads, we contribute to a more sustainable world and enjoy the benefits of a healthier, more self-sufficient lifestyle. As we move forward, sustainability principles can guide us in exploring even more ways to harness energy efficiently and sustainably, ensuring that our homesteads thrive for future generations.

Conservation Efforts

Conservation of natural resources plays a pivotal role in the journey toward a more sustainable lifestyle, especially within the confines of a backyard homestead. This section delves into practical and innovative strategies that homesteaders can employ to conserve water, soil, and biodiversity, thereby ensuring the health and productivity of their land for generations to come.

Water is a precious commodity in any garden or homestead. One of the most effective ways to conserve water is through rainwater harvesting. By installing rain barrels or designing a more complex rainwater catchment system, homesteaders can collect and store rainwater for irrigation purposes. This reduces reliance on municipal water supplies and decreases the energy footprint associated with water treatment and distribution. Additionally, employing drip irrigation systems or soaker hoses can significantly reduce water wastage by delivering water directly to the plant roots, where it's most needed.

Soil conservation is another critical aspect of sustainable homesteading. The health of the soil directly influences the health of the plants it sustains. Practices such as cover cropping, crop rotation, and applying organic mulches can protect soil from erosion, enhance its fertility, and maintain its moisture content. Cover crops, for instance, prevent soil erosion and fix nitrogen in the soil, reducing the need for synthetic fertilizers. Similarly, incorporating compost into the garden beds improves soil structure and provides a rich source of plant nutrients, promoting a more vibrant and resilient ecosystem.

Biodiversity conservation is equally important in a backyard homestead. A diverse ecosystem is more resilient and productive, offering a natural defense against pests and diseases while supporting many pollinators and beneficial insects. Creating habitats for wildlife, such as birdhouses, bee hotels, and butterfly gardens, can enhance biodiversity and contribute to the ecological health of the homestead. Moreover, planting various crops, including native plants, can support local wildlife and promote a balanced ecosystem.

In conclusion, conservation efforts in a backyard homestead are not just about sustaining the land and its resources; they're about creating a harmonious and self-sustaining ecosystem that thrives on the principles of sustainability and resilience. By adopting water and soil conservation practices and promoting biodiversity, homesteaders can play a crucial role in preserving the environment for future generations while enjoying the bounty and beauty of their land today. When combined with sustainable energy practices, these efforts lay the groundwork for a holistic approach to sustainable living, setting the stage for community involvement and education in the broader quest for environmental stewardship.

Community Involvement and Education

The role of community involvement and education in the journey toward sustainable living cannot be overstated. While individual efforts in conservation and sustainable practices are crucial, collective action and shared knowledge within a community can significantly amplify the impact. This section delves into how backyard homesteaders can engage with their communities to foster a culture of sustainability and self-reliance.

One of the most powerful steps a backyard homesteader can take is to become an advocate for sustainability within their local community. This can be achieved through various means, such as organizing workshops, participating in local farmers' markets, or starting a community garden. Workshops can cover various topics, from organic gardening and composting to rainwater harvesting and renewable energy solutions. These educational initiatives spread valuable knowledge and create a platform for exchanging ideas and experiences, fostering a sense of community and collective learning.

Participating in local farmers' markets is another effective way to engage with the community. By selling or donating produce grown on your homestead, you provide others with access to fresh, locally-grown food and raise awareness about the benefits of sustainable farming practices. It's an opportunity to demonstrate the viability of backyard homesteading and inspire others to consider similar practices.

Starting or joining a community garden is yet another avenue for involvement. Community gardens can serve as living classrooms, offering hands-on experience in gardening and sustainable living to people of all ages. They can also help to address food insecurity in the community by providing fresh produce to those in need. Moreover, community gardens can become hubs for social interaction, strengthening community bonds and fostering a shared sense of responsibility for the local environment.

Education plays a pivotal role in community involvement. By sharing knowledge and skills related to sustainable living, backyard homesteaders can empower others to make informed decisions about their lifestyle and consumption habits. This can be as simple as starting a blog or a YouTube channel focused on sustainable living practices or offering to speak at local schools and community centers. The goal is to ignite curiosity and passion for sustainable living in others, encouraging them to explore how they can contribute to a more sustainable future.

In conclusion, community involvement and education are essential components of sustainable living. By engaging with their communities, backyard homesteaders can extend the reach of their sustainability efforts, creating a ripple effect that encourages the widespread adoption of sustainable practices. Through workshops, participation in local markets, community gardens, and educational initiatives, homesteaders can play a crucial role in fostering a culture of sustainability and self-reliance. As we move forward, collective action and shared knowledge of communities will be key in navigating sustainable living challenges and ensuring a healthier, more sustainable future for all.

Living Off the Grid

Transitioning from a lifestyle that emphasizes community involvement and education, we delve into the essence of sustainable living through the lens of living off the grid. This approach embodies the principles of self-sufficiency and environmental stewardship and represents a profound commitment to reducing one's carbon footprint and living in harmony with nature.

Living off the grid in a backyard homestead involves a series of strategic and thoughtful adaptations aimed at creating a lifestyle that is self-sustaining and minimally dependent on external utilities. This encompasses energy production, water sourcing, waste management, and food production, each of which contributes to a holistic approach to sustainable living.

Energy production is often the first consideration for those looking to live off the grid. Solar panels and wind turbines can be integrated into the homestead to harness natural resources for electricity. This reduces reliance on fossil fuels and ensures that the homestead remains powered during outages or disruptions in the grid. Additionally, using energy-efficient appliances and lighting and thoughtful design choices that maximize natural light and insulation can significantly reduce energy consumption.

Water sourcing is another critical component of living off the grid. Rainwater harvesting systems can collect and store rainwater for household use, while greywater systems recycle water from sinks, showers, and washing machines for use in irrigation. For those in suitable locations, wells can provide a steady supply of fresh water, though it's important to consider purification methods to ensure water safety.

Waste management on an off-grid homestead involves composting organic waste and recycling as much as possible. Composting reduces the amount of waste sent to landfills and produces valuable compost that can enrich the soil in your garden. Some off-grid homesteaders also explore more advanced waste management systems, such as biogas digesters, which can convert organic waste into energy.

Food production is the most rewarding aspect of living off the grid. Homesteaders can produce a significant portion of their food by cultivating a vegetable garden, raising livestock, and perhaps keeping bees. This reduces the carbon footprint associated with food transportation and ensures that the food is fresh, nutritious, and free of harmful chemicals. Moreover, preserving food through canning, drying, and fermenting can ensure a steady food supply year-round.

Living off the grid on a backyard homestead has its challenges. It requires a significant investment of time, resources, and energy. However, the rewards of a sustainable, self-sufficient lifestyle are immeasurable. It offers a profound sense of connection to the natural world, a deep appreciation for the resources we often take for granted, and the satisfaction of knowing that one is living in a way that is kind to the planet.

Chapter Summary

- Sustainable living on a backyard homestead emphasizes reducing waste through reducing,

reusing, recycling, and composting, transforming our perspective on resources.
- Conscious purchasing decisions, such as choosing items with minimal packaging and made from sustainable materials, are key to reducing waste.
- Reusing items, such as repurposing glass jars for storage or old T-shirts for rags, fosters a culture of resourcefulness and innovation.
- Effective recycling requires understanding local programs and prioritizing easily recyclable materials to avoid contaminating the recycling stream.
- Composting kitchen scraps and yard waste closes the loop by returning nutrients to the soil, enhancing garden health, and reducing landfill waste.
- Eco-friendly homestead products, including tools made from sustainable materials and natural pest control methods, support a healthier ecosystem.
- Sustainable energy practices, like installing solar panels and wind turbines, reduce carbon footprints and can offer long-term savings and environmental benefits.
- Community involvement and education amplify the impact of sustainable living efforts, fostering a culture of sustainability and self-reliance through workshops, local markets, and community gardens.

12
HOMESTEAD PLANNING AND MANAGEMENT

A sustainable farm with solar panels and wind turbines.

Year-Round Planning

Establishing a backyard homestead requires a passion for self-sufficiency and a strategic approach to planning and management that spans the entire year. Year-round planning is the backbone of a successful homestead, ensuring every season brings its own set of tasks, goals, and rewards. This approach allows homesteaders to maximize their resources, manage their time effectively, and achieve a sustainable lifestyle.

The essence of year-round planning lies in understanding the cyclical nature of farming and homesteading activities. Each season has unique demands, from planting and harvesting to maintenance and preparation for the coming months. Spring is often the busiest season, filled with planting and early harvesting. It's a time to start seedlings, prepare garden beds, and set the foundation for the year's productivity. Summer follows its peak growth and harvest periods, requiring diligent care, watering, and pest management to ensure the health of crops and livestock. Fall brings another harvest season, alongside the need to preserve the bounty and prepare the homestead for the colder months. Winter, while seemingly quieter, is crucial for planning the following year's crops, repairing equipment, and focusing on indoor projects.

Effective year-round planning also involves understanding your local climate and ecosystem. For instance, knowing the first and last frost dates is vital for planting schedules. Similarly, being aware of local wildlife and their habits can help you plan defenses for your crops and livestock. Additionally, understanding the natural resources available on your land can guide decisions on water management, soil conservation, and sustainable energy sources.

To implement a successful year-round plan, homesteaders should start with a comprehensive calendar outlining the necessary tasks for each season. This calendar should include agricultural activities, infrastructure maintenance, financial planning, and personal learning goals. Regularly reviewing and adjusting this plan is essential, as it allows for incorporating new knowledge, adaptation to unexpected challenges, and optimizing processes.

Moreover, year-round planning is not just about the physical aspects of homesteading; it also encompasses the financial and emotional well-being of the homesteader. Balancing the demands of the homestead with personal health, family time, and community involvement is crucial for long-term sustainability. This holistic approach ensures that the homestead is not just a place of work but also a source of joy, fulfillment, and connection to the natural world.

In conclusion, year-round planning is dynamic and integral to managing a backyard homestead. It requires a deep understanding of the land, a commitment to sustainable practices, and a willingness to adapt and learn. By embracing this approach, homesteaders can achieve their goals of self-sufficiency and sustainability and enrich their lives and the environment around them. As we move forward, the next logical step in ensuring the success of our homestead is to delve into the intricacies of budgeting and managing expenses, ensuring that our endeavors are not only environmentally sustainable but financially viable.

Budgeting and Expenses

Transitioning from strategic considerations to practical budgeting and expenses is essential for effective homestead management. The financial health of your backyard homestead influences daily operations and future project feasibility, so managing your budget is crucial.

Start by creating a clear budget, listing all income sources and anticipated expenses. Be realistic in your estimates to avoid financial strain. This involves considering income from produce, eggs, honey, handmade goods, and expenses like seeds, feed, and maintenance.

Keeping a detailed record of expenses is vital for staying within budget and identifying cost-reduction areas. Use a spreadsheet or budgeting software designed for small-scale farming. Update this record regularly to reflect expenses and income, adjusting your budget as needed.

Prioritize investments that offer long-term benefits, such as quality tools and perennial plants. Over time, these can be more cost-effective than cheaper alternatives or annuals that need replanting each season. This approach ensures sustainability and efficiency.

If considering debt, proceed with caution. Loans or credit can fund significant investments like greenhouse construction but ensure the return justifies the borrowing cost. This strategy should enhance productivity and sustainability.

Building a reserve fund is critical for managing unexpected expenses, such as emergency repairs. This financial cushion ensures unforeseen costs don't compromise operations. It's an essential part of financial planning.

Adopt cost-effective practices like composting, rainwater harvesting, and seed saving. DIY projects can save money, provided you have the skills and resources. These practices reduce expenses and promote sustainability.

Consider diversifying your income streams to increase revenue potential and provide a buffer against failure. Exploring different markets, offering workshops, or venturing into online sales can enhance financial stability. Diversification is critical to resilience.

In conclusion, disciplined and strategic financial planning is foundational to the success and sustainability of your backyard homestead. As we discuss time management and efficiency, remember the close tie between financial health and effective time management. This approach ensures the growth and resilience of your homestead for years to come.

Time Management and Efficiency

In backyard homesteading, mastering the art of time management and efficiency is akin to discovering the secret garden of productivity. It's about making the most of the daylight hours, ensuring that every task, no matter how small, contributes to the overarching goal of self-sufficiency. This section delves into strategies and practices to transform your homestead from a demanding taskmaster into a well-oiled machine of productivity and satisfaction.

Firstly, understanding the rhythm of your land and its cycles is paramount. Nature operates on its timetable, and successful homesteaders align their activities with these natural cycles. This means planting and harvesting by the seasons, caring for animals based on their natural behaviors and needs, and even performing maintenance tasks when the weather and season dictate their necessity. By syncing your activities with these natural rhythms, you work more efficiently and increase the yield and health of your plants and animals.

Creating a prioritized task list is another cornerstone of effective time management. Not all tasks are created equal, and it is essential to recognize which tasks are critical and which can wait. Prioritization should be based on factors such as seasonality, the needs of plants and animals, and the sustainability of your homestead. For instance, planting or transplanting seedlings may take precedence in the spring, while harvesting and preservation dominate the autumn months.

Moreover, the implementation of systems and routines significantly enhances efficiency on a homestead. Systems can range from composting setups that reduce waste and nourish your soil to rainwater collection systems that ensure your plants are watered even in dry spells. Routines, such as regular feeding times for animals and daily garden inspections, help in the early detection of issues before they escalate, saving time and resources in the long run.

Another aspect often overlooked is the power of delegation and community. Homesteading is not a solitary journey. Involving family members in daily tasks lightens the load and instills a sense of responsibility and connection to the land. Furthermore, engaging with the wider homesteading community through cooperative purchasing, skill swaps, or collective labor efforts can significantly enhance efficiency and productivity.

Lastly, embracing technology and innovation can lead to substantial time savings and increased efficiency. Technology can be a powerful ally in managing a homestead, from drip irrigation systems that save water and time to apps that help track planting schedules and livestock health. However, it's essential to balance the benefits of technology with the principles of sustainability and self-sufficiency that lie at the heart of homesteading.

In conclusion, time management and efficiency in backyard homesteading are not about rushing through tasks or cutting corners. Instead, they are about thoughtful planning, understanding the natural rhythms of your environment, and leveraging both community and technology to work smarter, not harder. By adopting these practices, you can transform your homestead into a model of productivity and a source of deep personal satisfaction.

Record Keeping and Documentation

In transforming your backyard into a thriving homestead, meticulous record-keeping and documentation are indispensable tools. Often overlooked in the initial excitement of planting seeds and raising livestock, this practice is the backbone of efficient homestead management. It ensures that your efforts are fruitful but also sustainable and scalable.

At its core, record-keeping involves tracking various aspects of your homestead operations. This includes, but is not limited to, planting schedules, harvest yields, livestock health records, equipment maintenance logs, and financial expenditures and income. The purpose of maintaining such records is twofold. Firstly, it provides a clear snapshot of your homestead's current status, allowing for informed decision-making. Secondly, it offers invaluable insights into trends and patterns over time, which can inform future planning and improvements.

Starting with the garden, a simple journal can be transformative. Documenting what you plant, when, and where, alongside notes on weather conditions, pest issues, and harvest dates, can help refine your planting strategy year after year. This historical data becomes a guide, helping you to understand which crops thrive in your specific conditions and how to rotate them to maintain soil health.

For those raising livestock, health and productivity records are crucial. Tracking vaccinations, feed types and amounts, breeding cycles, and any health issues ensures your animals' well-being and impacts the quality and quantity of the produce they provide. Over time, these records can highlight patterns in health issues or productivity dips, enabling preemptive measures rather than reactive ones.

Financial documentation, though perhaps less appealing, is equally vital. Keeping detailed accounts of all income generated from your homestead, be it from selling produce, eggs, or handmade goods, as well as all expenses, offers a clear picture of your homestead's economic health. This financial clarity is essential for sustainability, allowing you to identify profitable ventures, cut unnecessary costs, and plan for future investments.

In today's digital age, numerous tools and software are available to simplify this process. From mobile apps designed for garden planning to comprehensive farm management software, technology can streamline record keeping, making it less daunting and more efficient. However, the charm and simplicity of a handwritten journal, with its sketches and personal notes, still hold value for many homesteaders.

As your homestead grows, these records become the foundation for scaling up. They allow you to assess the feasibility of expanding certain areas of your homestead, introduce new ventures with a clear understanding of the required resources and potential challenges, and ensure that growth is managed sustainably without compromising your land's or livestock's health.

In essence, diligent record-keeping and documentation are not mere administrative tasks but strategic tools that empower you to nurture a thriving, sustainable homestead. By embracing this practice, you lay the groundwork for meeting your current goals and expanding your vision for the future.

Scaling Up Your Homestead

As your backyard homestead begins to flourish, you may contemplate the following steps to expand your operations. Scaling up your homestead is exciting, but it requires careful planning and management to ensure success. This section will guide you through the considerations and strategies for effectively scaling up your backyard homestead.

Firstly, assess your current capacity and resources. Understand the limitations and potentials of your space, time, and budget. Expansion doesn't always mean acquiring more land; it can also mean optimizing your current space through vertical gardening, companion planting, or integrating more efficient systems like drip irrigation.

Next, set clear goals for scaling up. Are you looking to increase your food production, diversify the types of crops and livestock, or start a small-scale agricultural business? Specific objectives will help you plan the steps and resources required to achieve them.

Financial planning is crucial when scaling up. Consider the initial investment needed for additional resources, such as seeds, tools, livestock, or infrastructure improvements. It's also wise to project the potential return on investment, especially if you plan to sell your produce or products.

Creating a detailed budget will help you manage expenses and assess the financial viability of your expansion.

Expanding your homestead may also require additional knowledge and skills. Whether learning about new crop varieties, animal care, or sustainable farming practices, investing in your education will pay dividends. Consider attending workshops, joining local farming groups, or seeking mentorship from experienced homesteaders.

As you plan your expansion, think about the long-term sustainability of your homestead. Incorporate practices that enhance soil health, conserve water, and promote biodiversity. Scaling up offers an opportunity to deepen your commitment to sustainable and regenerative agriculture.

Finally, be prepared to adapt. As you implement your plans, you may encounter unexpected challenges or opportunities. Stay flexible and open to adjusting your strategies as needed. Remember, scaling up is a journey that requires patience, perseverance, and a willingness to learn and grow.

By thoughtfully planning and managing the scaling up of your backyard homestead, you can increase your self-sufficiency, contribute to your community, and enjoy the rewards of a thriving homestead. Remember that expansion should enhance your homesteading experience, not overwhelm it. With careful consideration and strategic planning, you can successfully scale up your backyard homestead and achieve your goals.

Dealing with Setbacks

Expanding and managing your backyard homestead will require setbacks. These challenges are inevitable, but you can overcome them with resilience and the right strategies. This section will guide you through common issues and provide practical advice to keep your homestead thriving.

Weather can be unpredictable, affecting your plants and livestock in various adverse ways. Droughts, floods, unexpected frosts, and heatwaves can all cause significant damage. Implement water-saving techniques like rainwater harvesting and drip irrigation to combat these issues. Using row covers and shade cloth and ensuring proper ventilation for animal housing can protect against frost and heat, and having an emergency plan for extreme weather is crucial.

Pests and diseases can quickly turn a healthy garden or flock into a struggling one. Employing Integrated Pest Management (IPM) strategies, which include biological controls, natural predators, and organic pesticides, can help manage these issues in an eco-friendly way. Regular health checks and quarantining new additions to your homestead can prevent outbreaks from taking hold.

As your homestead grows, so does the complexity of its management, potentially leading to operational overwhelm. Creating a robust system for tracking tasks, expenses, and yields can help manage this complexity. Automating repetitive tasks and delegating responsibilities can reduce pressure, allowing you to focus on strategic improvements.

Financial setbacks, such as unexpected expenses or market downturns, can impact your homestead's stability. Building a financial buffer, diversifying income streams, and applying lean management principles provide some security. Seeking out grants, loans, and subsidies, as well as maintaining meticulous financial records, can also aid in managing your budget effectively.

Change is constant in homesteading, whether due to evolving consumer preferences, new regulations, or climate shifts. Staying informed through continuous learning and networking with other homesteaders is vital. Being willing to adapt your strategies, whether by trying new crops or exploring alternative markets, can keep you ahead of these changes.

In conclusion, setbacks are a natural part of homesteading. They challenge you to be resilient and innovative and ultimately contribute to your success. By preparing for potential challenges and responding proactively, you can navigate these hurdles and maintain a sustainable and fulfilling backyard homestead.

Chapter Summary

- Year-round planning is essential for a successful backyard homestead, understanding the cyclical nature of farming activities and adjusting tasks seasonally.
- Effective planning requires knowledge of the local climate, ecosystem, and available natural resources to optimize planting schedules and manage resources sustainably.
- A comprehensive calendar outlining agricultural activities, infrastructure maintenance, and personal

goals is crucial, with regular reviews to adapt and optimize processes.
- Financial and emotional well-being, along with balancing homestead demands with personal health and community involvement, are key to sustainable homesteading.
- Budgeting and expense management are foundational, involving realistic income and expense estimates, prioritizing long-term investments, and maintaining a reserve fund for unforeseen costs.
- Time management and efficiency in homesteading rely on understanding land rhythms, prioritizing tasks, implementing systems and routines, and leveraging community and technology.
- Meticulous record-keeping and documentation of homestead operations are indispensable for informed decision-making and future planning.
- Scaling up a homestead requires assessing current resources, setting clear goals, financial planning, acquiring new knowledge, and adapting to challenges and opportunities.

THE FUTURE OF BACKYARD HOMESTEADING

Peaceful countryside with a greenhouse and chickens.

Reflecting on the Journey

As we stand at the threshold of the future, looking back on the journey of backyard homesteading, it's essential to pause and reflect on the path we've traversed. This journey, marked by the sweat of our brows and the dirt under our fingernails, has been more than just about cultivating land; it's been about cultivating life.

Backyard homesteading has transformed from a mere hobby or trend into a lifestyle that resonates with the core of sustainable living. It has taught us the value of self-reliance in an era where convenience often trumps sustainability. We've learned to appreciate the cycles of nature, understand the rhythm of the seasons, and respect the balance of life that thrives in our backyards.

This journey has not been without its challenges. There were days when the soil seemed too stubborn to till and seasons when the harvests were meager. Yet, these obstacles only strengthened our resolve and deepened our connection to the land. They reminded us that homesteading is not just about the yield but the process and the profound lessons learned along the way.

The future of backyard homesteading looks promising, with more individuals and families awakening to the joys and benefits of this fulfilling practice. Technology and innovation continue to open new avenues for sustainable living, making it more accessible and efficient. However, the essence of homesteading remains rooted in the timeless principles of hard work, patience, and stewardship of the earth.

As we move forward, let us carry the lessons of the past with us. Let us continue to share our knowledge and experiences with the community, fostering a spirit of cooperation and mutual support. The impact of our homesteading journey extends beyond the confines of our backyards, influencing our families, communities, and the environment in profound ways.

In embracing the future of backyard homesteading, we are

not just cultivating our gardens but nurturing a legacy of sustainability and resilience for generations to come. This journey, with its highs and lows, has been a testament to the human spirit's capacity for growth and adaptation. It is a journey worth celebrating, a journey worth continuing.

The Impact of Homesteading on Family and Community

As we delve into the essence of backyard homesteading, it becomes evident that its impact stretches far beyond the confines of one's property, weaving itself into the fabric of family life and community spirit. The journey of transforming a simple backyard into a thriving homestead is not just about cultivating the land; it's about nurturing relationships and building a sense of belonging and responsibility towards one another and the environment.

For families, the homesteading lifestyle offers a unique platform for learning and growth. It fosters a culture of self-reliance and problem-solving, where each family member can contribute their skills and learn new ones. Children raised in this environment often develop a profound understanding of the cycles of nature, the value of hard work, and the importance of sustainability. They witness firsthand the fruits of their labor, from planting seeds to harvesting crops, which instills a sense of pride and accomplishment in them. This hands-on approach to learning encourages curiosity and a deep appreciation for the natural world.

Moreover, backyard homesteading has the potential to strengthen family bonds. Working together towards a common goal creates opportunities for quality time and shared experiences. Families can connect on a deeper level in these moments, whether tending to the garden, caring for animals, or preserving the harvest. The challenges and triumphs experienced along the way become cherished memories and valuable life lessons passed down through generations.

The influence of backyard homesteading extends into the broader community as well. It can catalyze neighborhood collaboration and support. Homesteaders often share surplus produce, seeds, and plants with their neighbors, fostering a culture of generosity and mutual aid. This exchange helps build resilient local food systems, encourages social interaction, and strengthens community ties. Additionally, homesteading initiatives can inspire community projects, such as communal gardens, farmers' markets, and educational workshops, further enriching the area's social fabric.

Another significant contribution of backyard homesteading to the community is the revival of traditional skills and knowledge. Once commonplace, skills such as gardening, preserving food, and carpentry have faded in the modern era. Homesteading revives these practices, preserving them for future generations while promoting a more sustainable and self-sufficient lifestyle.

In essence, the impact of backyard homesteading on family and community is profound and multifaceted. It nurtures a sense of responsibility, fosters connections, and promotes a sustainable way of living that benefits the individual homesteader and the community as a whole. As we look toward the future of backyard homesteading, it's clear that its potential to transform lives and communities is immense. The journey of homesteading, with all its challenges and rewards, is a testament to the resilience and creativity of the human spirit, offering a path towards a more connected, sustainable, and fulfilling way of life.

Challenges and Rewards

The path of a backyard homesteader is only sometimes smooth; it is paved with obstacles that test resilience, adaptability, and commitment. Yet, these very challenges make the rewards even more gratifying.

One of the primary challenges faced by homesteaders is the steep learning curve. Whether mastering the art of vegetable gardening, understanding the nuances of animal husbandry, or learning how to preserve food, each skill requires time, patience, and a willingness to learn from mistakes. Nature's unpredictability adds another layer of complexity, with weather conditions, pests, and diseases posing constant threats to crops and livestock. Moreover, the initial financial investment and ongoing maintenance costs can be significant, requiring careful planning and budgeting.

Despite these hurdles, the rewards of backyard homesteading are immense and multifaceted. A profound sense of accomplishment comes from growing your own food, reducing dependence on commercial food systems, and living more sustainably. This lifestyle fosters a deep connection with the natural world, encouraging a rhythm of life that is more in tune with the seasons and cycles of the earth. The health benefits are also noteworthy, with access to fresh, organic produce and the physical activity involved in gardening and animal care contributing to overall well-being.

Furthermore, backyard homesteading offers invaluable self-reliance, problem-solving, and creativity lessons. It cultivates a spirit of innovation, as homesteaders often find themselves devising unique solutions to challenges, whether repurposing materials for garden beds or developing efficient systems for water conservation. Another significant reward is the sense of community that emerges within the family and with fellow homesteaders. Sharing knowledge, experiences, and the fruits of one's labor fosters a sense of belonging and mutual support that is increasingly rare in today's fast-paced world.

As we look to the future, it's clear that the challenges and rewards of backyard homesteading will continue to evolve. With technological advancements, new opportunities for efficiency and sustainability are emerging, promising to shape the next chapter of this enduring lifestyle. The journey of a backyard homesteader is one of constant learning and adaptation. Still, it is also a testament to the enduring human spirit's desire to connect with the earth and live in harmony with nature.

Advancements in Homesteading Techniques

Technology has become a surprising ally in the quest for sustainability and efficiency in recent years. Innovative gardening tools, for instance, have revolutionized how we approach the cultivation of our land. Soil sensors can now provide real-time feedback on moisture levels, pH balance, and nutrient content, allowing for precise adjustments to ensure optimal plant growth. This technology, once the purview of commercial agriculture, is becoming increasingly accessible to the everyday homesteader, enabling us to produce more with less effort and fewer resources.

Another significant advancement is in the realm of water conservation and management. Rainwater harvesting systems have evolved from simple barrels to sophisticated systems that can collect, filter, and store water for irrigation, reducing our reliance on municipal supplies or well water. Coupled with drip irrigation technology, which delivers water directly to the plant roots with minimal waste, these systems exemplify how modern innovations support sustainable homesteading practices.

Renewable energy sources have also found their place in the backyard homestead, further reducing our carbon footprint and enhancing self-sufficiency. Solar panels can power everything from water pumps to lighting; small-scale wind turbines can supplement energy needs. These renewable energy systems are becoming more affordable and user-friendly, making it feasible for homesteaders to harness the power of the elements.

Integrating aquaponics and hydroponics into backyard homesteading presents a leap forward in food production. These systems, which grow plants without soil, offer a sustainable alternative to traditional gardening, using significantly less water and space. Fish waste provides a natural nutrient source for the plants in aquaponics systems, creating a closed-loop ecosystem that mimics nature's efficiency. These systems yield a diverse array of produce and open the door to year-round gardening, irrespective of climate.

As we look to the future, it's clear that the potential for backyard homesteading is boundless. The advancements in techniques and technology not only make homesteading more accessible but also more impactful. By embracing these innovations, we can enhance our self-reliance, reduce our environmental impact, and cultivate a deeper connection with the land.

In embracing these advancements, we also pave the way for a legacy of sustainability. The knowledge and practices we develop and refine today will be the inheritance of future generations of homesteaders. As we continue to innovate and adapt, we ensure that the art of homesteading not only endures but thrives, fostering a resilient and sustainable relationship with our environment for years to come.

Sustaining Your Homestead for Future Generations

The essence of homesteading is not just in self-sufficiency but in creating a legacy that outlives our efforts, ensuring that the knowledge and skills we cultivate are passed down and built upon.

Sustaining your homestead for future generations begins with a commitment to eco-friendly practices. This involves adopting methods that replenish the resources we use rather than depleting them. Composting, rainwater harvesting, and renewable energy sources are just a few ways to minimize your homestead's environmental impact. By integrating these practices, you make your homestead more sustainable and teach the next generation the importance of living in harmony with nature.

Another critical aspect is the preservation of heirloom seeds and the cultivation of biodiversity. By choosing to plant heirloom varieties, you're not just growing food; you're preserving plant genetics passed down through generations. This biodiversity is crucial for resilience against pests, diseases, and changing climate conditions. Encouraging local wildlife to thrive by creating habitats and food sources also contributes to a balanced ecosystem on your homestead.

Education plays a pivotal role in sustaining your homestead for future generations. This doesn't necessarily mean formal education; instead, it means sharing knowledge and experiences with family, friends, and the community. Workshops, community gardens, and social media are powerful tools for spreading the wisdom of homesteading practices. By fostering a community of like-minded individuals, you ensure that the skills and values of homesteading are preserved and evolved.

Finally, it's essential to embrace innovation and adaptability. As we've seen in the advancements of homesteading techniques, staying open to new ideas and technologies can significantly enhance your homestead's efficiency and sustainability. Whether it's through adopting new gardening methods, water-saving technologies, or sustainable building materials, being adaptable ensures that your homestead can meet future challenges.

In conclusion, sustaining your homestead for future generations is a multifaceted endeavor that requires a commitment to environmental stewardship, education, community building, and adaptability. By embedding these principles into the fabric of your homesteading practices, you lay the groundwork for a legacy that nurtures the land and the community for future generations. As we move forward, let us carry with us the responsibility to reap the earth's benefits and enrich it, ensuring a prosperous and sustainable future for all who follow in our footsteps.

Final Thoughts and Encouragement

As we stand at the threshold of the future, looking back at the journey of backyard homesteading, it's clear that what we've embarked upon is not just a trend but a transformative lifestyle that reconnects us with the earth and our food sources. The path you've chosen or are considering is one of resilience, sustainability, and profound satisfaction. It's about taking control of your food supply, reducing your carbon footprint, and nurturing a deeper connection with nature.

The journey of a backyard homesteader is filled with trials and triumphs. There will be days when your garden's bounty exceeds all expectations and others when unforeseen challenges test your resolve. Remember, every setback is a learning opportunity, and every success, no matter how small, is a step towards self-sufficiency and environmental stewardship.

As you move forward, let your homestead evolve with you. Adapt and innovate as you learn more about sustainable practices and the unique needs of your land. The beauty of backyard homesteading is that it's not a one-size-fits-all model but a canvas for creativity and personal expression.

Encourage others to start their journey into homesteading by sharing your experiences and the benefits you've reaped. Whether through community workshops, social media, or casual conversations, your story can inspire and empower others to take steps towards a more sustainable lifestyle.

Lastly, remember to enjoy the journey. Take time to appreciate the simple pleasures of homesteading—the morning dew in your garden, the taste of freshly harvested produce, and the joy of sharing your bounty with loved ones.

These moments are the true essence of backyard homesteading.

As we look to the future, it's clear that the principles of backyard homesteading—sustainability, self-sufficiency, and community—will play a crucial role in shaping a more resilient and environmentally conscious society. Your commitment to this lifestyle is a beacon of hope and a testament to the positive change individuals can create in their corner of the world.

So, as you close this book and step back into your garden, remember that you are part of a growing movement towards a sustainable future. Your backyard homestead is not just a piece of land but a living, breathing testament to the change we wish to see. Keep nurturing it, keep growing, and keep inspiring those around you. The future of backyard homesteading is bright and in your hands.

HOW TO SURVIVE WHEN THE GRID GOES DOWN

THE ULTIMATE GRID-DOWN SURVIVAL GUIDE FOR THRIVING IN A WORLD WITHOUT POWER

INTRODUCTION TO GRID DOWN SURVIVAL

Understanding the Grid and Its Importance

In the modern world, the grid is an intricate web of electrical lines, substations, transformers, and power stations working harmoniously to deliver electricity to our homes, businesses, and institutions. This network is the backbone of contemporary society, powering everything from the smallest household appliances to the largest industrial machines. The importance of the grid cannot be overstated; it is the lifeline that fuels our daily operations, communications, healthcare, and entertainment. Without it, the societal structure as we know it would grind to a halt, literally and figuratively plunging us into darkness.

The grid's role extends beyond mere convenience. It supports critical infrastructure, including water purification systems, hospitals, emergency services, and transportation networks. These systems rely on a continuous electricity supply to function effectively and ensure public safety. In the event of a grid failure, the immediate impact would be felt across all sectors of society, highlighting the grid's central role in maintaining the rhythm of our daily lives.

Moreover, the grid represents human ingenuity, representing decades of technological advancement and innovation. It is a complex, interconnected system designed to meet the growing demands of an increasingly digital and electrified world. However, this complexity also makes the grid vulnerable to various threats, from natural disasters to cyber-attacks. Understanding these vulnerabilities is crucial for preparing for and mitigating the effects of grid failures.

In essence, the grid is more than just a network of cables and power stations; it is the foundation of modern civilization. Its importance cannot be understated: serving as a conduit for electricity and a critical support system for every facet of contemporary life. As we move forward, the grid's resilience and reliability will become even more critical, underscoring the need for continued investment in infrastructure and innovation to safeguard this indispensable asset.

Potential Causes for Grid Failures

The stability and functionality of the grid are paramount to our daily lives. The grid powers everything from the smallest household appliances to the largest industrial machines. However, this complex and interconnected system is not impervious to failure. Several potential causes can lead to widespread grid failures, each with unique challenges and implications. Understanding these causes is the first step in preparing for and mitigating the impacts of a grid-down scenario.

Introduction to Grid Down Survival

One of the most common causes of grid failure is natural disasters. Events such as hurricanes, earthquakes, floods, and severe storms can wreak havoc on the infrastructure that supports the grid. Power lines can be downed, substations flooded, and generation facilities damaged, leading to widespread outages. The severity of these disasters can vary greatly, but their capacity to disrupt the grid is undeniable.

Another significant threat to the grid comes from human-made causes, including cyber-attacks and physical sabotage. As our grid becomes increasingly digital and interconnected, the potential for cyber-attacks that could disrupt operations grows. Hackers could target anything from power generation facilities to distribution networks, causing widespread outages. Similarly, physical attacks on key infrastructure points could lead to significant disruptions. These threats highlight the importance of robust security measures to protect the grid from malicious actors.

Electromagnetic pulses (EMPs), whether from a solar flare or a man-made weapon, represent another potential cause of grid failure. An EMP could severely damage or destroy electrical and electronic equipment, leading to immediate and widespread grid failure. The likelihood of such an event is debated among experts, but the potential impact is significant enough to warrant consideration in any discussion on grid resilience.

Aging infrastructure also poses a significant risk to the grid's stability. Many of the grid's components, including power lines, transformers, and generation facilities, are decades old and nearing the end of their designed lifespan. Without proper maintenance, upgrades, and replacements,

Introduction to Grid Down Survival

these components are more susceptible to failure, which could lead to localized or even widespread outages.

Lastly, the increasing demand for electricity, coupled with the shift towards renewable energy sources, presents both challenges and opportunities for the grid. While renewable energy sources such as wind and solar power offer cleaner alternatives to fossil fuels, they also introduce variability and unpredictability into the grid. Balancing supply and demand becomes more complex, requiring advanced technologies and management strategies to ensure stability.

In summary, the potential causes for grid failures vary, ranging from natural disasters and human-made attacks to aging infrastructure and the challenges of integrating renewable energy sources. Each of these causes presents unique challenges that require careful consideration and preparation. As we move forward, understanding these potential causes and working to mitigate their impacts will be crucial in ensuring the resilience and reliability of the grid.

Immediate Effects of a Grid-Down Scenario

Understanding the immediate effects of a grid-down scenario is crucial for anyone concerned about their ability to survive and thrive in the face of such a crisis. When the power grid fails, the repercussions are swift and far-reaching, affecting every aspect of modern life. This section delves into these immediate effects, providing a comprehensive overview to help you prepare and respond effectively.

Firstly, the loss of electricity halts the operation of essential services. Water treatment plants, for instance, rely heavily on electricity to purify and pump water to homes and

Introduction to Grid Down Survival

businesses. Without power, the water supply quickly becomes unsafe for consumption, leading to a critical need for alternative potable water sources. Similarly, the cessation of sewage treatment facilities can result in sanitation issues, posing severe health risks.

Communication networks are another casualty of power grid failures. Cell towers, internet routers, and landline systems depend on electricity. The loss of these services disrupts the flow of information, making it challenging to obtain updates on the crisis or communicate with loved ones and emergency services. This lack of communication can exacerbate confusion and panic in the initial stages of a grid-down event.

The immediate effects on healthcare facilities can be particularly dire. Hospitals and clinics rely on power for life-saving equipment, refrigeration of medicines and vaccines, and lighting for surgeries and patient care. Backup generators may provide temporary relief, but these are short-term solutions and are dependent on fuel supplies that may quickly dwindle.

Transportation systems also grind to a halt as traffic lights go out, fuel pumps at gas stations cease to operate, and public transportation systems stop running. This not only hampers evacuation efforts but also impedes the delivery of essential goods, including food and medical supplies. The resulting shortages can lead to panic buying and hoarding, further depleting available resources.

Food preservation and safety become immediate concerns as well. Refrigerators and freezers no longer function, leading to the spoilage of perishable items. This not only wastes food resources but also increases the risk of foodborne illnesses.

The disruption in the food supply chain exacerbates this issue, as grocery stores are unable to restock their shelves due to transportation and communication breakdowns.

Lastly, the psychological impact of a grid-down scenario cannot be underestimated. The sudden loss of modern conveniences, coupled with the uncertainty and potential for societal breakdown, can lead to significant stress and anxiety. The fear of the unknown, along with concerns for personal safety and the well-being of loved ones, can have profound effects on mental health.

In summary, the immediate effects of a grid-down scenario are multifaceted and severe, impacting water and food supply, healthcare, communication, transportation, and psychological well-being. Understanding these impacts is the first step in preparing for and mitigating the consequences of such events, ensuring that you and your loved ones can navigate the challenges.

Long-Term Implications of Living Off-Grid

In the aftermath of a grid-down scenario, the immediate effects, such as loss of electricity, communication, and essential utilities, give way to a more profound and enduring challenge: adapting to a life off-grid. This transition, while daunting, is manageable. It requires a comprehensive understanding of the long-term implications of living without the conveniences and support systems that have become integral to modern life.

Living off-grid, by necessity, fosters a deep connection with the natural environment. This connection is not merely philosophical but practical. Water sourcing, for instance, has

Introduction to Grid Down Survival

become a daily concern. Without access to municipal water supplies, individuals must rely on natural sources such as rivers, lakes, or rainwater collection systems. This requires knowledge of water purification techniques and an understanding of sustainable water usage to avoid depleting local resources.

Food security is another critical aspect. The reliance on grocery stores and food supply chains is replaced by self-sufficiency through gardening, foraging, hunting, and fishing. This shift necessitates learning about crop rotation, soil health, seasonal planting, and food preservation for leaner times. Moreover, it underscores the importance of community and cooperation, as sharing knowledge and resources can significantly enhance survival prospects.

Energy production and management become central to off-grid living. Solar panels, wind turbines, and hydroelectric systems can provide renewable energy, but their implementation requires technical knowledge and upfront investment. Energy conservation has become a daily practice, as resources are finite and must be managed judiciously.

Healthcare, too, transforms. Without immediate access to hospitals and pharmacies, basic medical knowledge becomes invaluable. Herbal medicine, first aid, and preventative care take on new significance, emphasizing the need for education and preparedness in these areas.

The psychological impact of this transition cannot be understated. The shift from a life of convenience to self-reliance requires mental resilience and adaptability. The sense of community becomes more pronounced as individuals rely on each other for support, knowledge, and companionship in ways that were previously taken for granted.

In conclusion, the long-term implications of living off-grid extend far beyond the initial loss of utilities and conveniences. They touch every aspect of daily life, from water and food to energy, healthcare, and community. Adapting to this new reality requires practical skills and knowledge and a profound shift in mindset. While challenging, it is a journey that can lead to a deeper understanding of self-reliance, sustainability, and the importance of community.

1

WATER PROCUREMENT AND PURIFICATION

Finding Water Sources

In a grid-down scenario, finding reliable water sources becomes a paramount concern for survival. Whether urban or rural, the landscape around you holds various potential water sources, but knowing where to look and how to access these sources safely is crucial. This section delves into practical strategies for locating water in environments that may initially seem devoid of this essential resource.

Natural water sources include rivers, streams, lakes, and ponds. These are often the most visible and accessible sources. However, their water quality can vary significantly depending on the surrounding environment and upstream activities. When approaching natural water sources, it's important to assess the area for signs of contamination, such as discolored water, unnatural odors, or dead wildlife. In wilderness areas, moving water, such as streams and rivers, is generally preferable to stagnant water, as it is less likely to harbor pathogens and parasites.

Rainwater is a relatively clean water source, making it ideal for collection and use. Setting up a rainwater collection system can be as simple as positioning clean containers outside during rainfall. Tarps or plastic sheets can funnel rainwater into containers for more efficient collection. Ensuring the collection surfaces and containers are clean is essential to avoid contamination.

Dew and condensation can provide small but vital amounts of water. Early morning, dew collects on vegetation, tarps, and other surfaces. Using a clean cloth or directly wringing out vegetation can yield drinkable water. Additionally, placing a clean cloth or plastic sheet over vegetation in the evening can capture condensation, which can be wrung out in the morning.

A solar still extracts water from the soil and vegetation using the sun's heat. Water evaporates from the soil by digging a hole, placing a container in the center, and covering it with a transparent plastic sheet. It condenses on the plastic, eventually dripping into the container. This method can be used in various environments, including arid regions, to collect drinkable water.

Water can often be found in water heaters, toilet tanks (not the bowl), and pipes in urban environments. After shutting off the main water valve to prevent contaminated water from entering the system, water can be drained from these sources. Additionally, rainwater collection methods can be adapted to urban settings by using rooftops and gutters.

Regardless of the source, all water found in a grid-down

situation should be considered potentially contaminated and purified before consumption, a process detailed in the following section. Practicing water conservation is also essential, prioritizing water usage for drinking and cooking over other activities.

Understanding how to locate water sources in various environments effectively can significantly increase your chances of survival in a grid-down scenario. Remember, the key to successful water procurement lies in knowing where to look and applying safe collection and purification methods to ensure the water is safe for consumption.

Methods of Water Purification

Once you have identified potential water sources, the next critical step is purifying the water to make it safe for consumption. Contaminated water can carry pathogens such as bacteria, viruses, and parasites, leading to severe illnesses. This section delves into various methods of water purification, each with its own set of advantages and considerations.

Boiling: Boiling is one of the most effective methods for purifying water. It kills most pathogens present in the water. To properly boil water, bring it to a rolling boil for at least one minute at sea level, adding one minute for every 1,000 feet of elevation above sea level. Although boiling does not remove chemical contaminants, it is effective against biological hazards.

Chemical Purification: Chemical purifiers, such as iodine or chlorine tablets, are convenient and lightweight options for treating water. Follow the manufacturer's instructions for the correct dosage and wait time. It's important to note that some pathogens, like Cryptosporidium, are resistant to chemical treatments. Additionally, these chemicals can leave an aftertaste, which can be mitigated by aerating the water or adding a pinch of salt.

UV Light Purification: Portable UV light purifiers are effective against bacteria, viruses, and protozoa. These devices work by exposing contaminated water to UV light, disrupting the DNA of pathogens and rendering them harmless. UV purification requires clear water so that pre-filtering may be necessary. It's also dependent on batteries or solar power, which could be a limitation in a grid-down scenario.

Filtration Systems: Water filters come in various forms, including pump filters, gravity filters, and straw filters. They physically remove pathogens and, depending on the pore size of the filter, can also eliminate chemicals and heavy metals. It's crucial to choose a filter that meets the EPA water purification standards and maintain it according to the manufacturer's guidelines.

Solar Disinfection (SODIS): This method involves filling clear plastic bottles with water and placing them in direct sunlight for at least six hours. The UV radiation from the sun kills pathogens. SODIS is a simple and cost-effective method, but it requires clear skies and relatively clear water. It's less effective in cloudy conditions or areas far from the equator.

Distillation: Distillation involves boiling water and then condensing the steam back into liquid. This process removes pathogens, heavy metals, salts, and contaminants. However, distillation requires a significant amount of fuel for boiling and a setup to condense the steam, making it less practical in some situations.

Each of these methods has its place in a comprehensive water purification strategy. The choice of method will depend on the specific circumstances, including the type and level of contamination, available resources, and the volume of water needed. In many cases, a combination of methods may be the most effective approach to ensure the safety of your water supply.

Storing and Conserving Water

Once you have procured and purified your water, the next critical step is to store and conserve it effectively. This ensures a sustainable supply, safeguarding against both contamination and scarcity. The strategies outlined here are designed to maximize your water reserves, ensuring they last as long as possible while remaining safe for consumption.

Choosing the Right Containers: The first step in storing water is selecting appropriate containers. Food-grade plastic containers with tight-fitting lids are ideal, as they are lightweight, durable, and do not impart harmful chemicals into the water. Glass containers are another safe option. However, they are heavier and more prone to breaking. Regardless of the material, ensure all containers are thoroughly cleaned and sanitized.

Location Matters: Store your water in a cool, dark place to prevent algae growth and keep the water from becoming too warm. Avoid direct sunlight and areas with significant temperature fluctuations. Basements or cellars can be ideal, but ensure containers are elevated off the ground on pallets or shelves to prevent contamination from flooding or spills.

Rotating Supplies: Water, while seemingly inert, can become stale or contaminated over time if not stored properly. To ensure freshness, label containers with the date of storage and rotate them regularly, using the oldest water first. This is especially important if you're using chlorine or other purification methods that diminish over time.

Mindful Usage: In a grid-down scenario, every drop counts. Be mindful of water usage, prioritizing drinking, cooking, and basic hygiene. Avoid wasting water on non-essential tasks. Simple habits, such as turning off the water while brushing your teeth or washing your hands with a minimal amount, can significantly extend your reserves.

Reusing Water: Consider ways to reuse water whenever safe and possible. For instance, water used for washing vegetables can be reused to water plants. Similarly, collecting rainwater can supplement your reserves, though it should be purified before drinking.

Leak Prevention: Regularly check your storage containers and any plumbing you may use for leaks. Even a small drip can result in significant water loss over time. Ensure all containers are tightly sealed and any hoses or faucets are turned off when not used.

Innovative Conservation Techniques: Explore innovative ways to conserve water, such as using water-saving devices or creating a rainwater collection system. Techniques like dew collection or solar stills can provide additional water sources in arid environments.

By implementing these storage and conservation strategies, you can ensure that your water supply remains robust and resilient, even in the most challenging grid-down scenarios. Water is life, and managing it wisely is paramount to survival.

Recognizing and Avoiding Contaminated Water

Ensuring the safety of your water supply is crucial to prevent severe illness and ensure survival. Water contamination can occur through biological, chemical, and physical pollutants, each posing unique risks. It's essential to understand the specific considerations for safe water consumption for each type of contaminant.

Biological contaminants include pathogens such as bacteria, viruses, and parasites, often found in water sources near populated areas or agricultural lands. Since signs of biological contamination are not always visible, it is best to treat any untreated water as potentially unsafe. Cloudy water, which has an unusual color or that contains organic material, should be treated with suspicion.

Chemical contaminants can enter water sources through industrial runoff, agricultural chemicals, and household waste. These contaminants may alter the taste, odor, or color of the water. Due to potential chemical pollution, it's advisable to avoid water from near industrial areas, mines, or agricultural fields.

Physical contaminants like sediments and metals can also pollute water. These are only sometimes harmful but can complicate water treatment. If water appears cloudy or has visible particles, it should be filtered before any disinfection process.

To avoid contaminated water, start by selecting water

sources that are flowing and appear clear, ideally away from potential contamination sources. Always inspect the water visually for clarity, color, and floating materials. Although clear water is not a guarantee of safety, it is a preferable starting point for treatment.

Performing a smell test can also help avoid water with an unusual or strong odor, as it may be contaminated with chemicals or decaying organic matter. Tasting water to determine its safety is not recommended due to the risk of ingesting contaminants. If water tastes bad after treatment, it's safer to discard it and find an alternative source.

Always treat water from natural sources before consumption, regardless of its appearance or location. Boiling, filtration, and chemical disinfection are effective methods to make water safe. Be aware of your surroundings and potential upstream sources of contamination, as even remote streams can be affected by animal waste.

In urban environments, extra caution is needed with water from rivers, ponds, or lakes, which can accumulate pollutants from various sources. Understanding these risks and applying these guidelines can significantly reduce the risk of waterborne illness and ensure a safer water supply.

Rainwater Collection Techniques

Collecting rainwater is a sustainable method to achieve a reliable water source, providing relatively pure water and reducing dependence on potentially contaminated natural water bodies. The simplest form of rainwater collection involves using catchment areas such as roofs, followed by a conveyance system to direct the water into storage containers.

It's crucial to ensure the catchment surface is made of non-toxic materials to avoid leaching harmful substances into the water. Metal roofs or those treated with non-toxic materials are ideal. The conveyance system, typically comprising gutters and downspouts, should be regularly cleaned to prevent blockages and contamination.

A first flush diverter is recommended to improve the quality of collected rainwater. This device diverts the initial flow of rainwater, which may contain contaminants from the catchment surface, away from the storage container. After the initial, most contaminated water is diverted, the cleaner water is allowed to flow into the storage system. This simple mechanism significantly enhances the purity of the collected water.

Food-grade barrels or tanks should be used to prevent chemicals from leaching into the water for storage. These containers must be covered to prevent mosquito breeding and debris entry. It's also advisable to place storage containers in a shaded area to inhibit algae growth. Non-scented household bleach (approximately 1/8 teaspoon per gallon) can be disinfectant for long-term storage. However, the treated water should stand for at least 30 minutes before use.

Even though rainwater is relatively clean, it can still be contaminated by airborne particles or materials from the catchment surface. Therefore, purification before consumption is essential. Boiling is the most effective method to kill pathogens. Alternatively, filtration systems can remove both particulates and microorganisms. Simple filters can be constructed using sand, charcoal, and gravel layers. For additional safety, chemical disinfectants like iodine or chlorine tablets can be used, following the manufacturer's instructions regarding dosage and contact time.

Regular maintenance of the rainwater collection system is crucial to ensure a safe water supply. This includes cleaning the catchment area, gutters, and storage containers. It's also essential to monitor the quality of the collected water, especially after prolonged dry spells or significant pollution events.

Implementing these rainwater collection techniques provides a sustainable solution to water procurement in a grid-down scenario. By understanding and applying these methods, individuals can secure a vital resource, ensuring their resilience and survival in challenging conditions.

Chapter Summary

- In a grid-down scenario, finding and purifying water is crucial for survival, with strategies varying by environment.
- Natural water sources like rivers and lakes can be used, but their quality must be assessed for contamination.
- Rainwater collection is a clean and simple method that uses containers or tarps to collect water.
- Dew and condensation offer small but vital water sources, which are collectible via clean cloths or plastic sheets.
- Solar stills can extract water from soil and vegetation using the sun's heat, making them suitable for arid regions.

- Urban environments offer water sources such as water heaters, toilet tanks, and rooftop rainwater collection.
- Water purification methods include boiling, chemical treatment, UV light, filtration systems, solar disinfection (SODIS), and distillation.
- Proper storage and conservation of water through mindful usage, reusing, and preventing leaks are essential for maintaining a sustainable supply.

2

FOOD ACQUISITION AND STORAGE

Hunting and Trapping for Food

Hunting and trapping are vital skills for survival. These methods allow you to procure meat from the environment, a valuable source of protein and other nutrients essential for maintaining your strength and health.

Hunting involves pursuing wild animals for food. It requires knowledge of animal behavior, tracking skills, and the ability to effectively use weapons such as firearms or bows. Safety is paramount, not only in handling weapons but also in ensuring that you are hunting legally and ethically. Before a disaster strikes, please familiarize yourself with local wildlife species, their habits, and the best times for hunting them. Also, practice your shooting skills regularly and maintain your equipment to ensure reliability when it counts.

Trapping is another effective method for securing food. It can be more passive than hunting, allowing you to set up multiple traps that work for you while you attend to other survival tasks. Traps can be simple snares for small animals like rabbits and squirrels or more complex systems for larger game. Learning to set snares and traps requires practice, as improper setup can lead to failure in capturing the animal or, worse, injuring it without a humane outcome. It's also important to check your traps regularly to avoid suffering animals.

Both hunting and trapping demand a deep respect for nature and wildlife. They require patience, persistence, and a significant amount of knowledge. It's crucial to understand the laws that govern these activities in your area and to follow them strictly. In a survival situation, while you might need to rely more heavily on these skills, your responsibility is to manage resources sustainably. Overhunting or overtrapping can deplete local wildlife populations, making it even harder to find food in the future.

In addition to acquiring food through hunting and trapping, you must also know how to process and store the meat to ensure it lasts as long as possible without refrigeration. Techniques such as smoking, curing, and drying meat can preserve it for weeks or months. These methods provide a way to store food safely and add variety to your diet, which can be a welcome change in a prolonged survival scenario.

Remember, the key to effective hunting and trapping is preparation. Invest time in learning and practicing these skills before they become a necessity. This preparation will boost your confidence and increase your chances of success in a grid-down world where self-sufficiency is the key to survival.

Foraging for Edible Plants

While hunting and trapping provide a valuable source of protein, foraging for edible plants is equally important as it supplements your diet with essential vitamins and minerals. Identifying edible plants accurately is crucial, as misidentification can lead to consuming toxic species, posing severe health risks. It's beneficial to start by familiarizing yourself with the flora in your region, focusing on easily recognizable and abundant species. Utilizing field guides specific to your area, which include color photographs and detailed descriptions, can be invaluable. Participating in local foraging workshops or hikes led by experienced foragers can enhance your skills.

Key plant identifiers include leaf shape, flower color and structure, fruit appearance, and growth patterns. It's important to cross-reference multiple identifiers to ensure accuracy, and while digital applications for plant identification can be helpful, they should be different from traditional knowledge and reference materials. When harvesting, it's vital to practice sustainability to ensure that plant populations remain healthy and viable for future use. This includes harvesting only what you need, using clean, sharp tools for precise cuts, and being mindful of the surrounding ecosystem.

Safety is paramount in foraging. You should never consume a plant unless you are 100% certain of its identification and are aware of potential allergic reactions. Avoid foraging near busy roads or industrial areas to prevent contamination from pollutants, and always wash all foraged foods thoroughly.

Focusing on a few common species like dandelion, wild

garlic, wild onions, and blackberries can provide a solid foundation for your foraging efforts. These plants are widely found and easily identifiable and add flavor and nutritional benefits to meals. Once harvested, these edible plants can be incorporated into your diet in various ways. Leaves and greens can be used in salads or cooked, roots may be boiled or roasted, and berries and fruits can be eaten raw or used in jams and preserves.

In conclusion, foraging for edible plants is a valuable skill that enhances food security in a grid-down scenario. With the proper knowledge, identification skills, and safety precautions, the natural environment offers abundant nutritional resources. As we move forward, we will explore methods of preserving these and other foods without electricity, ensuring a varied and sustainable diet over the long term.

Preserving Food Without Electricity

Preserving food without the luxury of electricity becomes a paramount skill for survival. Traditional methods used for centuries help keep food safe and edible for extended periods, ensuring a stable food supply while maintaining nutritional value and taste. One of the oldest and most energy-efficient methods of food preservation is drying, which involves removing moisture from food to inhibit the growth of bacteria, yeast, and mold.

Fruits, vegetables, meats, and herbs can all be dried using sun drying, the simplest method suitable for hot, dry climates, or oven drying for those in less ideal climates. The key to successful drying is ensuring that all moisture is removed, which can be tested by the brittleness or leathery texture of the product. Smoking is another traditional method that preserves food and imparts a unique flavor, particularly suitable for meat and fish.

The smoking process involves hanging the food in a smoker or over a smoky fire for hours to days. This technique slowly cooks the food at low temperatures, helps dry it out, and adds an antimicrobial layer that protects against spoilage. Salting, or curing with salt, is another preservation method that draws moisture out of the food through osmosis, creating an environment inhospitable to microbial growth.

This method is especially effective for meats and fish, using either dry-curing with salt directly applied to the surface or wet-curing by soaking in a brine solution. Fermentation relies on converting carbohydrates to alcohol or organic acids using microorganisms under anaerobic conditions, preserving the food, enhancing its nutritional value, and introducing probiotics into your diet. Common fermented foods include sauerkraut, kimchi, yogurt, and pickles, with successful fermentation depending on maintaining the correct temperature and salt concentration.

Root cellaring is a simple and effective way to store fruits and vegetables using the earth's natural insulation to maintain a consistent, cool, and humid environment. Vegetables like potatoes, carrots, beets, and fruits like apples and pears are well-suited for this method, with critical considerations including ventilation, temperature control, and humidity management. While traditional canning requires a heat source to process the jars, methods exist to preserve high-acid foods like fruits, tomatoes, and pickles without electricity using an open kettle and water bath canning over an open fire.

Incorporating these age-old preservation techniques into your survival strategy diversifies your food storage options and connects you to a heritage of self-sufficiency and resilience. Each method has advantages and challenges, and mastering them can significantly enhance your ability to sustain yourself and your loved ones in a grid-down scenario.

Creating a Survival Garden

A survival garden is essential for long-term food security in a grid-down scenario. It involves practical steps to create a garden that sustains and thrives, ensuring a steady food supply regardless of external circumstances. The first critical step is selecting an optimal site for your survival garden, which should receive at least six to eight hours of sunlight daily and have level ground to prevent water pooling. Container gardening or vertical gardening techniques can help maximize the growing area if space is limited.

Soil health is paramount in a survival garden. Start by testing the soil pH, aiming for a range between 6.0 and 7.0, and amend the soil with organic matter like compost to improve its structure, nutrient content, and water retention. Tilling the soil to a depth of at least 12 inches ensures that roots can penetrate deeply without obstruction.

Choosing suitable crops involves considering factors such as climate zone, growing season length, and the nutritional value of the plants. Focus on high-yield, nutrient-dense crops like potatoes, beans, squash, and leafy greens, and consider adding perennial crops like asparagus and berries for long-term yields. Heritage or heirloom varieties often provide better disease resistance and adaptability to local conditions.

Implement companion planting to maximize space, deter pests, and enhance growth, such as planting marigolds among tomatoes to repel harmful insects. Utilize succession planting by staggering planting dates or planting fast-growing crops between rows of longer-growing ones to ensure a continuous harvest. Efficient water management is crucial, especially in areas with limited water resources. Collect rainwater for irrigation and consider using drip irrigation or soaker hoses to minimize water waste.

Opt for organic methods for pest and disease control, introduce beneficial insects like ladybugs, and practice crop rotation to prevent soil-borne diseases. Regularly inspect plants and remove any signs of disease or infestation to prevent the spread. Harvest crops at their peak for the best nutritional value, save seeds from your best-performing plants to ensure a supply for the next planting season, and develop plant strains well-adapted to your garden conditions.

Creating a survival garden is a proactive step towards self-sufficiency, requiring planning, effort, and patience. The rewards include fresh, nutritious food and a deeper connection to the land, cultivating resilience and ensuring that you and your loved ones can thrive in the face of challenges.

Livestock and Animal Husbandry Basics

Understanding the role of livestock and animal husbandry is crucial for a sustainable food supply during grid-down scenarios. Transitioning from the cultivation of a survival garden, selecting the right livestock involves considering the size of your land, the climate, and your ability to provide for the animals. Chickens, rabbits, and goats are ideal for small-scale operations, providing eggs, meat, and dairy, while larger animals like cows and pigs might be feasible for those with more land.

Livestock requires appropriate shelter to protect it from the elements and predators, with the complexity varying by animal. For example, chickens need a coop, while goats and cows require sturdier structures like barns. Ensuring that animals have enough space to move and graze is also essential, as overcrowding can lead to disease and behavioral issues.

Feeding and nutrition are critical in a grid-down scenario where a self-sustaining approach is necessary. Animals like goats and cows can mainly graze but might need supplementary feed, including fodder crops from your garden, stored hay, or homemade feeds. Chickens and rabbits can benefit from kitchen scraps and garden waste, reducing the reliance on commercial feed.

Basic veterinary knowledge is essential for anyone raising livestock, including understanding common diseases and how to treat minor injuries. Establishing a relationship with a local veterinarian before a crisis is advisable, as is stockpiling essential veterinary supplies. Additionally, sustainable livestock management includes breeding and population control to ensure a continuous supply of animal products and maintain genetic diversity.

Integrating livestock with your survival garden can create a beneficial relationship where animals provide manure for compost and help control pests. However, it's essential to manage this integration to prevent crop damage. Livestock and animal husbandry are invaluable for a comprehensive food strategy in grid-down scenarios, requiring preparation, knowledge, and a commitment to animal well-being.

Chapter Summary

- Hunting and trapping are essential survival skills that provide a source of protein through the pursuit of wild animals and setting up traps for food.
- These activities require knowledge of animal behavior, legal and ethical considerations, and skills in weapon handling and trap setting, along with sustainable management of wildlife resources.
- Foraging for edible plants complements hunting and trapping by providing essential vitamins and minerals, emphasizing the importance of identifying and safely consuming wild edibles.
- Traditional food preservation methods without electricity, such as drying, smoking, salting, fermentation, and root cellaring, are vital for long-term food security.
- Establishing a survival garden with the right location, soil preparation, and crop selection ensures a steady food supply, focusing on high-yield, nutrient-dense crops.
- Efficient water management and organic pest control in gardening are essential, along with harvesting practices and seed saving for future planting.

- Livestock and animal husbandry, including selecting appropriate animals, providing shelter and nutrition, and managing health and breeding, complementing plant-based food sources.
- Integrating livestock with survival gardening creates a symbiotic relationship, enhancing soil fertility and pest control and contributing to a comprehensive food acquisition and storage strategy.

3

SHELTER AND SECURITY

Choosing a Safe Location

Finding and securing a safe location for shelter is essential. This decision can significantly impact your survival chances, affecting your immediate safety and your ability to gather resources, signal for help if necessary, and protect yourself from environmental hazards and potential threats.

When choosing a location for your shelter, the first factor to consider is the environmental conditions. Ideally, your shelter should be situated in an area that offers natural protection from the elements. Look for natural land formations such as hills or caves that shield you from strong winds, heavy rainfall, and extreme temperatures. However, be wary of locations that could become hazards themselves, such as flood plains or areas prone to landslides.

Accessibility to water is another critical factor. Your shelter should be within a reasonable distance from a freshwater source. However, it's crucial to balance proximity with safety, as water sources can attract both animals and other survivors. Ensure your shelter is not directly visible from the water source to maintain stealth and security.

Visibility to others is a double-edged sword. While being wholly hidden can offer security, it may also hinder rescue efforts in scenarios where you seek to be found. Opt for a location that allows you to observe your surroundings without being easily spotted. Techniques such as camouflage or using natural vegetation for cover can be beneficial.

Consider the proximity to resources. Your shelter location should allow easy access to materials for building, firewood, and food sources. However, these resources should not be so close that they attract other people or wildlife directly to your shelter.

Lastly, consider the location's long-term viability. In a prolonged grid-down situation, you may need to stay in this shelter for an extended period. Assess the area for potential threats, including wildlife, environmental hazards, and human activity. A location that initially seems safe may become dangerous as conditions change or other survivors move into the area.

Choosing a safe location for your shelter is a critical decision that requires careful consideration of multiple factors. By prioritizing safety, accessibility to resources, and strategic visibility, you can significantly increase your chances of survival in a grid-down scenario. Once a suitable location has been identified, the next step is to build a temporary shelter that can protect you from the elements and provide a base for your survival efforts.

Building Temporary Shelters

This section delves into practical methods for building temporary shelters that can protect you from the elements and provide a degree of security in uncertain times. The focus here is on utilizing readily available materials and simple techniques that do not require advanced skills or tools.

The first approach to constructing a temporary shelter involves leveraging the natural resources around you. Look for natural formations such as caves, large rock overhangs, or dense foliage that can offer immediate protection without the need for significant alteration. If such natural shelters are not available, the environment often provides materials such as branches, leaves, and vines that can be used to construct a rudimentary shelter.

A simple lean-to shelter can be made by leaning branches against a fallen log or a sturdy, low-hanging branch of a living tree. The framework should then be covered with smaller branches, leaves, or any available foliage to create a windbreak and to insulate against the cold. Ensure the shelter is small enough to retain body heat but large enough to lie comfortably.

Consider improvised materials for shelter construction in urban environments or situations where natural materials are scarce. Tarps, blankets, and even large trash bags can be invaluable in creating a protective space. A tarp or a large piece of plastic can be tied between trees to form a simple tent-like structure that can shield you from rain and wind. Blankets can be used for additional warmth or as a ground cover to insulate from the cold earth.

Regardless of the materials used, insulation and

waterproofing are vital considerations for any temporary shelter. In colder climates, insulation can be improved by piling leaves, grass, or even snow around and on top of your shelter. For waterproofing, ensure that the slope of any coverings allows rainwater to run off and not pool, potentially causing the shelter to collapse or become uninhabitable.

When constructing a temporary shelter, always consider your security. The shelter should be discreet, blending into the environment as much as possible to avoid drawing attention. It should also offer good visibility of the surrounding area, allowing you to see any approaching threats while remaining relatively concealed. Keep the shelter close to a water source but elevated to avoid flooding.

Building a temporary shelter in a grid-down scenario is about balancing the need for quick, adequate protection with the limitations of your environment and materials. Understanding and applying these basic principles can increase your chances of survival in the initial days following a disaster. Remember, the primary goal of any temporary shelter is to keep you safe and dry until you can either return home or transition to a more permanent habitat.

Constructing Long-Term Habitats

Transitioning from temporary shelters to constructing long-term habitats is the next logical step for survival. This section delves into the practicalities of building durable, secure, and sustainable living spaces that can support life for an extended period. The focus here is on selecting suitable locations, utilizing available materials, and incorporating renewable resources to create a stable environment.

Similarly to building a temporary habitat, the first step in constructing a long-term habitat is choosing an appropriate location. Factors to consider include proximity to water sources, elevation to avoid flooding, and natural barriers for protection against elements and potential threats. Assessing the land for agricultural potential is vital, ensuring that the soil can support crop cultivation for sustained food supply.

Utilizing locally available materials reduces the need for long-distance transportation and ensures that the habitat blends with the natural surroundings, offering camouflage against potential threats. Wood, stone, and earth are common materials that can be used effectively. Techniques such as timber framing, cob construction, and stone masonry are valuable skills to master, providing durable structures that can withstand harsh weather conditions.

In a grid-down situation, traditional utilities are no longer reliable. Renewable energy solutions such as solar panels or wind turbines can provide essential lighting, cooking, and heating power. Rainwater harvesting systems and gravity-fed water supplies can ensure a consistent water source, while water purification methods are crucial to ensure the water is safe for consumption.

Building with thermal mass in mind can help regulate indoor temperatures, keeping the habitat warm in the winter and cool in the summer. Materials like stone and earth absorb heat during the day and release it at night, reducing the need for external heating sources. Insulation is equally important, and natural materials such as straw bales or sheep's wool can be used effectively to prevent heat loss.

While the primary focus of a long-term habitat is sustainability and comfort, security should not be overlooked.

Designing the habitat with a single, easily defendable entrance, incorporating hidden or disguised storage areas for supplies, and ensuring that windows are reinforced or situated to prevent easy access from the outside are all critical considerations.

Finally, constructing long-term habitats often requires a community effort. Sharing skills, labor, and resources can make the building process more efficient and foster a sense of community and mutual support, which is invaluable in a grid-down scenario. Establishing communication, trade, and defense agreements with nearby habitats can enhance security and resource availability.

Constructing a long-term habitat in a grid-down scenario is complex but achievable. By carefully selecting a location, utilizing available materials, incorporating sustainable solutions, and focusing on security, survivors can create a stable and secure environment that supports long-term survival and well-being.

Home Fortification Techniques

Fortifying your long-term living space is crucial against potential threats. This section delves into practical home fortification techniques that can be implemented with minimal resources and technical know-how.

The first line of defense against intruders is to reinforce doors and windows. For doors, consider installing deadbolts and strike plates with longer screws to anchor them securely into the frame. A door barricade bar can also provide an additional layer of security. A simple but effective measure for sliding doors is to place a sturdy bar or a piece of wood in the track to prevent the door from being forced open.

Windows can be fortified by applying security film, which makes the glass more challenging to break. Installing window bars may also be necessary, especially in ground-level rooms. However, ensure that these measures do not trap occupants in case of a fire or other emergencies requiring quick evacuation.

To create a safe room, identify a room within your home that can be converted into a safe room. This room should have few or no windows and be accessible to all household members. Reinforce the door as you would the main entrance and stock the room with essential supplies, such as water, non-perishable food, a first aid kit, and a means of communication. This room can be a refuge during an extreme threat until help arrives or the situation stabilizes.

Improve visibility and deterrence. Good exterior lighting can deter would-be intruders. Solar-powered lights are ideal for grid-down situations, as they require no electricity. Position lights around the perimeter of your home, focusing on entry points and dark corners.

Consider also the strategic placement of security cameras. Even non-functional cameras can act as a deterrent. However, real-time monitoring capabilities can be advantageous if power solutions, such as solar panels or generators, are available.

Utilize natural and physical barriers. The landscape around your home can offer natural fortifications. Thorny bushes or dense hedges under windows can discourage attempts to break in. Similarly, a sturdy fence can serve as a physical barrier. While a high fence is beneficial, ensure that it does not provide cover for intruders to work unseen. The use of gravel in driveways and paths can alert you to visitors' approach due to the noise it generates when walked on.

Finally, in a grid-down scenario, there is strength in numbers. Collaborate with neighbors to establish a neighborhood watch or mutual aid agreements. Sharing information and resources can significantly enhance the security of your home and the community.

By implementing these home fortification techniques, you can create a safer and more secure environment for you and your family in the face of uncertainty. The next step in ensuring your safety involves developing comprehensive security measures and perimeter defense strategies to protect your fortified home further.

Security Measures and Perimeter Defense

With the basic fortification of your home addressed, the focus must now shift towards establishing a robust perimeter defense. This involves a combination of physical barriers, surveillance, and strategic planning to deter potential threats and ensure the safety of inhabitants.

Physical Barriers: The first line of defense in perimeter security is the creation of physical barriers. These can range from simple obstacles like fences and walls to more sophisticated ones like trenches or natural barriers like thick hedges. The key is to create a barrier that is difficult to cross unnoticed. Fences should be tall enough to deter climbers and include features like barbed wire to discourage attempts to breach them. On the other hand, walls offer more durability and can be reinforced with materials that make them difficult to penetrate.

Surveillance: In a grid-down situation, traditional electronic surveillance systems may not be reliable. However, alternative methods of surveillance can be employed. Setting up observation posts at strategic points around the perimeter allows for continuously monitoring the surroundings. These posts should be well-camouflaged and manned by individuals trained in spotting and assessing potential threats. Additionally, using mirrors or reflective surfaces can help extend the field of view around corners or over obstacles.

Alarm Systems: While electronic alarms may be inoperative, improvised alarm systems can be valuable to your security measures. Simple tripwires connected to noisy objects can be an early warning system against intruders. Cans filled with pebbles or bells attached to strings can create enough noise to alert defenders without requiring any power source.

Natural Surveillance: Utilizing the natural landscape can significantly enhance perimeter defense. Clearing foliage and potential hiding spots near your shelter eliminates cover for would-be intruders. Conversely, planting thorny bushes or other natural barriers can provide an eco-friendly deterrent that requires minimal maintenance.

Access Control: Controlling access to your shelter is crucial. This means establishing secure entry and exit points that can be easily monitored and defended. Gates should be sturdy and lockable, with reinforced hinges and locks that are difficult to tamper with. Ideally, the shelter should have a single, well-defended entrance, with all other potential access points securely sealed.

Community Coordination: In situations where multiple shelters are nearby, coordinating with neighboring shelters can create a mutual defense network. Sharing surveillance duties and establishing standard alarm signals can enhance the security of all involved. This collective approach distributes the workload and creates a more robust defense against external threats.

Training and Drills: Finally, the effectiveness of any security measure is only as good as the people implementing it. Regular training sessions and drills should be conducted to ensure that all inhabitants are familiar with security protocols, surveillance techniques, and emergency response procedures. This preparation ensures that in the event of an actual threat, everyone knows their role and can act swiftly and efficiently to secure the shelter.

By implementing these security measures and perimeter defense strategies, you can significantly enhance the safety and security of your shelter in a grid-down scenario. Remember, the goal is to deter potential threats and provide peace of mind for the inhabitants, knowing that measures are in place to protect them in uncertain times.

Fire Safety and Management

Fire is great. It's a crucial tool for warmth, cooking, and signaling. But, fire can become a devastating force if not properly managed. Especially when conventional emergency services are unavailable. This section delves into the essential fire safety and management practices to ensure your shelter remains a safe haven during challenging times.

First and foremost, selecting the appropriate location for your fire is critical. When outdoors, choose a spot that is clear of overhead hazards, such as tree branches, and at least 15 feet away from tent walls, shrubbery, and other flammable materials. Creating a perimeter of rocks or digging a small pit can help contain the fire and prevent it from spreading. For indoor fires, such as those in a fireplace or wood stove, ensure that the structure is well-ventilated to avoid smoke and carbon monoxide buildup. Regular inspection and cleaning of chimneys and flues are imperative to prevent blockages and reduce the risk of chimney fires.

Equally important is the selection of fuel for your fire. Dry, seasoned wood burns more efficiently and produces less smoke than green or wet wood. In a grid-down situation, conserving resources is critical, so use your fuel judiciously. Start with smaller kindling to get the fire going before adding larger logs to maintain it. This method reduces waste and minimizes the risk of creating an uncontrollably large fire.

Fire extinguishing practices are another critical component of fire safety. Always have a plan for extinguishing your fire quickly and safely. Keeping a bucket of water, sand, or dirt nearby for outdoor fires can allow for rapid response if the fire spreads. In an indoor setting, ensure you have a functional fire extinguisher within reach and that all occupants are familiar with its operation. Before leaving a fire unattended, whether indoors or out, ensure it is completely extinguished. Coals can remain hot and reignite for hours or even days after the flames have died.

Lastly, fire safety education is an invaluable tool. Familiarize yourself and your group with basic fire safety practices, such as "stop, drop, and roll," and establishing clear escape routes during a fire. Regular drills and discussions about fire safety help ensure everyone knows how to act swiftly and safely should a fire emergency arise.

In conclusion, while fire is an indispensable survival tool, its potential for destruction necessitates a disciplined approach to safety and management. By selecting appropriate fire locations, using fuel efficiently, practicing safe extinguishing methods, and prioritizing fire safety education, you can significantly reduce the risks associated with fire in a grid-down scenario, ensuring your shelter remains a secure and safe environment for all occupants.

Chapter Summary

- Choosing a safe location for shelter is crucial for survival in a grid-down scenario.
- Use natural resources and improvised materials to build shelters that protect from the elements.
- Transition to long-term habitats by selecting suitable locations and using local materials.
- Reinforce doors and windows to secure your home against threats.
- Establish a robust perimeter defense to ensure the safety of inhabitants.
- Practice fire safety by choosing appropriate locations and having extinguishing plans.
- Strategic location selection and resource accessibility are essential for survival and security.
- Emphasize community effort in constructing long-term habitats and fortifying homes.

4

HEALTH AND FIRST AID

Basic First Aid Skills

In grid-down survival, a foundational understanding of basic first aid skills is not just beneficial but crucial. The ability to respond effectively to common injuries and illnesses can mean the difference between a minor inconvenience and a life-threatening situation. This section aims to equip you with the knowledge and confidence needed to handle such scenarios, ensuring you're prepared for various medical emergencies that might arise when professional medical help is not immediately accessible.

First and foremost, it's essential to understand the principles of assessing a situation before diving into action. Always ensure the scene is safe for both the responder (you) and the victim. This means checking for any ongoing dangers, such as fire, toxic gas, or unstable structures. Once it's safe to proceed, assess the victim's condition by checking their responsiveness, airway, breathing, and circulation—often called the ABCs of first aid.

For unresponsive individuals, immediate action may be required. CPR (Cardiopulmonary Resuscitation) may be necessary if they are not breathing. It's crucial to be trained in performing CPR correctly, as improper technique can do more harm than good. Remember, CPR for adults differs from that for children and infants, so specialized training for each category is advisable.

Bleeding is another common issue that can arise in various situations, from minor cuts to severe wounds. The primary goal is to control the bleeding. Apply direct pressure to the wound with a clean cloth or bandage. If the bleeding does not stop, elevate the wound above the heart level and continue applying pressure. It's important to keep the person calm and still, as movement can exacerbate bleeding.

Burns, ranging from minor to severe, require specific care. For minor burns, cool the area under running water for at least 10 minutes to reduce pain and swelling. Avoid using ice, as it can cause further damage to the skin. Cover the burn with a sterile, non-adhesive bandage or cloth. For more severe burns, do not apply water. Instead, cover the burn with a clean, dry cloth and seek medical attention immediately.

Immobilization is key in cases of fractures or sprains. Use splints made from available materials to stabilize the affected area and prevent further injury. Ensure the splint is not too tight, as this can impede circulation. The RICE method (Rest, Ice, Compression, Elevation) can effectively reduce swelling and pain for sprains.

Recognizing the signs of common illnesses is also vital. Symptoms such as fever, vomiting, diarrhea, or rash may indicate various conditions that require different approaches. Hydration is crucial, especially in cases of vomiting and diarrhea. Monitor the person's temperature and provide over-the-counter medications if appropriate and available.

Lastly, always remember the importance of personal protection. Utilize gloves if available when dealing with blood or bodily fluids to minimize the risk of infection. Wash your hands thoroughly before and after providing first aid.

By mastering these basic first aid skills, you'll be better prepared to handle common injuries and illnesses, providing crucial care in the critical moments that often precede professional medical treatment. This knowledge enhances your survival capabilities and empowers you to assist others in need, embodying the essence of preparedness and resilience in grid-down scenarios.

Handling Common Injuries and Illnesses

Without access to professional medical facilities, primary healthcare responsibility falls squarely on the shoulders of individuals and communities. This section delves into practical strategies for managing various health concerns likely to arise, emphasizing a hands-on approach to care.

Cuts, from minor to severe, are among the most common injuries. Immediate and proper care is essential to prevent infection and ensure healing. Begin by washing your hands to minimize the risk of introducing bacteria into the wound. If available, wear gloves for additional protection. Clean the wound gently with water and mild soap, avoiding the use of harsh chemicals that can irritate the injury. Apply direct pressure with a clean cloth to stop bleeding. Once bleeding has ceased, cover the wound with a sterile bandage. Change the dressing daily or whenever it becomes wet or dirty. Watch for signs of infection, such as redness, swelling, or pus, and take steps to address these symptoms promptly.

Sprains and strains frequently occur during physical activity, especially in uneven or unfamiliar terrain. A sprain affects ligaments, the fibrous tissue connecting bones, while a strain involves muscles or tendons. The RICE method (Rest, Ice, Compression, Elevation) is a time-tested approach to treatment. Rest the injured area, apply ice to reduce swelling (wrapped in a cloth to avoid skin damage), use a compression bandage to provide support, and elevate the injury above heart level when possible. Limit movement until healing has progressed, and gradually reintroduce activity to avoid stiffness and encourage strength rebuilding.

Burns, whether from fire, sun exposure, or contact with hot objects, require careful attention. For minor burns, cool the area under running water for several minutes to reduce pain and swelling. Do not apply ice directly, as this can cause further damage to the skin. Cover the burn with a sterile, non-adhesive bandage or cloth. Avoid ointments or butter, which can trap heat and worsen the injury. For more severe burns characterized by extensive damage or charring of the skin, seek professional medical help immediately.

Dehydration and heat exhaustion are serious risks, particularly in hot climates or during strenuous activity. Symptoms include thirst, dizziness, fatigue, and confusion. Prevent dehydration by drinking plenty of water, even before feeling thirsty. For someone experiencing heat exhaustion, move them to a cooler place, encourage them to drink water or electrolyte solutions, and cool their body with wet cloths or a bath. Rest is crucial until recovery is evident.

In situations where sanitation is compromised, gastrointestinal issues can become common. Preventative measures include practicing good hygiene and ensuring water and food safety. For mild cases of diarrhea, maintain hydration with small, frequent sips of water or oral rehydration solutions. Avoid solid foods until symptoms improve. If symptoms persist or are severe, especially in children or the elderly, seek ways to access professional medical advice.

The ability to adapt and apply basic healthcare principles is invaluable in a grid-down scenario. While this guide covers managing common injuries and illnesses, it's important to continue learning and practicing these skills. Knowledge, preparation, and calm can significantly impact health outcomes in challenging situations.

Natural Remedies and Alternative Medicines

When conventional medical treatments are inaccessible, natural remedies and alternative medicines become essential. These traditional healing practices and plant-based treatments have been used for centuries. Practical, accessible, and effective natural remedies that can be cultivated or foraged provide a crucial lifeline when modern healthcare is unavailable.

Herbs are pivotal in traditional medicine across cultures, treating everything from minor headaches and digestive issues to inflammation and infections. Due to its salicin content, Willow bark, which is often called nature's aspirin, helps alleviate pain, reduce fever, and ease inflammation. Lavender is valued for its calming effects and antiseptic properties, and it is helpful for stress relief and treating cuts. Peppermint effectively addresses digestive problems and headaches. Echinacea is commonly used to bolster the immune system and combat respiratory infections.

In addition to cultivated herbs, many wild plants like dandelion, plantain, and yarrow offer medicinal benefits. Dandelions are nutritious and support liver health, plantain leaves soothe skin irritations and cuts, and yarrow is essential for first aid, capable of stopping bleeding and reducing fever. The effectiveness of these natural remedies largely depends on their proper preparation and usage. Infusions and decoctions extract medicinal properties from plants, while tinctures provide a potent, preserved form of herbal remedies.

However, using natural remedies requires caution. Accurate plant identification is critical to avoid harmful mistakes, and proper dosages ensure safety. Awareness of potential allergies and interactions with other medications is also necessary. In conclusion, natural remedies and alternative medicines are valuable for maintaining health and treating ailments when conventional options fail. By learning about herbal and plant medicine, individuals can enhance their resilience and self-sufficiency, preparing to care for themselves and their loved ones in challenging times.

Maintaining Hygiene and Sanitation

Maintaining hygiene and sanitation when the grid is down is crucial to prevent disease. Personal hygiene is essential; wash your hands regularly with soap and water, especially before eating, after using the toilet, and when handling food. If water is scarce, use alcohol-based hand sanitizers or a homemade solution of 1 part bleach to 9 parts water.

Try to bathe regularly using minimal water; sponge baths can be an effective way to conserve water while still cleaning the skin. If functioning toilets are unavailable, create a restroom away from living areas and water sources. Dig a deep hole for waste and cover it with soil after each use to reduce odor and deter flies, or use a bucket lined with a plastic bag indoors, sealing and disposing of it properly.

Proper disposal is critical; separate organic waste from recyclables and non-biodegradable materials. Compost organic waste reduces volume and creates beneficial soil while storing non-biodegradable waste securely until proper disposal is possible. Avoid burning waste due to pollution and fire risks.

Safe drinking water is necessary; boil water for at least one minute to kill pathogens or use purification tablets or household bleach if boiling isn't possible. Store purified water in clean, covered containers. Food safety is also essential; cover food to protect it from pests, cook thoroughly, and rely on non-perishable items like canned goods and dried foods. Wash fruits and vegetables with purified water before consumption.

Control pests by keeping living areas clean, sealing gaps, and using traps or natural repellents. Mosquito nets can offer protection during sleep. Be vigilant for signs of illness and isolate sick individuals early to prevent spread. Use natural remedies and over-the-counter medications for minor issues, and seek medical help for severe conditions when possible.

Following these guidelines can significantly reduce disease risk and create a safer environment.

Preventing and Treating Waterborne Diseases

Waterborne diseases such as cholera, dysentery, and typhoid pose significant health risks, notably lacking sanitation and hygiene. Practical strategies for preventing and treating these diseases include water purification, recognizing symptoms, and understanding basic treatment methods. Ensuring that drinking water is free from pathogens is crucial for prevention. Boiling water is a highly effective method; it should be brought to a rolling boil for at least one or three minutes at higher altitudes to kill most pathogens. Alternatively, chemical disinfectants like chlorine dioxide or iodine tablets can be used, though they may not eliminate all pathogens and could alter the water's taste.

For a sustainable approach, consider installing a rainwater collection system or using a high-quality water filter to remove contaminants. Clear water isn't necessarily safe for consumption and must be treated. Early recognition of waterborne disease symptoms such as diarrhea, vomiting, fever, and abdominal cramps is vital for effective treatment. Dehydration is a significant concern, indicated by symptoms like thirst, reduced urination, dry skin, fatigue, and dizziness. Recognizing these signs early can facilitate quicker treatment and recovery.

The primary treatment for waterborne diseases involves rehydration. For mild dehydration, consuming clean, purified water is crucial. In more severe cases, oral rehydration solutions (ORS) are essential and can be life-saving. ORS packets are practical for medical kits, but a homemade solution can also be made from salt, sugar, and treated water. Medical intervention with antibiotics or other medications may be necessary for persistent or severe symptoms, but these should be administered under professional guidance to avoid complications such as antibiotic resistance. In summary, managing waterborne diseases effectively requires proper water treatment, prompt recognition of symptoms, and immediate rehydration. These measures are crucial to maintaining health and resilience in challenging conditions.

Mental Health and Coping Mechanisms

An often overlooked aspect of survival is mental health and well-being. The psychological impact of such events can be profound, affecting individuals' ability to make rational decisions, maintain relationships, and ultimately survive. This section delves into the significance of mental health and coping mechanisms that can be employed to navigate through the psychological challenges of a grid-down situation.

Mental health challenges in a grid-down scenario can range from acute stress reactions to more prolonged disorders such as depression and post-traumatic stress disorder (PTSD). The loss of normalcy, the uncertainty of the future, and the potential for significant lifestyle changes or losses can trigger these responses. Recognizing the signs of mental health distress in oneself and others becomes a critical skill. Symptoms may include persistent sadness, excessive worry, changes in sleep patterns, withdrawal from social interactions, and increased irritability or aggression.

Establishing a routine can provide a sense of normalcy

and control to mitigate these challenges. Even in chaos, a structured daily schedule that includes time for physical activity, rest, meals, and social interaction can help maintain mental balance. Physical exercise, in particular, is beneficial not only for physical health but also for mental well-being, as it can reduce symptoms of anxiety and depression.

Social support plays a pivotal role in coping with stress and trauma. Building and maintaining a trust network with fellow survivors can provide emotional comfort and practical assistance. Sharing experiences and feelings with others who understand the situation can alleviate isolation and help process emotions.

Practicing mindfulness and relaxation techniques can also effectively manage stress and anxiety. Techniques such as deep breathing, meditation, and progressive muscle relaxation can help calm the mind and reduce the physiological responses to stress. These practices can be particularly beneficial in situations where the environment is beyond one's control, helping individuals focus on the present moment and reduce anxiety about the future.

In addition to these self-help strategies, it's important to recognize when professional help is needed. In a grid-down scenario, access to mental health professionals may be limited, but utilizing any available resources, such as counselors or support hotlines, can be crucial for those experiencing severe mental health difficulties.

Lastly, engaging in purposeful activities that contribute to the community's well-being can enhance one's sense of purpose and belonging. Whether participating in rebuilding efforts, teaching valuable skills to others, or simply offering a listening ear, being part of something larger than oneself can provide a powerful counterbalance to the feelings of despair and helplessness that may arise.

In conclusion, while the challenges of surviving a grid-down scenario are manifold, the importance of mental health cannot be overstated. Individuals can bolster their psychological resilience by employing a range of coping mechanisms, from maintaining routines and exercising to seeking social support and engaging in community activities. This, in turn, enhances their overall capacity to navigate the complexities of a post-grid-down world, ensuring survival and a path toward recovery and rebuilding.

Chapter Summary

- Understanding basic first aid skills is crucial for survival in grid-down scenarios. These skills enable individuals to handle medical emergencies when professional help is unavailable.
- Key first aid principles include scene safety and the ABCs (Airway, Breathing, Circulation); CPR may be necessary for unresponsive individuals, with different techniques for adults, children, and infants.
- Controlling bleeding involves applying direct pressure, elevating the wound, and keeping the injured person calm. Depending on the severity of the burn, it requires cooling with water or covering with a clean cloth.
- Fractures and sprains need immobilization and possibly the RICE method (Rest, Ice,

- Compression, Elevation); recognizing common illness signs and ensuring hydration is vital.
- Personal protection, like using gloves and washing hands, is important when providing first aid to minimize infection risk.
- Handling common injuries like cuts, sprains, burns, and addressing dehydration, gastrointestinal issues, and ensuring hygiene and sanitation are emphasized for health maintenance in grid-down situations.
- Natural and alternative medicines, including herbal and medicinal plants, offer viable treatment options when conventional healthcare is unavailable. They also have safety considerations for identification, dosages, and allergies.
- Mental health is as crucial as physical health, with coping mechanisms such as establishing routines, exercising, seeking social support, practicing mindfulness, and engaging in community activities highlighted for psychological resilience.

5

ENERGY AND POWER ALTERNATIVES

Solar Power Basics

Solar power is great, particularly in scenarios where traditional power grids are no longer reliable. This section delves into the fundamentals of harnessing solar energy, which converts the sun's rays into usable electricity, offering a lifeline in times of energy scarcity. At the heart of solar power systems are solar panels composed of photovoltaic (PV) cells. These cells are designed to capture sunlight and convert it into direct current (DC) electricity. The efficiency of this conversion process is a critical factor, influenced by the quality of the solar panels, the angle at which they are installed, and the amount of sunlight they receive. For optimal performance, panels should be positioned to face true south (in the Northern Hemisphere) and tilted at an angle equal to the latitude of their location, though adjustments may be necessary to account for seasonal variations in the sun's path.

Once generated, the DC electricity must still be prepared for typical household use. Most homes and appliances operate on alternating current (AC), necessitating an inverter. This device converts DC into AC, making the electricity compatible with the grid and suitable for everyday consumption. Modern inverters also have monitoring capabilities, allowing users to track their system's performance and energy output in real time.

For those living off-grid or in areas prone to power outages, energy storage is a crucial component of a solar power system. Batteries enable the storage of excess electricity produced during peak sunlight hours for use at night or on cloudy days. Lead-acid and lithium-ion batteries are the most common types, each with advantages and considerations regarding capacity, lifespan, and maintenance.

Implementing a solar power system requires careful planning and consideration of several factors, including location, energy needs, and budget. Initial costs can be significant, but various incentives and rebates governments and utilities offer can help offset these expenses. Moreover, the long-term benefits—reduced reliance on the grid, lower electricity bills, and a smaller carbon footprint—make solar power an increasingly attractive option for those seeking energy independence.

In embracing solar power, individuals secure a reliable energy source for themselves and contribute to a larger movement towards sustainable living. As we transition to the next section, we'll explore another form of renewable energy that complements solar power, offering further resilience and self-sufficiency in a grid-down scenario.

Wind Energy Fundamentals

Wind energy is a sustainable and reliable energy source in a grid-down scenario. This section delves into the fundamentals of harnessing wind power, a resource that has been utilized for centuries but remains underexploited in modern survival strategies.

Wind energy is generated by converting kinetic energy from wind into mechanical power or electricity. This process is facilitated by wind turbines, which consist of blades mounted on a tower to capture wind energy. When the wind blows, it turns the turbine's blades around a rotor, which spins a generator to produce electricity.

The feasibility of wind power as a survival energy source hinges on several factors, including location, wind speed, and the availability of suitable technology. Wind speeds vary greatly depending on geographic location, terrain, and altitude. Generally, an area with average wind speeds of at least 10 miles per hour (mph) is suitable for small-scale wind power generation. It's crucial to thoroughly assess local wind resources to determine the viability of wind energy in a specific location.

Small wind turbines can be a practical option for those in areas conducive to wind power. These turbines can be installed on properties to generate electricity for individual homes or small communities. A wind turbine's capacity is measured in kilowatts (kW), with systems typically ranging from 1 kW to 10 kW for residential use. The amount of electricity a turbine can generate depends on its capacity, the wind speed, and the turbine's efficiency.

When considering the installation of a wind turbine, the

initial costs, which include the turbine, tower, inverter, and installation, must be taken into account. Despite these upfront expenses, wind energy can be a cost-effective solution over time, particularly in off-grid scenarios where traditional power sources are unavailable or unsustainable.

Maintenance is another critical aspect of wind power. Regular inspections and upkeep are necessary to ensure the longevity and efficiency of the system. This includes checking the turbine's components for wear and tear, ensuring the blades are free of obstructions, and verifying that electrical connections are secure.

Incorporating wind energy into a grid-down survival plan offers several advantages. It provides a renewable and clean source of electricity, reduces dependence on fossil fuels, and can be combined with other renewable energy sources, such as solar power, to create a more robust and reliable energy system.

As we transition from discussing the potential of solar energy, it's clear that wind power represents another vital component in the arsenal of renewable energy options for sustainable living in times of crisis. By understanding the fundamentals of wind energy, individuals and communities can better prepare for and adapt to the challenges of a grid-down scenario, ensuring access to essential power when it's most needed.

Hydro Power Options

Hydropower is a viable and often underutilized energy source in sustainable and off-grid living. It involves converting the energy from flowing or falling water into electricity, using a simple principle: water turns a turbine, which spins a generator to produce electricity. The implementation of this principle varies based on available water sources, geographic conditions, and specific energy needs.

One accessible form of hydropower for off-grid living is the micro-hydro system, which generates power from small streams or rivers. These systems consist of an intake where water is diverted, a penstock (pipe) leading the water to the turbine, the turbine itself, a generator, and a tailrace where water returns to the stream. Micro-hydro provides continuous, reliable power and requires relatively low maintenance, making it ideal for those near suitable water sources.

Selecting the right site for a hydropower installation is crucial. To maximize power output, a sufficient water flow must be combined with a significant drop in elevation. Environmental and regulatory factors must also be considered, as water diversion and construction may impact ecosystems and require permits. For DIY enthusiasts, building a hydropower system can be rewarding, using off-the-shelf components and online tutorials for guidance. Safety measures such as proper grounding and waterproofing are essential.

Integrating hydropower into an off-grid system often involves using a battery bank for electricity storage, allowing the system to provide power during low water flow and meet varying demands. Components like charge controllers and inverters manage and convert the electricity for household use. In conclusion, hydropower is a promising alternative for those seeking grid independence or supplementing their energy sources sustainably, playing a pivotal role in off-grid living and emergency preparedness.

Manual Power Generation Techniques

This section delves into the practical and innovative techniques of manual power generation, offering a lifeline in scenarios where conventional energy sources are unavailable or have been compromised.

Hand Crank Generators: These devices convert human mechanical energy into electrical energy by turning a crank. Hand crank generators are invaluable for charging small devices such as radios, flashlights, and mobile phones. Their efficiency, however, is directly proportional to the physical effort exerted, making them more suitable for low-power applications or as a temporary solution during energy shortages.

Bicycle Generators: A step up from hand crank generators, bicycle generators harness the power of pedaling to produce electricity. By attaching a stationary bike to a generator, individuals can produce more power and be capable of charging larger batteries or running small appliances. The setup usually involves a motor used as a generator, a belt drive, and a charge controller to regulate the energy produced. This method not only provides a sustainable source of power but also promotes physical fitness.

Manual Treadmill Generators: Similar in concept to the bicycle generator, manual treadmill generators convert kinetic energy from walking or running into electrical power. Though the initial setup might require some technical adjustments, the energy output can be significant, making it a viable option for powering essential devices in a grid-down scenario.

Hand-Powered Flashlights and Radios: These devices have built-in generators activated by squeezing a handle or winding a crank. They are particularly useful in emergency kits, providing light and access to information without the need for external power sources. Their ease of use and portability make them indispensable tools for survival situations.

DIY Wind Turbines: For those with a knack for engineering and access to basic materials, constructing a DIY wind turbine can effectively generate power manually. Individuals can create a wind power system capable of charging batteries and powering small appliances using salvaged parts such as motorbike alternators, PVC pipes for blades, and repurposed batteries for storage. While this requires a higher level of technical skill, the payoff for renewable energy production can be substantial.

Incorporating these manual power generation techniques into your survival strategy ensures a degree of independence from the grid and prepares you for a wide range of emergency scenarios. Each method offers unique advantages and challenges, allowing for customization based on individual needs, physical capabilities, and available resources. As we move forward, the next logical step in ensuring a comprehensive energy solution in grid-down situations is to explore practical battery storage and management strategies, ensuring that the power generated through these manual methods is stored efficiently and ready for use when needed.

Battery Storage and Management

Storing and managing power efficiently is as crucial as generating it, especially when traditional power sources are unavailable. Understanding the different types of batteries available is the first step in mastering battery storage. The most common types include lead-acid, lithium-ion, nickel-cadmium (NiCd), and nickel-metal hydride (NiMH).

Lead-acid batteries are the oldest type of rechargeable battery. They are widely used due to their cost-effectiveness and high surge capability. However, they are heavy and have a lower energy density. Lithium-ion batteries are known for their high energy density and lightweight, making them prevalent in modern electronics and electric vehicles. They charge faster and have a longer lifespan than lead-acid batteries but are more expensive.

Nickel-cadmium batteries can deliver full power until completely discharged and withstand extreme temperatures and rough handling. However, they suffer from the "memory effect" and contain toxic materials. Nickel-metal hydride batteries offer a higher energy density than NiCd without toxic components. They are less prone to the memory effect but have a shorter lifespan in high-drain devices.

Proper storage extends the life of batteries and ensures they are ready when needed. Storing batteries in a cool, dry place helps maintain performance, as extreme temperatures can degrade them. Lithium-ion batteries should be kept at a 40-50% charge state for long-term storage, while lead-acid batteries should be fully charged and topped off every three to six months.

A Battery Management System (BMS) is crucial for monitoring and managing the health and performance of a battery pack. It performs cell balancing, overcharge and over-discharge protection, and temperature monitoring. These functions help prolong the battery's lifespan and prevent damage.

A battery bank is an effective strategy for maintaining a substantial power reserve. This involves connecting multiple batteries in series or parallel to increase voltage or amp-hour capacity. It is essential to use batteries of the same type, age, and capacity to prevent imbalance and to use proper cabling and connectors to ensure efficient power flow.

In conclusion, understanding and implementing adequate battery storage and management practices are pivotal in ensuring a reliable energy supply in grid-down scenarios. One can significantly enhance their energy resilience by selecting the appropriate battery types, adhering to storage best practices, utilizing a BMS, and carefully designing a battery bank. Integrating these storage solutions into a broader renewable energy plan is the next step toward achieving sustainable, off-grid power independence.

Creating a Renewable Energy Plan

Creating a renewable energy plan is a matter of convenience and survival. This section delves into the practical steps and considerations in establishing a renewable energy system that can sustain your needs during extended periods without grid power.

First and foremost, it's essential to assess your energy needs accurately. Begin by listing all the essential devices and appliances, such as refrigeration for food preservation, lighting, heating or cooling systems, and communication devices. For each item, note its power consumption in watts and estimate how many hours per day it will be used. This exercise will give you a rough estimate of your daily energy requirements in watt-hours (Wh) or kilowatt-hours (kWh), which is crucial for designing an appropriately sized renewable energy system.

Once you have a clear understanding of your energy needs, the next step is to explore the feasible renewable energy options for your location. Solar power is the most accessible and widely applicable option, but wind, hydro, and pedal power could be viable depending on your circumstances. Each energy source has advantages and limitations, which must be carefully considered. For instance, solar panels require significant sunlight exposure, making them less effective in areas with prolonged periods of cloud cover or during the winter months in higher latitudes.

The choice of renewable energy sources will directly influence the equipment you need. For solar power, this includes photovoltaic (PV) panels, inverters to convert the DC electricity generated by the panels into AC electricity usable by household devices, and mounting hardware. Wind power systems require turbines, towers, and, again, inverters. If you're considering multiple energy sources, you'll also need a controller to manage the input from each source efficiently.

Integration with your battery storage system is the next critical step. The energy generated by your renewable sources must be stored effectively when the source isn't actively generating power (e.g., solar panels at night). This involves selecting batteries with sufficient capacity to meet your energy needs and configuring them for optimal charge and discharge cycles. The connection between your renewable energy generation and battery storage must be carefully managed to prevent overcharging or excessive depletion, which can significantly reduce the lifespan of your batteries.

Maintenance and monitoring are ongoing requirements for

a renewable energy system. Regular checks will ensure that your equipment is functioning correctly and efficiently. This includes cleaning solar panels or wind turbine blades to remove dust and debris, checking connections for corrosion or wear, and monitoring system output to identify any issues promptly.

Finally, it's important to consider redundancy and backup options. No system is fail-proof, and having alternative means of meeting your essential energy needs can provide peace of mind and additional security in a grid-down scenario. This could be as simple as having portable solar chargers for small devices, manual tools to replace electric ones, or even a backup generator for critical needs, though the latter relies on fuel that may also be in short supply.

Creating a renewable energy plan is a significant undertaking that requires careful planning, investment, and ongoing management. However, its independence and security in a grid-down situation make it an essential component of any comprehensive survival strategy. By assessing your needs, choosing the right mix of renewable sources, and ensuring proper integration and maintenance, you can establish a resilient energy system that sustains your essential needs when the grid is down.

Chapter Summary

- Solar power basics highlight the importance of solar panels and photovoltaic (PV) cells in converting sunlight into electricity, emphasizing the need for optimal panel positioning and

inverters to convert DC to AC electricity for household use.
- Energy storage, particularly through batteries like lead-acid and lithium-ion, is crucial for off-grid solar systems to provide electricity during the night or cloudy days, with incentives and rebates available to offset initial costs.
- Wind energy is presented as a sustainable alternative, with wind turbines converting kinetic energy from wind into electricity, dependent on factors like location, wind speed, and technology for feasibility.
- Small wind turbines offer a practical solution for individual homes or communities in suitable areas, with considerations for initial costs, maintenance, and the benefits of renewable, clean electricity.
- Hydropower, especially micro-hydro systems, is discussed for its continuous power supply capability. Site selection and DIY options are explored for off-grid living and emergency preparedness.
- Manual power generation techniques, including hand crank generators, bicycle generators, and manual treadmills, are explored as vital for resilience and self-sufficiency in grid-down scenarios.
- Battery storage and management are critical for maintaining a reliable energy supply, with details on different battery types, storage best practices, and the importance of a Battery Management System (BMS).

- Creating a renewable energy plan involves assessing energy needs, exploring renewable options like solar, wind, and hydropower, integrating with battery storage, and ensuring system maintenance and redundancy for grid-down resilience.

6
COMMUNICATION AND NAVIGATION

Basic Signaling Techniques

When the grid goes down, traditional communication methods may fail, making it essential to revert to basic signaling techniques for conveying messages or attracting attention in emergencies. These methods are crucial for survival, finding help, or indicating your location. Visual signals are straightforward, ranging from creating smoke during the day to using mirrors or reflective surfaces to catch sunlight. Smoke signals are produced by starting a fire and covering it with green vegetation to generate smoke, ensuring the smoke contrasts with the background. Mirrors or reflective surfaces can be used to flash sunlight in a specific direction, requiring practice to aim accurately.

Sound signals become more effective when visibility is poor, or distances are great. These can include blowing a whistle, banging metal objects together, or using a horn to create a noise distinct from natural background sounds.

Especially useful in dense forests or at night, the universal distress signal involves three blasts of sound, such as three whistle blows or three gunshots, repeated every few minutes to enhance the chances of being heard. Additionally, marking your path when moving through unfamiliar territory or needing to retrace your steps is vital. This can be achieved by tying fabric to branches, stacking rocks, or marking trees with chalk or charcoal, ensuring these markers are noticeable and consistent.

Nature also offers indicators for navigation, such as moss growing on the northern side of trees in the northern hemisphere or using the position of the sun and stars for guidance. Reading these natural signs is invaluable when other navigation aids are unavailable. While these signaling techniques may seem simple, practice dramatically enhances their effectiveness. Familiarizing yourself with these methods before they are needed ensures efficient and effective use in survival situations, with regular practice sessions refining these skills. In conclusion, mastering basic signaling techniques is fundamental to survival in a grid-down scenario, enabling communication over distances, attracting attention in emergencies, and navigating unfamiliar territories, significantly increasing your chances of survival and rescue.

Using Radios for Communication

Maintaining communication with your group or reaching out for help is crucial in a grid-down scenario. With conventional communication means like cell phones and the internet unavailable, radios become an essential lifeline. This section explores the practical use of radios for communication, focusing on different types, operations, and best practices to ensure connectivity during crises.

Handheld radios or walkie-talkies are compact and user-friendly for short-range communication within a group. They operate on various frequencies, including the Family Radio Service (FRS) and General Mobile Radio Service (GMRS) bands. FRS radios are accessible without a license and suitable for general use. GMRS radios, offering a longer range, require a license from the Federal Communications Commission (FCC) in the United States.

Ham radios are unmatched for long-distance communication. They can operate on multiple frequencies, enabling communication across towns, states, or even internationally under certain conditions. However, using a ham radio requires a license obtained by passing an exam that covers radio theory, operating practices, and regulations. Citizen Band (CB) radios also provide short-to-medium-range communication without a license. Truckers commonly use them, making them a valuable tool for survival communication.

Ensure your radios have a reliable power source, such as AA or AAA batteries or rechargeable battery packs. Consider solar or hand-crank chargers to keep your radios operational when traditional power sources fail. Understanding the frequencies your radio can access and any legal restrictions is also essential. Privacy can be a concern since others can listen to your communications, use privacy codes if available, and be cautious about the information you share.

The range of your radio can be significantly affected by its antenna. In some cases, upgrading to a higher-quality antenna or setting up a base station with an external antenna for ham radios can significantly extend your reach. Establish clear communication protocols within your group, use call signs to identify each member, and agree on specific frequencies and times for check-ins. Keep transmissions brief and to the point to conserve battery life and minimize the chance of interception.

Familiarize yourself with your radio equipment and practice using it regularly to ensure efficient operation in an emergency. Maintain radio discipline by transmitting only when necessary and keeping communications concise to conserve battery life and maintain operational security. Develop a comprehensive communication plan that includes primary and secondary frequencies, rendezvous points, and protocols for message passing, ensuring every group member understands and can execute the plan.

In conclusion, radios are vital tools for communication in a grid-down situation. By selecting the appropriate type of radio, understanding its operation, and adhering to best practices, you can maintain a lifeline between your group and the outside world, even when other forms of communication are unavailable.

Navigating Without GPS

Reliance on technology, especially GPS for navigation, has become second nature in the modern world. However, in a grid-down scenario, these conveniences may no longer be available, necessitating a return to more traditional methods of finding one's way. This section delves into the essential skills and knowledge required to navigate without GPS, ensuring you can confidently move from point A to point B without needing electronic devices.

The foundation of navigation without GPS lies in understanding the basic principles of direction and location. Your primary guides are the cardinal directions—north, south, east, and west. Familiarizing yourself with the sun's position at different times of the day can provide a rudimentary method of determining direction. Remember, the sun rises in the east and sets in the west. At noon, when the sun is at its highest point, it will be directly south in the Northern Hemisphere and north in the Southern Hemisphere.

Nature provides an abundance of indicators that can help in navigation. For instance, moss often grows on the northern side of trees in the Northern Hemisphere due to reduced exposure to sunlight. Similarly, observing the stars can be a reliable method for night-time navigation. The North Star, Polaris, remains relatively fixed in the sky and indicates true north. Learning to recognize constellations such as the Big Dipper, which points towards Polaris, can be invaluable.

Creating an improvised compass is a practical skill when traditional navigation tools are unavailable. One method involves using a needle, magnetizing it by rubbing it against silk or wool and then floating it on a leaf in a water bowl. The needle will align with the Earth's magnetic field, pointing towards the magnetic north. While this method may not be as accurate as a standard compass, it can provide a general sense of direction.

Identifying and using landmarks is a crucial skill in navigation without GPS. Natural landmarks such as mountains, rivers, distinctive rock formations, and artificial structures can serve as points of reference to maintain orientation and track progress. Wayfinding involves choosing landmarks in the direction of travel and moving from one to the next, ensuring that you stay on course.

Developing the ability to create mental maps of your surroundings is essential for navigation without electronic aids. This involves paying close attention to the environment and noting changes in terrain, vegetation, and other features. Keeping a mental note of the direction and distance traveled from known points can help maintain a sense of location and direction.

In conclusion, while the absence of GPS and other electronic navigation aids in a grid-down scenario may initially seem daunting, navigating effectively using traditional methods is possible. You can confidently find your way in any environment by understanding basic navigation principles, utilizing natural indicators, improvising tools, and developing keen observation skills.

Map Reading and Land Navigation

When GPS and digital maps are unavailable, the ability to read a map and navigate the land becomes invaluable. This section equips you with the knowledge to find your way in an uncertain world. A map is more than just a piece of paper; it's a scaled-down representation of the Earth's surface. The first step in mastering map reading is to familiarize yourself with the map's scale, legend, and symbols. The scale indicates the relationship between distances on the map and the actual distances on the ground. At the same time, the legend, or key, deciphers the symbols and colors used on the map, representing various physical features such as rivers, roads, and terrain types. To use a map effectively, you must orient it to the surrounding environment by aligning the map so that its north corresponds with true north or magnetic north, which can be done using a compass or by identifying landmarks. A compass is an essential tool for navigation, especially when traversing unfamiliar terrain. It points toward magnetic north, which, combined with a correctly oriented map, allows you to determine your direction of travel. Maps also depict terrain features that can help or hinder your movement, including contours, vegetation, water bodies, and artificial structures. Learning to read these features enables you to choose the best path of travel and anticipate potential challenges.

Once you've oriented your map and identified your current location and destination, the next step is to plot a course by determining the direction and distance between the two points. Consider natural obstacles and terrain features that may require detours, use the map's scale to estimate distances, and plan your route accordingly. Pacing and dead reckoning help you navigate without landmarks by counting steps to estimate the distance traveled and navigating from a known position to a new one using estimated speeds, elapsed time, and bearing. These methods require practice to develop accuracy but can be invaluable in featureless terrain.

The key to successful navigation is knowing how to find your way and avoid getting lost. Always keep track of your position on the map, check against landmarks regularly, and adjust your course as needed. If you are disoriented, stop, reassess your location using the map and compass, and retrace your steps if necessary. You can confidently navigate the landscape in a grid-down scenario by understanding the basics, orienting the map, using a compass, recognizing terrain features, plotting a course, and employing pacing and dead reckoning. Remember, the key to effective navigation is practice; the more you use these skills, the more proficient you will become.

Creating and Using Codes

Effective communication becomes paramount in a grid-down scenario where conventional means might be compromised, monitored, or unavailable. This necessitates the development of alternative methods to convey messages securely, such as creating and using codes. Codes are a powerful tool for maintaining privacy and ensuring that critical information is shared only with intended recipients.

The first step in creating a code is to decide on the type that best suits your needs. Simple substitution codes can be effective for basic messages. At the same time, more sophisticated methods like the Vigenère cipher are suitable for complex or sensitive information. The code must be complex enough to deter unintended deciphering but simple enough for all intended recipients to understand and use without confusion.

Codes can be used to encode locations of supply caches, detail rendezvous points, or convey status updates and requests for assistance. They can be transmitted through written notes, discreet signals, or digitally if some electronic communication remains operational. Practicing encoding and decoding messages with your group is crucial to ensure proficiency and identify potential issues with the code system.

The effectiveness of a code can diminish over time, especially if there's a risk it has been compromised. Protocols for regularly updating or changing codes are essential, which might involve setting predetermined intervals for changes or implementing a system to trigger an immediate change if there's suspicion of compromise.

Without conventional communication methods, codes offer a secure alternative for conveying important information. By carefully creating and practicing codes, you can enhance your group's ability to communicate effectively and securely in a grid-down environment. The goal is to prevent outsiders from understanding your messages and ensure that your team can communicate efficiently under stress and in challenging conditions. Maintaining operational security will be our next focus, building on the foundation of secure communication established through effective coding practices.

Maintaining Operational Security

Maintaining operational security (OPSEC) is important, especially when it comes to communication and navigation. In this context, OPSEC refers to the measures and protocols you put in place to prevent unauthorized access to your plans, movements, and communications. It ensures that sensitive information remains within your trusted circle, safeguarding you and your group from potential threats.

It's crucial to understand that every piece of information, no matter how trivial it might seem, could be valuable to someone with malicious intent. Therefore, the first step in maintaining operational security is identifying sensitive information and limiting its exposure. This includes details about your location, resources, routes, and communication methods.

When discussing sensitive information, do so in a secure environment. Avoid open spaces or areas where you could be easily overheard. If you're using electronic devices, ensure they are secure and protected against unauthorized access. This might involve encrypting your communications or using secure, dedicated channels for sensitive discussions.

Another key aspect of OPSEC is being aware of your surroundings and understanding that information can be inadvertently leaked through non-verbal cues. For instance, packing your vehicle in a manner that suggests you're leaving for an extended period could attract unwanted attention. Similarly, a sudden change in your daily routine might signal to observant eyes that something is amiss. Be mindful of these non-verbal cues and strive to maintain a low profile.

Regarding navigation, operational security means moving discreetly and avoiding predictable patterns. If you need to scout or travel, do so at times and through routes that minimize your visibility and exposure. Vary your routes and schedules to avoid establishing patterns that could be easily tracked.

Communication discipline is also a critical component of OPSEC. This involves knowing when to communicate and what medium to use. For instance, radio communications should be kept brief, encrypted, and only used when necessary. The same principle applies to any form of electronic communication. Always assume that your communications could be intercepted and plan accordingly.

Lastly, trust is a cornerstone of operational security. Be

cautious about who you share sensitive information with. Even within your group, operate on a need-to-know basis. The fewer people who know the details of your plans and movements, the less likely it is for that information to fall into the wrong hands.

In summary, maintaining operational security in a grid-down scenario requires vigilance, discipline, and a thorough understanding of the potential risks associated with communication and navigation. By implementing these principles, you can significantly reduce your vulnerability and enhance your chances of safely navigating challenging times.

Chapter Summary

- Basic survival signaling techniques include visual signals (e.g., smoke, mirrors), sound signals, trail marking, and using natural navigation indicators.
- Regularly practicing signaling methods improves effectiveness, aiding long-distance communication, emergency attention, and navigation.
- Radios (handheld, ham, CB) are crucial in grid-down scenarios; knowledge of their operation, power sources, and privacy is necessary.
- Effective radio use requires understanding frequencies, enhancing range with antennas, establishing protocols, and practicing discipline for security and battery conservation.
- Navigating without GPS involves mastering natural indicators, improvising tools like

compasses, and honing observation skills.
- Map reading and land navigation require understanding map fundamentals, compass use, recognizing terrain, and employing pacing and dead reckoning techniques.
- Creating and using codes for secure communication in grid-down scenarios is essential, emphasizing clarity, simplicity, and regular updates.
- Maintaining operational security (OPSEC) includes protecting sensitive information, practicing discreet communication and movement, avoiding predictability, and limiting information sharing.

7

SURVIVAL GEAR AND TOOLS

Essential Survival Gear

In grid-down survival, a well-curated selection of essential survival gear forms the backbone of your survival strategy, enabling you to navigate, sustain, and protect yourself in an environment stripped of modern conveniences and services. The following items are considered indispensable for anyone preparing for a failed grid scenario.

Water Filtration and Purification Devices: Access to clean drinking water is paramount. In the absence of tap water, you must have the means to purify natural water sources. Portable water filters, purification tablets, or a simple boiling setup can make the difference between hydration and dehydration, health, and illness.

Durable Multi-Tool and Fixed-Blade Knife: A high-quality multi-tool can perform numerous tasks, from repairing gear to preparing food. Complement this with a sturdy fixed-blade knife, invaluable for heavier tasks such as chopping wood or building shelter.

Fire Starting Tools: The ability to start a fire is critical for warmth, cooking, and morale. Your kit should include waterproof matches, ferro rods, and lighters. Practice using these tools in various conditions to ensure you can reliably produce fire when needed.

First Aid Kit: A comprehensive kit tailored to your group's specific needs and any known medical conditions is essential. Beyond the basics, include prescription medications, a tourniquet, and trauma shears. Knowledge of first aid practices is equally important, so consider taking courses to enhance your skills.

Shelter and Warmth Items: Exposure to the elements can be life-threatening. Compact, lightweight options such as emergency bivvy bags, tarps, and space blankets can provide immediate shelter and help retain body heat.

Light Sources: Reliable light sources such as headlamps, flashlights, and lanterns, along with an ample supply of batteries or alternative charging methods (solar, hand-crank), are crucial. These tools aid in navigation and camp setup and can signal for help in emergencies.

Communication Devices: Traditional communication methods may be unavailable in a grid-down scenario. Hand-crank or solar-powered radios can receive weather and news updates, while two-way radios can facilitate communication with your group or nearby allies.

Navigation Tools: GPS devices may be unreliable or unavailable, making traditional navigation tools like maps and compasses indispensable. Familiarize yourself with their use and keep local and regional maps in your kit.

Food Supplies: While long-term food storage is a broader topic, your immediate survival gear should include high-calorie, nutrient-dense foods that require minimal preparation, such as energy bars, nuts, and ready-to-eat meals.

Personal Hygiene Items: Maintaining personal hygiene prevents infections and diseases. Include items such as hand sanitizer, soap, toothbrush, and toothpaste, along with a small towel.

Each item in your survival gear must be carefully chosen, considering its utility, durability, and weight. Regularly review and maintain your gear, ensuring everything is in working order, and consumables are within their use-by dates. Familiarity with your equipment is as crucial as the gear itself; practice using each item in various conditions to ensure you can rely on it when the situation demands.

Choosing and Maintaining Tools

In grid-down survival, the importance of selecting the right tools cannot be overstated. These tools need to be durable and versatile and also maintainable with limited resources. The process of choosing and maintaining your survival tools is a critical skill that can significantly impact your ability to navigate challenging times.

When selecting tools, prioritize those made from high-quality materials. Stainless steel, for example, is renowned for its rust resistance and overall durability, making it an excellent choice for knives, multi-tools, and other gear. However, it's also essential to consider the tool's weight and size, as you may need to transport your gear over long distances. Opt for tools that offer multiple functions in a single design to reduce the need to carry extra items.

After choosing your tools, the next crucial step is familiarizing yourself with their proper maintenance. Regular cleaning and sharpening can significantly extend the life of your tools. For instance, a knife should be cleaned after each use and sharpened regularly to ensure it remains effective for cutting and carving tasks. Learning to sharpen your tools with a whetstone or sharpening rod is a valuable skill that will serve you well.

Rust prevention is another critical aspect of tool maintenance. Applying a light coat of oil to metal parts can prevent rust and corrosion, especially in humid environments. Be sure to use an oil safe for all your tools' materials, including any handles made from wood or synthetic materials.

Storage plays a significant role in maintaining the condition of your tools. Tools should be stored in a dry, clean place to prevent damage when not in use. If you're on the move, consider using protective sheaths or cases to safeguard your tools from the elements and accidental damage.

Lastly, it's worth noting that the ability to repair your tools can be just as important as maintaining them. Familiarize yourself with common repair techniques, such as replacing tool handles or tightening loose components. A basic repair kit that includes items like screws, nuts, bolts, and adhesives can be invaluable in extending the life of your tools.

In conclusion, selecting and maintaining your survival tools are foundational aspects of preparedness for a grid-down scenario. By choosing durable, versatile tools and committing to their regular maintenance and repair, you can ensure that your gear remains reliable and effective, no matter the challenges you face.

DIY Survival Tools

The ability to adapt and create your tools from available resources can be a game-changer. This section delves into the world of DIY survival tools, offering practical advice on how to craft essential gear using minimal resources. The focus here is on creating tools from scratch and repurposing and improvising with what you have, ensuring you remain resilient and resourceful in the face of adversity.

A knife is one of the most versatile tools in any survival situation. Creating a basic survival knife from natural materials can be your first DIY project if you find yourself without one. Look for a piece of flint or obsidian for the blade, which can be knapped or chipped away to create a sharp edge. A sturdy piece of wood secured to the stone blade with strips of leather, cloth, or even strong plant fibers will suffice for the handle.

Securing food is a priority in survival situations, and fish can be an excellent source of nutrition. A fishing spear can be made by selecting a long, straight branch of hardwood, sharpening one end into a point, or splitting the end into four prongs and sharpening each for a more effective tool. Heating the points over a fire can harden them, making your spear more durable and significantly increasing your chances of catching fish in shallow water.

Clean water is crucial, and knowing how to construct a basic filtration system can save your life—using a container, such as a bottle with the bottom cut off, layer charcoal from your fire, sand, and small stones. Pouring water through this makeshift filter can remove significant particulates and improve water quality before boiling or purification. However, this method doesn't purify water; it is a preliminary step to remove larger debris.

Your ability to construct a shelter from natural materials can protect you from the elements and improve your chances of survival. A simple lean-to can be made by leaning branches against a fallen tree or rock, creating a frame, and covering this frame with smaller branches, leaves, and debris for insulation and protection from wind and rain. The key is creating a space that retains heat and protects you from the environment.

Fire is essential for warmth, cooking, and morale. Without matches or a lighter, creating a fire using friction is a primitive but effective method. The bow drill method, which involves rapidly spinning a wooden spindle against a fireboard to create an ember, is one of the most efficient friction-fire techniques. It requires patience and practice but ensures you can create fire without modern conveniences.

Crafting DIY survival tools is an invaluable skill in any grid-down scenario. These examples are just the beginning. With creativity and resourcefulness, almost anything can be repurposed into a useful tool. Remember, the key to survival is not just your gear but your knowledge and ingenuity in using what's available to you. As we move forward, we'll explore how everyday items can be transformed into multi-use survival tools, further expanding your ability to adapt and thrive in any situation.

Multi-Use Items for Survival

In grid-down survival, the efficiency of your gear can mean the difference between thriving and merely surviving. This section delves into the critical importance of multi-use items in your survival toolkit, emphasizing their role in ensuring you're well-prepared for various scenarios without overburdening your pack.

One of the quintessential multi-use items is the paracord. Known for its strength and versatility, paracord can secure shelters, repair gear, fish, set traps, and even be a makeshift tourniquet. Its lightweight nature and the ability to unravel it into thinner strands make it indispensable in any survival situation.

Another invaluable multi-use tool is the bandana. Beyond its primary use as headwear to protect against the sun, a bandana can serve as a filter for water before purification, a sling for injured limbs, a signal flag, and even a tinder for starting fires. Its compact size allows multiple bandanas to be easily carried without taking up significant space.

The multi-tool, embodying the essence of versatility, is a must-have for any survival kit. With various built-in tools such as pliers, knives, screwdrivers, and can openers, a sturdy multi-tool can tackle many tasks, from gear repair to food preparation. Opting for a high-quality multi-tool ensures durability and reliability when needed.

A stainless steel water bottle offers more than just hydration. When empty, it can boil water, making it safe to drink or cook simple meals. Stainless steel's durability also means it can withstand the rigors of outdoor survival situations, providing a reliable container for water storage and more.

Lastly, duct tape's reputation for fixing nearly anything holds true in survival scenarios. Its uses are only limited by one's creativity, including repairing gear, sealing containers, making emergency bandages, and even crafting makeshift shoes. A roll of duct tape takes up minimal space but offers endless utility.

Incorporating these multi-use items into your survival gear maximizes the utility of each item carried and significantly reduces the weight and bulk of your pack. This approach to selecting gear ensures you're prepared for various challenges, making your survival strategy efficient and effective.

As we transition from crafting and improvisation of DIY survival tools, understanding the significance of multi-use items sets a solid foundation for the next step: packaging and transporting your gear. Packing smartly and prioritizing items that serve multiple purposes is crucial in maintaining mobility and readiness in any grid-down scenario.

Packaging and Transporting Gear

How you package and transport your gear can significantly impact your mobility, efficiency, and, ultimately, your survival. This section delves into the essential considerations and strategies for effectively packaging and transporting your survival gear, ensuring that you remain agile and prepared.

Choosing the Right Containers: The first step in effectively packaging your gear is selecting the right containers. Waterproof, durable, and lightweight containers are ideal. Dry bags, for instance, offer an excellent solution for keeping your items dry and can be easily compressed to save space. Hard cases, while heavier, provide unmatched protection for delicate equipment such as communication devices or medical supplies. When selecting containers, consider the nature of the items you're packing and the conditions you expect to encounter.

Compartmentalization: Organizing your gear into categories and packing it into separate compartments or bags within your main pack can save precious time when you need to access specific items quickly. Use color-coded bags or labels to easily identify the contents without having to unpack everything. This method not only streamlines access but also helps maintain an inventory of your supplies.

Weight Distribution: Proper weight distribution is crucial when packing your gear, especially if carrying it on your back for extended periods. Heavy items should be packed closer to your body and in the middle of the pack to maintain balance and reduce strain. Lighter items can be placed on the outside or in external pockets. Testing the pack's weight and adjusting the distribution can prevent fatigue and injury.

Modularity: Adopting a modular approach to packing your gear can offer flexibility and adaptability in various scenarios. Modular packing involves grouping items into separate modules or kits based on their function (e.g., fire-starting, first-aid, food kit). This strategy allows you to quickly adapt to changing conditions by reconfiguring the modules you carry without repacking your entire gear.

Transport Methods: The method of transporting your gear will largely depend on the terrain, distance, and your physical condition. While backpacks are the most common choice for hands-free convenience, alternative methods such as carts, sleds, or even pack animals may be more suitable in certain situations. Each method has advantages and limitations, and choosing the right one can significantly enhance mobility and efficiency.

Practice and Preparedness: Finally, the best-laid plans for packaging and transporting gear can only be validated through practice. Regularly packing, carrying, and accessing your gear in a controlled environment can reveal shortcomings in your strategy and provide valuable insights for improvement. Additionally, practicing with your gear in various weather conditions and terrains can prepare you for the unpredictability of real-world scenarios.

In conclusion, how you package and transport your survival gear is critical to your preparedness strategy. By choosing suitable containers, compartmentalizing your supplies, focusing on weight distribution, adopting a modular approach, selecting the appropriate transport method, and practicing regularly, you can ensure that your gear enhances rather than hinders your survival capabilities.

Innovative Uses for Common Items

This section delves into innovative uses for everyday objects, transforming them into essential survival gear. The focus is not just on what to pack but on seeing the potential in what you already have.

Dental floss, often overlooked as merely a dental hygiene tool, is a strong and versatile thread perfect for survival. It can be used as a fishing line, a snare for small game, or to tie together shelter materials, making it an invaluable addition to any survival kit due to its strength and compact size. Plastic bottles, another common item, can be repurposed in numerous ways, such as containers for collecting water or makeshift scoops. When filled with water and left in the sun, clear plastic bottles can purify water through solar water disinfection, and they also serve as waterproof containers for storing sensitive items like matches or tinder.

Aluminum foil is a multifunctional material that is lightweight, compact, and moldable, ideal for survival scenarios. It can be used to cook food, create makeshift bowls, or enhance the fire signal by reflecting light, and in emergencies, it can be molded into a cutting tool or used as insulation. Sanitary pads and tampons, typically used for personal care, also have several survival applications; pads are highly absorbent and can be used as dressings for large wounds, while both can be used as fire-starting fuel or to filter debris from the water.

Eyeglasses can double as a tool for starting fires in sunny conditions by focusing sunlight onto a small point, similar to a magnifying glass. While requiring patience and precise angling, this method can be crucial when traditional fire-starting tools are unavailable. Steel wool, a common household item, also has unexpected survival uses; when touched by the terminals of a battery, it can ignite, providing a quick way to start a fire. It is also helpful for cleaning tools or making emergency repairs.

The ability to repurpose everyday items for survival enhances preparedness, saves space in your survival kit, and encourages creative problem-solving in challenging situations. By viewing everyday items through the lens of survival, you equip yourself with a versatile toolkit adaptable to various scenarios, significantly boosting your survival capabilities.

Chapter Summary

- Essential survival gear includes water filtration devices, multi-tools, fire-starting tools, first aid kits, shelter and warmth items, light sources, communication devices, navigation tools, food supplies, and personal hygiene items.
- Selecting and maintaining tools is crucial in a grid-down scenario, emphasizing the importance of durability, versatility, and the ability to maintain them with limited resources.
- DIY survival tools, such as a basic survival knife, fishing spear, water filter, shelter, and fire-making techniques, can be crafted from natural or available materials, enhancing adaptability and resourcefulness.
- Multi-use items like paracord, bandanas, multi-tools, stainless steel water bottles, and duct tape are emphasized for their versatility and efficiency in survival situations.
- Effective packaging and transporting of gear involve choosing suitable containers, compartmentalization, proper weight distribution, modularity, selecting appropriate transport methods, and regular practice.
- Innovative uses for everyday items, such as dental floss for fishing lines, plastic bottles for water

purification, aluminum foil for cooking, sanitary pads and tampons for wound care and fire starting, eyeglasses for fire starting, and steel wool for fire starting and repairs, showcase adaptability.

- The importance of creativity and ingenuity in using everyday items for survival purposes is highlighted, encouraging a mindset of seeing potential in common objects for various survival applications.

- The text underscores the significance of preparedness, knowledge, and the ability to adapt and improvise with specialized gear and everyday items in a grid-down scenario.

8

SELF-DEFENSE AND TACTICAL TRAINING

Basic Self-Defense Techniques

Knowing how to defend oneself is crucial in a grid-down scenario where societal norms may collapse. Self-defense encompasses a range of skills, from situational awareness to understanding legal implications. Still, we focus on basic techniques accessible to individuals of all fitness levels. These methods are practical, effective, and designed for quick learning, setting the groundwork for more advanced skills.

Understanding foundational self-defense principles is essential. The primary objective is to avoid confrontations, using de-escalation and evasion as first-line strategies. However, knowing how to protect oneself is vital when conflict is unavoidable.

A proper stance is fundamental in self-defense, providing stability, mobility, and readiness. Position your feet shoulder-width apart, one slightly ahead, with knees slightly bent. This stance allows for quick movements and helps maintain balance during physical confrontations.

Effective striking involves knowing which body parts can serve as weapons and targeting vulnerable areas of an attacker, such as the eyes, nose, throat, and groin. Use the heel of your palm, elbows, knees, and feet to deliver powerful strikes, aiming to incapacitate the attacker long enough to escape.

Blocking or parrying attacks helps avoid taking damage. Keep your hands up to protect your face and neck, using your arms to deflect blows. Observing the attacker's movements and reacting swiftly is crucial for effective defense.

If an attacker grabs you, knowing how to break free is crucial. Techniques depend on the nature of the hold but generally involve using leverage and quick movements to escape. For instance, twisting against an attacker's thumb when they grab your wrist can break their grip.

When defending yourself on the ground, protect your vital areas and use your legs to fend off attackers. Practice getting up quickly and safely, as being on the ground is a significant disadvantage.

Proficiency in these techniques requires practice. Enrolling in a self-defense class offers the opportunity to learn from experienced instructors and build the muscle memory needed for effective response under stress.

The ultimate goal of self-defense is personal safety and the protection of others. It's about preparation, awareness, and appropriate reaction in crises. Individuals can develop a comprehensive self-defense strategy tailored to their abilities and needs with these basic techniques.

Firearms Training and Safety

While basic self-defense techniques provide a foundation, introducing firearms into one's survival strategy significantly increases defensive capability and requires a complex set of responsibilities and skills. Firearms training and safety are critical components of self-defense and tactical training, requiring careful consideration and continuous practice.

First and foremost, understanding and respecting the fundamental rules of firearm safety is non-negotiable. These rules include treating every firearm as if it is loaded, never pointing a firearm at anything you are not willing to destroy, keeping your finger off the trigger until you are ready to shoot, and being aware of your target and what is beyond it. These principles form the bedrock of safe firearm handling and are applicable in every situation, whether in a controlled training environment or the unpredictability of a grid-down scenario.

Beyond basic safety, selecting the right firearm is a critical decision. Factors to consider include the firearm's purpose (self-defense, hunting, or perimeter security), the shooter's proficiency and comfort with the firearm, and the availability of ammunition. For many, a versatile and reliable rifle or shotgun, combined with a handgun for personal defense, provides a balanced approach. However, the specific choice should be tailored to the individual's situation and needs.

Training is where the theoretical knowledge of firearms safety and the practical shooting skills converge. Effective firearms training encompasses marksmanship, situational awareness, stress management, and decision-making under pressure. Regular practice at a shooting range can build proficiency, but scenario-based training exercises that simulate potential real-life situations are invaluable. These exercises help to prepare for the psychological and physiological effects of a high-stress encounter, teaching the shooter to maintain focus, make rapid decisions, and accurately deploy their firearm when necessary.

Maintenance and care of firearms are as crucial as the skills to use them. A well-maintained firearm is reliable, safe, and effective. This includes regular cleaning, proper storage, and the timely replacement of worn parts. Understanding the mechanical aspects of one's firearms ensures they function as expected when needed most.

Lastly, the legal and ethical considerations of using firearms for self-defense cannot be overstressed. Even in a grid-down scenario, the principles of lawful self-defense remain relevant. Lethal force is a grave responsibility and should always be considered a last resort. Understanding the legal framework surrounding self-defense and firearms use in one's jurisdiction before a crisis occurs is essential.

As we transition from the foundational aspects of firearms training and safety to the innovative realm of improvised weapons and tools, it's clear that self-defense in a grid-down world is multifaceted. Firearms play a critical role but are part of a broader strategy that includes a wide range of skills and considerations. The goal is always to ensure the safety and security of oneself and one's community through preparedness, training, and the ethical use of force.

Improvised Weapons and Tools

Mastering improvised weapons and tools is essential for survival in a grid-down scenario. Almost any object can be transformed into a means of self-defense if used with skill and determination. It's essential to evaluate items for their typical uses and potential in a survival context, considering factors like weight, balance, and durability.

Everyday items such as pens, pencils, keys, bottles, ropes, flashlights, and belts can all be repurposed as weapons. For instance, pens and pencils can be used for stabbing, keys can enhance the impact of a punch, and belts can serve as whips or binding tools. Additionally, creating tools is equally crucial; broken glass or sharp stones can serve as cutting tools, while boards or flat stones can be used for digging.

Training and practice are vital to utilize these improvised weapons and tools effectively. Understanding basic striking, cutting, and defensive techniques enhances proficiency. It's also important to consider any weapon's ethical and legal implications. These skills should only be used in self-defense to ensure safety and de-escalate conflicts. Integrating these principles into your survival strategy prepares you for emergencies and bolsters your adaptability and resourcefulness.

Tactical Movement and Camouflage

Moving stealthily and remaining undetected in a grid-down scenario are as crucial as self-defense skills. Tactical movement and camouflage are vital for navigating hostile environments while minimizing confrontation risks. This guide provides practical advice on blending into surroundings and moving without drawing attention.

Tactical movement involves efficiently transitioning from one location to another with minimal exposure. Fundamental principles include minimizing noise, avoiding silhouetting, using natural and artificial cover, and moving slowly and deliberately. To minimize noise, move slowly to reduce the sound of footsteps, wear soft-soled shoes, and avoid stepping on noisy underbrush.

Avoid silhouetting by being mindful of your background and moving through areas where your outline blends with the surroundings rather than open spaces. Differentiate between cover, which protects from projectiles, and concealment, which hides you from view, using both strategically. Rapid movements attract attention, so move slowly, pause often to observe and listen, and prioritize stealth over speed.

Camouflage involves using clothing, materials, and techniques to blend into the environment, making you less visible. Effective camouflage requires understanding how to manage shape, shine, shadow, silhouette, and spacing. Wear patterned clothing that mimics the environment and add natural elements to disrupt your outline. Cover or remove shiny objects, and be mindful of your shadow, especially in low light.

In addition to visual camouflage, securing loose gear minimizes odors and controls noise. Like any skill, effective camouflage requires practice. Spend time in various environments to observe how well you blend in and adjust your techniques accordingly.

Mastering tactical movement and camouflage improves your ability to navigate a grid-down world safely, enhancing your chances of avoiding confrontations and providing a strategic advantage where stealth is key to survival. The goal is to avoid detection, preserve safety, and conserve resources when necessary.

Situational Awareness and Threat Assessment

In grid-down survival, accurately assessing your surroundings and identifying potential threats before they become imminent dangers is an invaluable skill. This section delves into the critical concepts of situational awareness and threat assessment, providing the knowledge and techniques necessary to enhance your safety and security in uncertain times.

Situational awareness is the practice of being mindful of your environment and understanding what is happening around you at all times. It involves continuously observing the people, objects, and events in your vicinity and interpreting their significance for your safety. To develop situational awareness, start by honing your observational skills. Make a habit of scanning your environment, noting exits, potential hazards, and the behavior of individuals nearby. It's essential to remain discreet and avoid tunnel vision; focus on the big picture rather than fixating on a single element.

Another critical aspect of situational awareness is understanding baseline behaviors for the environments you frequent. Baselines are the norms or averages of behavior and conditions in a specific area. By recognizing when something deviates from the baseline, you can quickly identify potential threats. For example, an abrupt silence or a sudden gathering of people in a typically bustling market may indicate a problem or threat. Learning to detect these anomalies allows you to react swiftly and appropriately.

Threat assessment is identifying and evaluating potential threats to determine their severity and likelihood of becoming actual dangers. This involves recognizing immediate threats and anticipating future ones based on the information at hand. Effective threat assessment requires a combination of intuition, experience, and logical analysis. Start by categorizing potential threats based on their nature—human, environmental, or technological. Then, evaluate each threat based on its capability to harm you, its opportunity to do so, and its intent. This triad will help you prioritize which threats need immediate attention and which can be monitored or mitigated.

Incorporating situational awareness and threat assessment into your daily routine may seem daunting initially, but it becomes second nature with practice. Begin by consciously applying these principles in safe, familiar environments and gradually expand to more complex scenarios. Training exercises, such as scenario planning and role-playing, can also be beneficial in developing these skills. Remember, the goal is not to live in a state of paranoia but to cultivate a heightened awareness that empowers you to make informed decisions and take proactive measures to protect yourself and your loved ones.

By mastering situational awareness and threat assessment, you equip yourself with the tools necessary to navigate the unpredictable landscape of a grid-down scenario. These skills enhance your ability to avoid or mitigate dangers and contribute to the overall resilience and security of your survival strategy. As we progress, the emphasis will shift towards leveraging these individual skills to foster collective strength and security by building a cohesive survival team.

Building a Survival Team

Understanding the formation and structuring of a survival team is crucial. Ideally, this team acts as a cohesive unit capable of defending, providing for, and supporting each other during societal collapse. It's not just about gathering individuals; it's about assembling a team with complementary skills, a shared commitment to survival, and the ability to operate under stress with trust and efficiency.

The composition of your survival team is paramount and should include individuals with various essential skills. These skills include medical knowledge, self-defense and tactical training, food production and preservation, mechanical repair, and communication. Each member should bring a unique set of skills to the table, ensuring the team can address various challenges.

Trust and reliability form the bedrock of any effective survival team. Members must be able to rely on each other implicitly, as the stakes in a grid-down scenario are incredibly high. This trust is built over time through training, shared experiences, and developing interpersonal relationships. It's crucial to vet potential team members thoroughly.

Training together is an essential aspect of building a cohesive survival team. Regular, structured training sessions in self-defense, first aid, emergency communication, and other survival skills are crucial. These sessions improve individual and group proficiency and enhance team bonding and trust. Training scenarios should be as realistic as possible to prepare the team for a grid-down environment's physical and psychological challenges.

Leadership within the survival team should be clear yet flexible. While a designated leader can provide direction and make critical decisions, a rigid hierarchy can stifle initiative and adaptability. Leadership might rotate based on the situation or the specific skills required at the time, and decision-making should balance leveraging the leader's expertise with incorporating input from team members.

Effective communication is vital for a survival team's success. This includes tactical communication during operations and regular discussions about plans, challenges, and group dynamics. Conflict is inevitable in high-stress situations; therefore, the team must have strategies in place for conflict resolution, including mediation and structured discussions.

Finally, a survival team must be committed to continuous improvement. This means regularly reviewing and critiquing performance, learning from successes and failures, and staying informed about new survival strategies and technologies. The landscape of a grid-down scenario is ever-changing, and adaptability is critical to long-term survival. Building a survival team is a complex but crucial process that requires careful consideration of skills, trust, leadership, and continuous improvement. This will enhance the chances of survival and provide a support system that can make the ordeal psychologically bearable.

Chapter Summary

- Basic self-defense techniques are crucial in scenarios where society's structure collapses. They focus on practical, effective methods suitable for individuals of varying physical fitness.
- Foundational self-defense principles include avoiding confrontation, adopting a stable and ready stance, effective striking using body parts less prone to injury, and targeting vulnerable areas on an attacker.
- Techniques for blocking, parrying, breaking away from grabs, and ground defense are essential, with emphasis on leverage, swift movements, and protecting vital organs.
- Regular training and practice under experienced instructors are recommended to build proficiency and muscle memory for effective self-defense under stress.
- Firearms training and safety are critical, emphasizing respect for fundamental safety rules, selecting appropriate firearms, and continuous practice for skill proficiency and maintenance.
- Improvised weapons and tools from everyday items can be vital in self-defense, with training enhancing their effectiveness. Ethical and legal considerations remain paramount.
- Tactical movement and camouflage skills are essential for stealth and avoiding detection in hostile environments. They also focus on

minimizing noise, avoiding silhouetting, and blending into surroundings.
- Building a cohesive survival team involves assembling individuals with complementary skills, trust, and reliability, with continuous training, effective communication, and leadership flexibility being key to long-term survival.

9

PSYCHOLOGICAL PREPAREDNESS AND LEADERSHIP

Mental Resilience in Survival Situations

Mental resilience is not merely a beneficial trait but a crucial cornerstone of survival strategy in grid-down survival. Maintaining a positive outlook, managing stress effectively, and adapting to rapidly changing circumstances can significantly impact one's ability to navigate the challenges of a grid-down scenario. This section delves into the psychological aspects of survival, offering practical advice on cultivating mental resilience in the face of adversity.

First and foremost, understanding stress and its effects is vital. Stress, in survival situations, can be a double-edged sword. On one hand, it can heighten senses and improve reaction times, providing an edge in critical moments. On the other, prolonged stress can lead to mental fatigue, impaired decision-making, and a host of psychological issues, including anxiety and depression. Recognizing the signs of stress in oneself and others is the first step in managing it effectively.

Deep breathing exercises, meditation, and routine maintenance can help mitigate stress and promote mental well-being.

Adaptability is another critical component of mental resilience. Adjusting to new challenges and unfamiliar environments is essential in a grid-down situation. This involves physical adaptation and a mental willingness to accept change and work with it rather than against it. Cultivating a mindset that views challenges as opportunities for growth rather than insurmountable obstacles can significantly enhance one's adaptability and overall resilience.

While it may seem counterintuitive in dire situations, optimism plays a critical role in survival. A positive outlook can boost morale for the individual and those around them, fostering a sense of hope and motivation to persevere. This does not mean ignoring the realities of the situation but instead choosing to focus on what can be controlled and finding solace in small victories and progress.

Building a solid support network is also crucial for maintaining mental resilience. In a grid-down scenario, isolation can quickly lead to despair. Sharing experiences, offering support, and working together towards common goals provide a sense of purpose and belonging, essential for psychological well-being. This sense of community can be a powerful antidote to the mental strain of survival situations.

Lastly, preparing mentally for a grid-down scenario can significantly improve one's resilience when faced with the actual event. This involves educating oneself about potential challenges and solutions and practicing mental and emotional coping strategies. Scenario planning, stress inoculation training, and mental rehearsal of survival situations can help build a psychological toolkit that is invaluable when reality strikes.

In conclusion, mental resilience in survival is a multifaceted discipline that encompasses stress management, adaptability, optimism, community building, and mental preparedness. Individuals can significantly improve their chances of surviving and thriving in adversity by cultivating these qualities and skills. As we discuss effective leadership and team dynamics, it's important to recognize that mental resilience is not just a personal asset but a foundational element of decisive leadership and cohesive team function in survival scenarios.

Effective Leadership and Team Dynamics

The importance of effective leadership and team dynamics cannot be overstated in a grid-down scenario. As individuals grapple with the psychological strain of survival, the role of a leader evolves into something far more critical than in ordinary circumstances. This section delves into the nuances of leadership and team dynamics in a survival context, offering practical advice for those in positions of responsibility.

Leadership in a grid-down situation is characterized by the ability to make decisions under pressure, inspire confidence among team members, and maintain a clear vision of survival and recovery. A leader's first task is to assess each team member's skills, strengths, and weaknesses, integrating these into a cohesive plan that leverages individual capabilities for the collective good. This assessment should be ongoing, as the survival stress can affect individuals' performance, and roles may need to be adjusted accordingly.

Communication is the linchpin of effective leadership and team dynamics. Leaders must establish open, honest, and clear channels of communication. This involves disseminating information and orders and listening to team members' concerns, suggestions, and feedback. In a survival situation, every team member's input can be valuable, and fostering a culture of mutual respect and inclusivity can significantly enhance group cohesion and morale.

Another critical aspect of leadership in survival scenarios is adaptability. Conditions can change rapidly, and leaders must be prepared to alter plans and strategies at a moment's notice. This flexibility should be balanced with a steady commitment to the group's overarching goals and the well-being of its members. Demonstrating resilience in the face of adversity can inspire the same in others, making adaptability a shared strength rather than a source of uncertainty.

Effective leaders also recognize the importance of maintaining morale. In the challenging environment of a grid-down scenario, hope can be as crucial as any physical resource. Leaders should find ways to motivate and uplift their team through shared goals, recognition of achievements, or maintaining a positive outlook. This does not mean ignoring the realities of the situation but instead framing challenges as obstacles that can be overcome together.

Finally, leadership in a survival context is not about authoritarian control but rather about fostering a sense of shared responsibility and empowerment. Leaders can cultivate a sense of ownership and investment in the group's success by involving team members in decision-making processes. This collaborative approach not only leverages the team's diverse skills and perspectives but also strengthens the social bonds that are essential for psychological resilience.

In conclusion, effective leadership and team dynamics in a grid-down survival scenario hinge on clear communication, adaptability, morale maintenance, and collaborative decision-making. Leaders who embody these principles can navigate survival challenges with a cohesive, motivated, and resilient team. As we move forward, resolving conflicts and negotiating effectively will become increasingly important, building on the foundation of strong leadership and team dynamics to ensure the group's continued survival and well-being.

Conflict Resolution and Negotiation

Resolving conflicts and effective negotiation are crucial for maintaining group cohesion and ensuring survival in a grid-down situation. Conflicts may arise from various sources, such as resource allocation, task distribution, personal grievances, or stress. Identifying the root cause is the first step in conflict resolution, which involves active listening and an empathetic understanding of each party's perspective.

Once the root causes are understood, establishing a resolution framework is necessary. This includes setting ground rules for respectful communication and focusing discussions on finding solutions rather than assigning blame. Reminding all parties of the common goal of survival and well-being can help diffuse tensions and encourage a collaborative approach.

Negotiation in a grid-down environment requires

flexibility and creativity, as traditional bargaining may only sometimes be applicable. Interest-based negotiation can effectively address each party's underlying needs and interests. Techniques such as the "win-win" approach aim to find solutions that benefit all parties, requiring compromise but ensuring that core needs are met.

After reaching a resolution or agreement, it is crucial to implement it promptly and effectively. This involves defining the terms, assigning responsibilities, setting timelines, and conducting regular check-ins to ensure adherence and make necessary adjustments. A feedback mechanism and ongoing dialogue can prevent future conflicts and strengthen group dynamics.

Building a culture of collaboration and mutual respect within the group is essential. This can be achieved by resolving conflicts as they arise, preventing them through clear communication, equitable resource distribution, and fostering a sense of community. Regular group meetings to voice concerns, share ideas, and offer support are invaluable in maintaining this culture. In conclusion, mastering conflict resolution and negotiation is vital for navigating the challenges of a grid-down environment and maintaining group cohesion.

Stress Management Techniques

The psychological strain on individuals and groups can be immense in a grid-down scenario. If not managed properly, stress can undermine all survival survival efforts, leading to poor decision-making, conflict, and a breakdown in morale. Therefore, it is imperative that leaders and members of survival groups are equipped with effective stress management techniques to navigate these challenging times.

One of the first steps in managing stress is identifying and acknowledging its presence. Stress can manifest in various ways, including, but not limited to, physical symptoms such as headaches or fatigue, emotional symptoms like irritability or depression, and behavioral changes such as withdrawal or aggression. Recognizing these signs early on is crucial for addressing stress before it escalates.

Breathing exercises are a foundational tool in the stress management arsenal. Deep, controlled breathing can help calm the nervous system and reduce the physiological effects of stress. Techniques such as the 4-7-8 method, where you inhale for four seconds, hold your breath for seven seconds, and exhale for eight seconds, can be particularly effective. These exercises can be performed anywhere, anytime, making them an invaluable resource for immediate stress relief.

Physical activity is another vital stress management technique. Exercise improves physical health and has been shown to reduce anxiety and depression. Even in a grid-down scenario, simple activities like walking, stretching, or any form of manual labor can serve as effective stress relievers. The key is to integrate physical activity into daily routines to help maintain a level of normalcy and routine.

Mindfulness and meditation have gained recognition for reducing stress and improving overall well-being. Practicing mindfulness involves being fully present in the moment, aware of where we are and what we're doing, without being overly reactive or overwhelmed by what's happening around us. Guided meditations, focusing on a particular object, sound, or breath, can help achieve a calm state and reduce stress levels.

Journaling is another technique that can assist in managing stress. Writing down thoughts and feelings can provide an outlet for expressing emotions, reflecting on experiences, and identifying stressors. This practice can help individuals process their emotions and gain perspective on their situation, contributing to better mental health.

Lastly, fostering a supportive community is essential for stress management. Sharing experiences, concerns, and coping strategies within a group can provide emotional support and strengthen collective resilience. Encouraging open communication and building trust within the group can help mitigate stress and promote a sense of unity and purpose.

In conclusion, stress management in a grid-down scenario requires a multifaceted approach that includes recognizing stress, employing physical and mental techniques to reduce its impact, and fostering a supportive community. By integrating these strategies into daily life, individuals and groups can better navigate the psychological challenges of survival situations, maintaining their focus, decision-making capabilities, and, ultimately, their hope for the future.

Building Morale and Maintaining Hope

A group's psychological landscape can swiftly become as challenging as physical hardships. Building morale and maintaining hope are not just supplementary tasks but essential to survival. This section delves into practical strategies for fostering a positive group dynamic and ensuring hope remains a steadfast companion, even in the darkest times.

Communication as a Cornerstone: Open, honest communication establishes trust and prevents the spread of rumors that can quickly erode morale. Leaders should encourage regular meetings where concerns, ideas, and feelings are freely expressed. This transparency helps create a sense of community and shared purpose, reinforcing the idea that everyone works together towards a common goal.

Setting Small, Achievable Goals: Setting and achieving small goals can provide a sense of progress and control in a situation where the future is uncertain. These accomplishments, whether building a shelter, securing a day's food, or simply maintaining a fire, can significantly boost morale. Celebrating these victories, no matter how minor they may seem, reinforces a positive outlook and the belief that survival and eventual recovery are possible.

Maintaining Routines and Traditions: Establishing routines can impart a sense of normalcy and structure, which is comforting during times of chaos. Similarly, preserving or adapting traditions, such as meal times, storytelling, or even birthdays, can strengthen bonds within the group and serve as reminders of the humanity and culture that survive despite the circumstances.

Encouraging Personal Time and Space: While group cohesion is vital, recognizing the importance of personal time and space is equally crucial. Individuals should be encouraged to spend time alone, engage in hobbies, or reflect. This can help mitigate feeling overwhelmed and provide a mental break from the stresses of survival.

Fostering a Culture of Learning and Adaptability:

Encouraging the group to view the situation as an opportunity for learning and growth can transform challenges into valuable experiences. Sharing knowledge, skills, and even failures within the group enhances collective adaptability and reinforces the idea that every member has value and can contribute to the group's resilience.

Leading by Example: Leaders are critical in setting the tone for morale and hope. Even when faced with setbacks, demonstrating calmness, confidence, and compassion can inspire similar qualities in group members. Leaders should also be transparent about the challenges ahead but frame them in a way that emphasizes collective strength and the feasibility of overcoming obstacles together.

In conclusion, building morale and maintaining hope requires intention, effort, and creativity. They are about nurturing the human spirit as much as ensuring physical survival. By fostering a positive, cohesive group dynamic, leaders can help navigate the psychological complexities of a grid-down scenario, keeping despair at bay and paving the way for a resilient, hopeful community.

Training and Preparing Your Mind for Survival

During grid-down survival, the resilience of the human spirit is tested to its limits. Beyond the tangible necessities of food, water, and shelter lies the critical battlefield of the mind. Training and preparing your mind for survival is not just an option; it is necessary for those who aim to lead and thrive in the most challenging conditions.

The process of mental preparation for survival begins with understanding and acceptance. Acknowledge the potential severity of a grid-down scenario and its impacts on your life and community. This acceptance isn't about succumbing to fear but about recognizing the reality of the situation to better prepare for it. It's about building a mental framework that sees challenges as surmountable obstacles rather than insurmountable barriers.

Developing situational awareness is one of the first steps in training your mind for survival. This means being keenly aware of your environment and any changes, allowing you to anticipate problems and react swiftly and effectively. Regularly practice observing your surroundings, identifying potential threats, and imagining how you might deal with them. This exercise sharpens your awareness and enhances your ability to think on your feet—a crucial skill in any survival situation.

Another vital aspect of mental preparation is stress management. High-stress levels can cloud judgment, impair decision-making, and lead to panic—all detrimental in a survival scenario. Techniques such as deep breathing, meditation, and visualization can be powerful tools for maintaining a calm and clear mind. Regular practice of these techniques can help you develop the ability to stay composed under pressure, ensuring that you can make rational decisions when they matter most.

Resilience, the capacity to recover quickly from difficulties, is a trait that can be cultivated and strengthened over time. It involves maintaining a positive outlook, practicing gratitude, and embracing challenges as opportunities for growth. Encourage yourself and your team to view setbacks not as failures but as learning experiences. This mindset shift is pivotal in building the mental toughness required to navigate the uncertainties of a grid-down world.

Finally, leadership in such trying times hinges on inspiring and motivating others. A leader's confidence and calm demeanor can be contagious, helping to elevate the morale of the entire group. Therefore, part of your mental preparation should involve honing your communication skills and empathy. Listening actively, offering encouragement, and providing constructive feedback are all essential in fostering a cohesive and resilient team.

In conclusion, preparing your mind for survival is a multifaceted endeavor encompassing acceptance, situational awareness, stress management, resilience, and leadership. By dedicating time and effort to develop these mental skills, you equip yourself and those you lead with the psychological fortitude necessary to face the challenges of a grid-down scenario head-on. Remember, the body cannot go where the mind has not been. Therefore, let your mind venture into possibility, preparation, and unwavering resolve.

Chapter Summary

- Mental resilience is crucial in grid-down survival situations, involving stress management, adaptability, optimism, community building, and mental preparedness.
- Stress can sharpen senses and lead to mental fatigue; managing it involves recognizing signs, practicing deep breathing, meditation, and maintaining routines.

- Adaptability requires a mindset that views challenges as opportunities, emphasizing the importance of a positive outlook and building a solid support network.
- Preparing mentally for grid-down scenarios through education, scenario planning, and practicing coping strategies enhances resilience.
- Effective leadership in such scenarios involves decision-making under pressure, clear communication, fostering group cohesion, and maintaining morale.
- Conflict resolution and negotiation are essential for group cohesion. They focus on understanding root causes, establishing resolution frameworks, and implementing agreements fairly.
- Stress management techniques include: recognizing stress signs, engaging in physical activity, practicing mindfulness, and fostering a supportive community.
- Building morale involves open communication, setting achievable goals, maintaining routines, encouraging adaptability, and leading by example to nurture hope and resilience.

10

COMMUNITY BUILDING AND NETWORKING

Forming and Strengthening Community Ties

In a grid-down scenario, society as we know it would undergo a fundamental transformation. The reliance on digital communication, centralized governance, and a cash-based economy would quickly become untenable. In such times, a community's strength and resilience would hinge on its members' ability to form and strengthen ties based on mutual support, trust, and cooperation.

Forming and strengthening community ties in a grid-down situation requires a proactive approach. Initially, it involves identifying individuals within your vicinity who share a common goal of survival and mutual aid. These could be neighbors, friends, or even acquaintances willing to prepare for or aware of the challenges posed by such scenarios. The foundation of these community ties is the understanding that collective efforts are more likely to yield positive outcomes in times of crisis than solitary endeavors.

Communication plays a pivotal role in this process. Communities must revert to more traditional means without the luxury of electronic communication. Establishing a system of regular face-to-face meetings, using notice boards in communal areas, or even setting up a system of messengers can ensure that information flows effectively within the group. These meetings and communications should focus on immediate survival strategies, long-term sustainability, and security.

Trust is another cornerstone of strong community ties. Building trust requires transparency, consistency, and reliability among members. Sharing skills, knowledge, and resources openly can foster a sense of belonging and mutual respect. Community members need to engage in activities that build relationships beyond the immediate survival needs, such as communal meals, joint training sessions on survival skills, or group projects to improve the collective living conditions.

The concept of mutual aid is essential in forming and strengthening community ties. This involves creating a system where resources are pooled, and skills are shared for the benefit of all members. For instance, those with medical knowledge could be responsible for health and wellness, while those with gardening or farming skills could lead food production efforts. The key is to identify and utilize the unique skills and resources each member brings to the table, ensuring that everyone has a role and feels valued within the community.

Adapting and overcoming challenges as a unified community can significantly increase the chances of surviving and thriving in a grid-down scenario. The process of forming and strengthening community ties is ongoing and evolves as the situation changes. It requires patience, empathy, and a shared commitment to a common cause. By laying the groundwork for solid community networks, individuals can create a resilient support system capable of withstanding the uncertainties of a post-grid world.

As communities solidify these ties, the next logical step in ensuring sustainability and self-sufficiency involves leveraging the diverse skills and resources within the group. This leads to establishing a bartering system and emphasizing trade skills, which become invaluable in a world where traditional currency and economic systems may no longer sway.

Bartering and Trade Skills

The conventional monetary system may falter in a grid-down scenario, rendering traditional currency less useful or obsolete. This shift necessitates a return to more primal exchange methods, primarily bartering and using trade skills. This section delves into the intricacies of these practices, offering practical advice on navigating and leveraging them for survival and community resilience.

Bartering, at its core, is the exchange of goods and services without the intermediary of money. In a grid-down situation, the value of items shifts dramatically, with practical, life-sustaining goods and services becoming highly prized. To engage effectively in bartering, one must first assess their resources and skills, identifying what they can offer. Simultaneously, understanding the needs and desires of your community is crucial. Items like food, water purification methods, medical supplies, and fuel often become highly sought after, but so do less obvious commodities like seeds, tools, and even knowledge or expertise in specific areas.

Developing trade skills is another vital aspect of surviving and thriving in a post-grid world. Skills that contribute directly to the sustenance and protection of a community become invaluable. These can range from agriculture, animal husbandry, and blacksmithing to more modern skills like solar panel installation and repair or radio communication expertise. Learning and mastering these skills ensures survival and enhances your value within a bartering system.

When engaging in barter, it's essential to establish and maintain trust within your community. Clear communication and transaction fairness help build a reputation as a reliable and honest trader, which can be invaluable in long-term survival scenarios. Additionally, understanding the basic principles of negotiation can help ensure that exchanges benefit all parties involved.

Moreover, the organization of bartering networks or markets within a community can facilitate the efficient exchange of goods and services. These networks can range from informal agreements between neighbors to more structured gatherings at designated times and places. The key is ensuring these arrangements are secure, equitable, and accessible to all community members.

In conclusion, the revival of bartering and the emphasis on trade skills are survival strategies and opportunities to rebuild and strengthen community bonds. By fostering a culture of cooperation and mutual support, communities can more effectively navigate the challenges of a grid-down scenario, laying the foundation for a resilient and sustainable future.

Collaborative Survival Strategies

In a grid-down scenario, the importance of individual survival skills cannot be overstated. However, the true strength in enduring such challenging times often lies in a community's collective abilities and resources. Collaborative survival strategies are beneficial and essential for long-term sustainability and recovery, focusing on practical approaches and organizational structures that can enhance community resilience and mutual support during extended periods without the grid.

The first step in collaborative survival is forming alliances within your community based on mutual trust and the understanding that everyone has something valuable to contribute. It is crucial to identify individuals with essential skills—such as medical professionals, carpenters, and farmers. Organizing regular meetings to discuss plans, share knowledge, and distribute tasks helps create a comprehensive survival plan addressing food production, security, medical care, and communication.

One of the most effective ways to strengthen a community's survival capabilities is through skill-sharing workshops. These workshops can cover various topics, including first aid, food preservation, and basic carpentry. By leveraging the expertise within the community, members can learn from each other, reducing the community's overall vulnerability and ensuring that knowledge is continuously passed on.

In a grid-down situation, resources become exceedingly precious, making joint resource management essential to ensure equitable distribution of food, water, medicine, and fuel. Establishing a community store or bank where resources can be pooled and allocated according to need can prevent hoarding and conflict. This system requires transparent management and clear communication to maintain trust among community members.

Security becomes a paramount concern when the grid is down, and a community is more resilient to potential threats when it adopts a collective approach to defense. Organizing a neighborhood watch or a community patrol can deter threats and ensure the safety of all members. Training sessions on self-defense and discussions on non-violent conflict resolution should be part of the community's security strategy, along with establishing communication protocols for emergencies.

Access to hospitals and pharmacies is necessary for community health initiatives to become vital. Collaborating with medical professionals within the community to provide primary healthcare and emergency medical services is critical. Stockpiling essential medicines, organizing health education sessions, and creating natural remedies from locally available resources are all strategies that can improve the community's health resilience.

Collaborative survival strategies involve leveraging a community's collective strength and resources to withstand and recover from a grid-down scenario. By forming survival alliances, sharing skills, managing resources jointly, ensuring collective security, and prioritizing community health, a community can survive and lay the groundwork for rebuilding a sustainable way of life. The key to success lies in preparation, cooperation, and the willingness to support one another through the most challenging times.

Creating Mutual Aid Networks

As individuals, our ability to survive and thrive is significantly enhanced by forming strong, supportive networks. This is where the concept of creating mutual aid networks comes into play, serving as a cornerstone for resilient community building and networking. Mutual aid networks are collaborative structures that enable individuals and groups to pool resources, share skills, and support each other in times of need. This section delves into the practical steps for establishing these networks, ensuring they are effective, inclusive, and sustainable.

The first step in creating a mutual aid network is identifying potential members within your community who share a common interest in preparedness and resilience. This can include neighbors, friends, local businesses, and community organizations. The goal is to unite a diverse group of individuals with a wide range of skills, resources, and knowledge. Diversity in the network ensures a more comprehensive approach to problem-solving and resource allocation.

Once potential members have been identified, the next step is organizing an initial meeting to discuss the goals, expectations, and structure of the mutual aid network. This meeting is crucial for establishing trust, setting clear objectives, and determining each member's roles and responsibilities. It's important to create an environment of openness and inclusivity where every member feels valued and heard.

Effective communication is the backbone of any successful mutual aid network. Establishing reliable communication channels ensures members can coordinate efforts, share information, and provide support efficiently. These can include regular meetings, social media groups, email lists, or radio communication in more severe grid-down scenarios. The chosen methods should be accessible to all members and secure enough to protect the network's privacy and safety.

Resource pooling and skill sharing are fundamental aspects of mutual aid networks. Members can inventory their skills, tools, and resources, identifying what they can offer to the network and what they may need from others. These can range from practical skills like carpentry and gardening to resources like food, water, and medical supplies. The network can create a shared repository that enhances the community's collective resilience and self-sufficiency by pooling these resources.

Finally, it's essential to establish guidelines and protocols for how the network will operate during emergencies. This includes decision-making processes, resource allocation, and conflict resolution mechanisms. These guidelines ensure that the network can respond effectively and cohesively when faced with challenges.

Creating a mutual aid network is a proactive step towards building a resilient community capable of facing the uncertainties of a grid-down scenario. Individuals can enhance their ability to navigate such complexities through collaboration, shared resources, and mutual support. As we move forward, the principles of mutual aid can serve as a blueprint for fostering more robust, interconnected communities that are prepared to face any challenge together.

Legal and Ethical Considerations

In a grid-down scenario, society as we know it can be significantly altered. This brings the importance of community building and networking to the forefront. However, as we navigate these uncharted waters, we must remain vigilant about the legal and ethical considerations underpinning our actions and decisions. This awareness ensures that our efforts to rebuild and sustain communities are grounded in principles that promote fairness, respect, and dignity for all individuals involved.

Legal considerations in a grid-down scenario can be complex, given that existing laws can be temporarily unenforceable or subject to reinterpretation in emergency conditions. Despite these challenges, community leaders and members need to strive for adherence to the rule of law to the extent possible. This includes respecting property rights, upholding contractual obligations, and ensuring that any form of community governance or decision-making process is transparent and equitable. When the conventional legal system is not operational, communities may need to develop provisional codes of conduct or dispute resolution mechanisms, always with an eye toward eventual reintegration with broader societal norms.

Ethical considerations are equally paramount, as they guide our moral compass in times of crisis. The principles of beneficence (doing good), nonmaleficence (avoiding harm), autonomy (respecting individual freedom), and justice (ensuring fairness) become the cornerstones of community interactions. For instance, when establishing mutual aid networks, it is vital to ensure that resources are distributed based on need, without discrimination or favoritism. Similarly, decisions regarding community safety, resource allocation, and collaboration with neighboring groups must be made with a keen sense of ethical responsibility, recognizing the inherent worth of every community member.

Moreover, all community endeavors should emphasize transparency and accountability in the spirit of ethical conduct. This involves clear communication about the community's goals, challenges, and achievements and an openness to feedback and critique. By fostering an environment where ethical dilemmas are openly discussed and navigated collectively, communities can build a strong foundation of trust and mutual respect.

In navigating the legal and ethical landscapes of a grid-down scenario, we must consider the long-term implications of our actions. The decisions and precedents set during this period can have lasting effects on post-collapse communities' social fabric and governance structures. As such, a forward-thinking approach, coupled with a deep commitment to ethical principles and legal integrity, will be instrumental in laying the groundwork for resilient, just, and thriving communities in the aftermath of a crisis.

In conclusion, while the challenges of community building and networking in a grid-down scenario are manifold, they also present an opportunity to reaffirm our commitment to legal and ethical standards. By upholding these values, we not only navigate the immediate crisis with integrity but also contribute to creating a robust framework for the sustainable development of communities in a post-collapse world.

Chapter Summary

- In a grid-down scenario, communities must form and strengthen ties based on mutual support, trust, and cooperation, moving away from reliance on digital communication and centralized governance.
- Effective communication is crucial, requiring communities to use traditional means like face-to-face meetings and notice boards to ensure information flow.
- Trust and mutual aid are foundational, with community members sharing skills, knowledge, and resources and engaging in activities that build relationships beyond survival needs.
- Bartering and trade skills become essential as traditional currency may lose value; practical goods and services are highly prized, and trade skills directly contributing to community sustenance are invaluable.
- Collaborative survival strategies, including forming survival alliances, skill-sharing workshops, joint resource management, and collective defense, are essential for long-term sustainability and recovery.
- Creating mutual aid networks involves identifying community members with shared interests in preparedness, organizing meetings to set goals and roles, and establishing effective communication and resource pooling.

- Legal and ethical considerations remain essential, with communities striving to adhere to the rule of law and ethical principles like fairness and respect, even when conventional legal systems are not operational.
- Rebuilding and sustaining communities post-collapse requires effective communication, resource management, security measures, education and skill-sharing, healthcare provision, and establishing governance and leadership structures.

11

LONG-TERM SUSTAINABILITY AND SELF-SUFFICIENCY

Sustainable Agriculture and Permaculture

A pivotal component of long-term sustainability and self-sufficiency is the establishment of sustainable agriculture and the principles of permaculture. This approach ensures food security in a grid-down scenario and promotes ecological health and resilience. The foundation of sustainable agriculture and permaculture lies in understanding and working with natural ecosystems rather than against them. This section delves into practical strategies and techniques to implement these concepts effectively.

To begin with, sustainable agriculture focuses on producing food, fiber, and other plant or animal products using farming techniques that protect the environment, public health, human communities, and animal welfare. This form of agriculture enables us to produce healthy food without compromising future generations' ability to do the same. The key practices include crop rotation, which helps prevent soil depletion and pest buildup; organic farming, which avoids synthetic pesticides and fertilizers; and agroforestry, which integrates trees and shrubs into agricultural landscapes.

On the other hand, permaculture is a design system for creating sustainable human habitats by following nature's patterns. It involves creating a diversified, resilient ecosystem that mimics the dynamics observed in natural ecosystems. Permaculture principles include observing and interacting with the natural environment to design efficient systems, capturing and storing energy, obtaining a yield, and applying self-regulation and feedback. These principles guide the design of sustainable homesteads, where water harvesting, waste recycling, and energy efficiency are seamlessly integrated.

Soil health is one of the most critical aspects of implementing sustainable agriculture and permaculture. Healthy soil is the foundation of a productive garden or farm. Techniques such as composting, mulching, and no-till farming can improve soil structure, enhance microbial activity, and increase water retention. Composting organic waste creates a nutrient-rich soil amendment, reducing the need for chemical fertilizers. Mulching helps suppress weeds, conserve soil moisture, and prevent soil erosion. No-till farming avoids soil disturbance, preserves soil structure, conserves water, and builds organic matter.

Water management is another vital component. Efficient water use can be achieved through rainwater harvesting, drip irrigation, and the construction of swales and ponds to capture and store water in the landscape. These practices ensure that crops receive adequate water without wasting this precious resource.

Diversity is a hallmark of sustainable agriculture and permaculture. A diverse farm or garden is more resilient to pests, diseases, and weather fluctuations. Integrating a variety of crops, along with animals, beneficial insects, and native plants, creates a balanced ecosystem that supports itself. Crop rotation and intercropping (growing complementary plants together) can also improve yields and reduce pest problems.

Finally, integrating animals into the farm or garden ecosystem can provide multiple benefits. Chickens, for example, can offer natural pest control, manure for compost, and eggs. Bees can improve pollination, enhancing fruit and vegetable yields. The key is to create a symbiotic relationship between plants, animals, and humans, where each component supports and benefits the others.

In conclusion, sustainable agriculture and permaculture are not just farming practices but a philosophy of coexistence with nature. By adopting these practices, individuals and communities can build resilient, productive systems that meet their needs while enhancing the natural environment. This approach to food production and land management is crucial for navigating the challenges of a grid-down scenario, ensuring long-term sustainability and self-sufficiency.

Waste Management and Recycling

Managing waste and embracing recycling practices are crucial for long-term sustainability and self-sufficiency, especially without municipal waste services. Individuals and communities must adopt strategies that minimize waste production and repurpose materials whenever possible. This approach ensures health, safety, and resource conservation in a grid-down environment.

Effective waste management begins with segregation. It is essential to differentiate between organic waste, recyclables, and non-recyclable waste. Organic waste like food scraps and yard waste can be composted to create valuable fertilizer for gardens, thus closing the nutrient loop. At the same time, recyclables such as certain plastics, metals, glass, and paper should be cleaned and stored separately for repurposing.

Composting is a cornerstone of waste management in a grid-down scenario, allowing the conversion of organic waste into rich soil to enhance garden productivity. A simple compost pile or bin can be established with minimal effort, and maintaining a balance between nitrogen-rich materials and carbon-rich materials, along with regular turning, accelerates decomposition.

Recycling and repurposing materials extend their lifecycle and reduce the need for new resources. While melting down metals, glass, and certain plastics requires specific skills and equipment, repurposing or "upcycling" items is more accessible. For example, empty containers can be used for storage, and old clothing can be transformed into quilts or rags.

Reducing waste at the source is an effective strategy in a grid-down scenario. This involves mindful consumption and prioritizing durable, reusable products. Repairing broken items, choosing products with minimal packaging, and adopting a minimalist lifestyle can significantly reduce waste output.

Proper disposal of non-recyclable waste and hazardous materials is critical to prevent pollution and disease. Small landfills or incineration may be necessary in the absence of municipal services. Still, these methods must be cautiously approached to avoid contaminating water sources or creating health hazards. Regular cleaning and disinfection of waste storage areas help prevent pest infestations and maintain sanitary conditions.

Community initiatives enhance waste management and recycling efforts. Organizing community clean-up days, establishing shared composting facilities, and pooling resources for recycling projects can improve efficiency and foster a sense of solidarity. Education and awareness campaigns are also vital in promoting sustainable waste practices within the community.

In conclusion, effective waste management and recycling are critical components of living sustainably in a grid-down scenario. By adopting practices that reduce, reuse, and recycle waste, individuals and communities can mitigate environmental impact, conserve resources, and maintain health and safety standards. As we transition to discussing building and maintaining infrastructure, the principles of sustainability and resourcefulness continue to guide our approach to creating resilient, self-sufficient communities in the face of adversity.

Building and Maintaining Infrastructure

The importance of building and maintaining robust infrastructure cannot be overstated in the journey toward long-term sustainability and self-sufficiency, especially in scenarios where the grid has gone down. This infrastructure is not just about the physical constructs but also the systems and processes supporting a resilient and self-sufficient community.

The first step in building adequate infrastructure is to assess the community's needs. This involves identifying critical systems such as water supply, food production, shelter, and energy. Each system requires a different approach, but the overarching goal is to ensure they are resilient, sustainable, and independent from external inputs.

Water supply, for instance, can be secured through the collection and purification of rainwater, the digging of wells, or the development of spring-fed water systems. Each method has its advantages and challenges, but the key is to establish a reliable system that can be maintained with the resources and skills available within the community.

Food production is another critical area. Developing sustainable agriculture practices, such as permaculture, can help ensure a steady food supply. This involves not just cultivating crops but also integrating livestock, recycling nutrients, and conserving water. Community gardens and cooperative farming can also play a significant role in enhancing food security.

Shelter is about more than just building homes. It's about creating energy-efficient, durable structures made from locally sourced or recycled materials. Techniques such as earthbag construction, straw bale building, and the use of cob can be effective in many environments. Moreover, the design of living spaces should consider the efficient use of energy, with passive solar design and incorporating renewable energy systems being key considerations.

Energy infrastructure is one of the most challenging to address post-grid. However, developing microgrids, solar panels, wind turbines, and small-scale hydroelectric systems can provide sustainable energy solutions. The key is to design these systems for scalability and flexibility, allowing them to grow or change as the community's needs evolve.

Infrastructure maintenance is as critical as its construction. This involves regular checks and repairs, as well as a proactive approach to managing resources. It also requires the development of skills within the community, ensuring that there are individuals capable of repairing, improving, and innovating as needs and technologies change.

In conclusion, building and maintaining infrastructure in a grid-down scenario is about more than just survival. It's about creating a foundation for a sustainable, self-sufficient community that can thrive in the long term. This requires careful planning, a commitment to sustainability, and a willingness to learn and adapt. By focusing on the essentials of water, food, shelter, and energy and ensuring that these systems are well-maintained, communities can build a resilient infrastructure supporting a high quality of life even in challenging circumstances.

Education and Skill Sharing for Self-Sufficiency

Communities striving for long-term survival and prosperity focus on transferring knowledge and skills among all members. This approach emphasizes practical education and skill sharing tailored to self-sufficiency, covering agriculture, carpentry, mechanical repair, and medical care. The aim is to equip every community member with diverse skills to enhance flexibility and resilience.

Skill sharing is facilitated through workshops, mentorship

programs, and hands-on projects. Workshops target specific skills like water purification or solar panel construction. Mentorship programs allow for personalized learning under the guidance of experienced individuals. Hands-on projects provide practical learning experiences and contribute directly to community infrastructure.

However, implementing these educational initiatives can be challenging due to needing more resources, varying participant skill levels, and the need to juggle educational activities with daily survival tasks. Communities can address these challenges by being resourceful, creating teaching materials, tailoring classes to accommodate different skill levels, and integrating learning with essential daily activities.

Children and youth are vital to the community's future sustainability. By involving them in practical, hands-on learning, they become equipped to contribute meaningfully to the community while developing a strong sense of responsibility and belonging. This early engagement helps integrate education seamlessly into their everyday lives.

The dynamic nature of a grid-down scenario necessitates continuous learning and adaptability. Communities should cultivate an environment that encourages questioning, experimenting, and innovating to adapt to changing circumstances. This continuous improvement culture helps the community survive, thrive, and evolve.

In conclusion, effective education and skill sharing are the foundations of a resilient, self-sufficient community in a grid-down scenario. By focusing on practical skills, structuring educational programs effectively, and promoting an adaptive learning environment, communities can ensure their resilience and continued prosperity. This strategic focus on education empowers individuals to meet their needs while collectively strengthening the community.

Chapter Summary

- Sustainable agriculture, including permaculture, focuses on long-term ecological health and food security using crop rotation and agroforestry methods.
- Permaculture uses natural ecosystem principles to create sustainable habitats, emphasizing diversity and energy efficiency.
- Soil health is enhanced by composting, mulching, and no-till farming to improve fertility.
- Efficient water management techniques include rainwater harvesting and drip irrigation to ensure adequate supply without waste.
- Renewable energy sources like solar, wind, and micro-hydro are crucial for self-sufficiency and energy conservation, especially in off-grid scenarios.
- Water conservation is vital, involving efficient use and purification techniques to secure a dependable water supply.
- Waste management in off-grid situations involves segregation, composting, and repurposing to reduce environmental impact.
- Community resilience relies on building infrastructure and promoting education and skill sharing for adaptation and self-sufficiency.

12

ADAPTING TO A NEW WORLD

Embracing Change and Overcoming Challenges

In a grid-down scenario, adapting to the new world requires resilience and a profound willingness to embrace change and overcome the challenges that arise. This adaptation journey is not merely about survival but redefining our relationship with the environment, our communities, and the very essence of day-to-day living.

The initial shock of finding ourselves in a situation where the conveniences and supports of modern infrastructure are stripped away can be overwhelming. However, it's crucial to recognize that within this crisis lies an opportunity for profound personal growth and community strengthening. Embracing change in this context means acknowledging the loss of what was once familiar while being open to the possibilities of forging a new path.

One of the first steps in this journey is to assess our immediate environment and resources with fresh eyes. What was once taken for granted may now be a critical asset. For example, natural water sources, previously overlooked in favor of tap water, have become invaluable. Similarly, understanding local flora and fauna can transform from a hobbyist's interest to a vital skill in foraging for food and medicinal plants.

Overcoming challenges in a grid-down world also demands a shift in mindset from individualism to collective survival. The strength of a community can often be the deciding factor between merely surviving and truly thriving. Sharing skills, resources, and responsibilities becomes not just beneficial but essential. Those with knowledge in first aid, gardening, mechanical repair, or construction find their skills in high demand, and teaching others these skills helps to build a more resilient community.

Innovation plays a key role in adapting to this new world. Without access to conventional tools and materials, improvisation becomes a critical skill. The ability to repurpose materials or devise new methods for old tasks can significantly improve quality of life. For instance, creating a gravity-fed water filtration system from salvaged materials or developing a community barter system to distribute goods and services evenly.

Mental and emotional resilience are equally important. The stress and uncertainty of a grid-down scenario can take a toll on even the most robust individuals. Cultivating a mindset that focuses on solutions rather than problems, finds joy in small victories, and maintains hope and positivity in the face of adversity is crucial. When shared within a community, this mental resilience creates an atmosphere of mutual support and encouragement that can weather the most challenging times.

As we navigate the challenges of adapting to a grid-down world, we must remember that our greatest resource is our collective human spirit. By embracing change, fostering community, innovating solutions, and maintaining resilience, we can survive and build a foundation for a new way of living that could redefine our future for the better.

Innovative Problem Solving

Thinking outside the box is a critical survival skill. The world as we know it transforms, and with it, our daily challenges. This section delves into the essence of innovative problem-solving, a skill that not only aids in adapting to new circumstances but also in thriving amidst them.

Innovative problem-solving in a post-grid world involves creativity, practicality, and resourcefulness. It's about looking at what you have through a different lens and imagining how it can serve a purpose it was never intended for. This mindset shift is vital for overcoming challenges when traditional systems and supports are no longer available.

One of the first steps in cultivating this skill is to assess your environment and resources with fresh eyes. Everything around you has potential. For instance, consider the natural resources at your disposal. A fallen tree isn't just an obstacle; it's a source of firewood, a potential shelter structure, or even raw material for tools and utensils. Similarly, an abandoned vehicle can be a source of metal, glass, and other materials that can be repurposed in countless ways.

Another aspect of innovative problem-solving is the ability to improvise. This means using available materials and knowledge to create solutions on the fly. For example, if you're facing a water purification challenge, understanding the basics of filtration and disinfection can help you devise a makeshift purification system using charcoal, sand, and sunlight. This improvisational skill hinges on a solid foundation of knowledge across various domains, highlighting the importance of a well-rounded skill set in survival situations.

Collaboration plays a significant role in innovative problem-solving. Pooling knowledge and skills with others broadens the range of potential solutions and fosters a sense of community and mutual support, which is invaluable in challenging times. Through collaboration, individuals can combine their strengths and compensate for each other's weaknesses, leading to more effective and sustainable solutions.

Finally, embracing a mindset of continuous learning and adaptation is essential. The post-grid world is dynamic, with new challenges and opportunities emerging regularly. Staying curious, open to new ideas, and willing to experiment can lead to discoveries that significantly improve your quality of life in a grid-down scenario.

In conclusion, innovative problem-solving is a multifaceted skill encompassing creativity, improvisation, collaboration, and continuous learning. By developing this skill, individuals can better navigate the uncertainties of a post-grid world, turning challenges into opportunities for growth and innovation. As we move forward, the role of technology in this new landscape will be a critical factor to consider, offering both challenges and solutions in our journey of adaptation.

The Role of Technology in a Post-Grid World

The collapse of the power grid and the subsequent failure of conventional communication, transportation, and utility infrastructures compel us to reassess our relationship with technology. This section delves into how we can adapt and leverage technology in a post-grid world, ensuring our survival and facilitating the rebuilding of society.

Initially, it's crucial to understand that not all technology is rendered obsolete in the absence of a power grid. Solar panels, wind turbines, and other renewable energy sources become invaluable assets. These technologies can power essential devices, from communication tools to medical equipment, providing a lifeline in the aftermath of a grid collapse. Adaptation involves the use of these technologies and the knowledge to maintain and repair them. Community workshops and shared knowledge bases become critical for preserving these skills.

Communication technology, in particular, is undergoing a significant shift. Without the internet and cellular networks, alternative forms of communication, such as shortwave radios and satellite phones, gain prominence. These tools enable communities to stay informed, share resources, and coordinate recovery efforts. The knowledge of operating these devices, often overlooked in a grid-dependent world, becomes a vital skill set.

Moreover, the role of technology in purifying and managing water supplies cannot be overstated. Simple yet effective technological solutions like solar water disinfection (SODIS) methods and manually operated water purifiers ensure access to clean water, a critical component of survival.

The innovation lies in adapting these technologies to local conditions and materials available, underscoring the importance of ingenuity in a post-grid world.

Agriculture and food production also see a technological transformation. Techniques such as permaculture, aquaponics, and vertical farming, powered by renewable energy sources, offer sustainable ways to produce food. These methods not only ensure food security but also contribute to the regeneration of the ecosystem. The knowledge of these technologies and traditional farming practices form the backbone of a resilient food system.

In healthcare, technology plays a pivotal role in maintaining community health. Portable diagnostic tools powered by renewable energy enable the monitoring of health conditions, while telemedicine practices, adapted to work over radio or other basic communication networks, allow for the sharing of medical knowledge and advice. Creating and distributing essential medicines and treatments, relying on modern and traditional methods, has become a community-driven effort.

Adapting to a new world where technology must be reimagined and repurposed is challenging. It requires a shift in mindset from consumption to conservation, from dependence to self-sufficiency. The resilience of technology in a post-grid world lies not in its complexity but in its adaptability and the community's ability to innovate and preserve knowledge. This transition ensures survival and lays the foundation for a future where technology, powered by renewable energy and driven by community needs, plays a central role in rebuilding and enhancing society.

Preserving Knowledge and Culture

In a grid-down scenario, where modern technology and conveniences are inaccessible, preserving knowledge and culture is crucial. The loss of digital infrastructure would significantly impact access to knowledge, making it essential to prioritize the preservation of physical books, documents, and other educational materials. Establishing community libraries or archives can serve as central points for knowledge storage and sharing, focusing on a wide range of subjects such as agriculture, medicine, engineering, and history to ensure a well-rounded knowledge base is available.

Workshops and apprenticeships should also encourage and document the practice of traditional skills and crafts. These can facilitate the transfer of practical knowledge from basic carpentry and metalwork to more complex skills like weaving and pottery. Such skills preserve cultural heritage and provide communities with the means to rebuild and sustain themselves without relying on modern industrial processes.

Culture, encompassing language, art, traditions, and social practices, is the soul of a community, and its preservation becomes a communal effort in a world without the grid. Oral traditions, such as storytelling, songs, and folklore, play a vital role in passing down history, moral lessons, and cultural identity from one generation to the next. Additionally, creating and maintaining physical records of cultural practices, including written records, drawings, paintings, and other forms of art that depict cultural events, traditional clothing, and architecture, is essential. Encouraging the continued practice of cultural festivals and ceremonies can help maintain a sense of community and continuity.

Education will be the cornerstone of preserving knowledge and culture, requiring communities to adopt more flexible and adaptive forms of education. This might include community-led classes, mentorship programs, and practical, hands-on learning experiences directly relevant to life in a post-grid world. In this context, everyone has something to teach and something to learn, making sharing knowledge across generations a communal responsibility, with elders passing down wisdom and younger members contributing fresh ideas and innovations.

Preserving knowledge and culture in a post-grid scenario is not merely about survival; it's about ensuring that the essence of who we are as a species is not lost. By proactively safeguarding our collective knowledge and cultural heritage, communities can lay the foundation for a resilient, sustainable future where the human spirit thrives even in the face of adversity. This endeavor will aid in the practical aspects of rebuilding society and ensure that the richness of human culture continues to inspire and guide future generations.

Environmental Stewardship

The immediate aftermath of a grid-down scenario may have us focused on survival, but as we adapt to a new world, environmental stewardship becomes not just a moral imperative but a practical necessity. This section delves into the principles and practices of sustaining and nurturing the environment in times of crisis, ensuring that our survival strategies are aligned with the health of our planet.

The cornerstone of environmental stewardship in a grid-down world is the sustainable management of resources.

Water, soil, and air—the essential elements of life—must be protected and preserved with utmost care. Water conservation becomes critical; methods such as rainwater harvesting, dew collection, and greywater recycling for agricultural purposes should be implemented. Soil health can be maintained through composting, crop rotation, and avoiding chemical fertilizers, which may be scarce or unavailable. Air quality, though less immediately controllable, benefits from reducing industrial pollutants and carefully managing biomass burning.

Biodiversity is another critical aspect of environmental stewardship. A grid-down scenario likely disrupts ecosystems, making protecting native species and habitats more important than ever. Establishing and maintaining seed banks ensures the preservation of plant diversity, which is crucial for food security and ecological balance. Similarly, protecting wildlife by avoiding overhunting and preserving natural habitats helps maintain the balance of ecosystems upon which human survival ultimately depends.

Renewable energy sources become invaluable in a world without the grid. Solar, wind, and hydropower can provide sustainable energy solutions, reducing our dependence on fossil fuels and minimizing our ecological footprint. Implementing renewable energy systems not only addresses immediate energy needs but also sets a foundation for the long-term sustainability of communities.

Waste management is transformed in a grid-down scenario. Communities must adopt zero-waste practices without the infrastructure for waste collection and disposal. This involves the reduction of waste production, the reuse of materials, and the recycling or composting of organic and inorganic waste. Such practices reduce environmental impact and turn waste into valuable resources.

Finally, environmental education plays a pivotal role in sustaining these efforts. Knowledge about sustainable living practices passed down through generations, becomes a cornerstone of community resilience. Workshops, hands-on demonstrations, and community projects can foster a culture of environmental stewardship, ensuring that sustainability principles are ingrained in the fabric of society.

In adapting to a new world, our survival is intricately linked to the health of our environment. By embracing the principles of environmental stewardship, we ensure our immediate survival and lay the groundwork for a sustainable future. This holistic approach to living in harmony with our planet is not just a strategy for survival; it is a testament to our resilience and commitment to preserving the world for future generations.

Chapter Summary

- Adapting to a grid-down world involves embracing change, assessing resources anew, and fostering community strength.
- Overcoming challenges requires shifting from individualism to collective survival, sharing skills, and innovating solutions.
- Mental and emotional resilience, focusing on solutions, and maintaining positivity are crucial in a grid-down scenario.

- Innovative problem-solving is key, involving creativity, practicality, resourcefulness, and collaboration.
- Technology plays a transformative role, with renewable energy sources and alternative communication methods becoming vital.
- Preserving knowledge and culture through community libraries, traditional skills workshops, and education ensures continuity for future generations.
- Environmental stewardship is essential, focusing on sustainable resource management, biodiversity protection, and renewable energy.
- Planning for future generations emphasizes education in practical skills, healthcare knowledge, and building resilient communities.

THE PATH FORWARD

Reflecting on Lessons Learned

As we navigate the closing pages of our journey through the uncharted territories of a world without the grid, it becomes imperative to pause and reflect on the myriad lessons that have emerged from the shadows of this new reality. The transition from a life of convenience and instant connectivity to one of self-reliance and resilience has not been without its trials. Yet, within these challenges lie invaluable insights that prepare us for a future of uncertainties and enrich our understanding of what it means to persevere truly.

One of the most profound lessons learned is the undeniable importance of preparedness. The initial shock accompanying the loss of the grid serves as a stark reminder of the fragility of our modern infrastructure. It underscores the necessity of having a well-thought-out plan that encompasses not just the immediate needs of survival, such as water, food, and shelter, but also long-term sustainability through skills like gardening, foraging, and renewable energy sources. The journey from dependence to independence is paved with the knowledge and skills acquired before necessity becomes the master.

Adaptability, too, has proven to be a cornerstone of surviving and thriving in a grid-down scenario. The ability to adjust to new challenges, innovate with the resources at hand, and abandon preconceived notions of living is crucial. This adaptability extends beyond the physical to the psychological, where mental resilience becomes just as important as any survival skill. The capacity to maintain hope, find joy in simplicity, and persevere through adversity ultimately defines the human spirit in the face of collapse.

Equally important is the lesson of self-sufficiency, yet it is within this lesson that a paradox emerges. While the initial focus may be on individual or familial survival, it becomes increasingly clear that true self-sufficiency is intertwined with the community's well-being. Individuals' skills, resources, and strengths can be pooled to create a collective resilience far greater than the sum of its parts. Through this synergy, the foundation for a sustainable future is laid, one where mutual aid and cooperation become the pillars of a new society.

Reflecting on these lessons, it is evident that the path forward is not one of isolation but of connection. The challenges faced in a world without the grid have illuminated the intrinsic value of community, the strength derived from shared hardship, and the profound impact of collective action. As we stand at the threshold of this new world, this spirit of collaboration and unity will light the way.

The Importance of Community and Collaboration

In a grid-down scenario, the significance of individual preparedness cannot be overstated. However, as we have navigated through the complexities and challenges of surviving without our usual infrastructures, one truth has emerged with undeniable clarity: the importance of community and collaboration. This realization is a byproduct of hardship and a fundamental principle that can guide us toward a more resilient future.

The concept of self-sufficiency is often romanticized, conjuring images of a lone survivor braving the elements with nothing but their wits and willpower. While individual skills and preparedness are crucial, they are but one piece of the survival puzzle. Humans are inherently social beings; our strength lies in our ability to work together, share knowledge, and support each other through adversity.

Community and collaboration offer several advantages in a grid-down situation. Firstly, they allow for the pooling of resources. When individuals come together, they can combine their supplies, leading to a more efficient use of resources and reducing the risk of shortages. This pooling is not limited to physical resources but extends to skills and knowledge. In a community, individuals can specialize in certain tasks, leading to more efficient work and better outcomes.

Secondly, collaboration enhances security. In times of crisis, threats can come from environmental challenges, scarcity of resources, or even other people. A community can organize collective defense measures, create warning systems, and establish protocols that a single individual or a small family unit would struggle to implement independently.

Moreover, the psychological benefits of being part of a community cannot be overlooked. The stress and mental strain of surviving a grid-down scenario can be overwhelming. A support network provides emotional comfort and can be critical to maintaining mental health and resilience.

However, building and maintaining a community in such challenging times has its challenges. It requires trust, communication, and a willingness to put the group's needs alongside, if not before, individual desires. Leadership and decision-making become more complex but also more critical. Establishing clear roles, responsibilities, and rules can help manage these challenges.

As we look toward the future, the lessons learned about the value of community and collaboration should be remembered. These principles should be integrated into our preparedness plans from the outset. Building strong, supportive networks now, based on mutual aid and respect, can significantly enhance our collective resilience in the face of future crises.

In conclusion, while individual preparedness is essential, the power of community and collaboration stands out as a beacon of hope and strength. By fostering these relationships and networks, we increase our chances of survival in a grid-down scenario and pave the way for a more connected and resilient society. As we move forward, let us carry with us the understanding that together, we are stronger, and it is through collaboration that we can build a path to a more secure and sustainable future.

Continued Learning and Adaptation

Understanding the pivotal role that community and collaboration play in navigating the challenges of a grid-down scenario, it becomes evident that our journey does not end with merely establishing connections and fostering teamwork. The essence of truly thriving in such situations lies in our ability to engage in continued learning and adaptation. This process is not just about acquiring new skills or knowledge but about evolving our mindset to be more resilient, resourceful, and responsive to the changing dynamics of our environment.

Continued learning encompasses a broad spectrum of activities in the context of grid-down survival. It involves staying informed about the latest survival techniques, understanding the advancements in sustainable living practices, and keeping abreast of the developments in renewable energy sources. This knowledge enhances our ability to sustain ourselves without the grid and empowers us to make informed decisions that can significantly improve our quality of life in such circumstances.

Moreover, adaptation is a critical component of this learning process. It's about taking the knowledge we've acquired and applying it to our unique situations. This might mean modifying a solar panel setup to work more efficiently in your specific geographic location or adapting a water purification technique to better suit your resources. The key is to be flexible and open to experimenting with different solutions to find what works best for your community and environment.

This journey of continued learning and adaptation also

involves significant trial and error. Only some ideas will be successful, and only some plans will unfold as expected. However, each attempt, whether successful or not, is a valuable learning experience that contributes to our collective knowledge pool. Sharing these experiences with the community helps refine our strategies and strengthens the bonds within the community, as everyone benefits from the shared wisdom.

Embracing a mindset of continued learning and adaptation also means being proactive in seeking new information and growth opportunities. This could involve participating in workshops, joining online forums, or organizing community learning events. The goal is to create a culture of continuous improvement, where everyone is encouraged to share their knowledge and experiences for the betterment of the community.

In conclusion, as we navigate the path forward in a grid-down world, continued learning and adaptation principles stand as beacons of hope. They remind us that our ability to thrive in such scenarios is not fixed but is an ever-evolving process that requires dedication, curiosity, and a willingness to embrace change. By committing to this journey of continuous growth, we not only enhance our chances of survival but also pave the way for a future where we can live in harmony with our environment, resilient and self-sufficient, regardless of the challenges we may face.

Staying Prepared for Future Uncertainties

Understanding the importance of staying prepared for future uncertainties is paramount in preparing for grid-down scenarios. This mindset does not merely involve accumulating supplies or mastering survival skills; it encompasses a holistic approach to readiness that evolves with time and the changing nature of threats.

First and foremost, it is crucial to maintain a vigilant watch on the world's socio-economic and environmental trends. The nature of threats is ever-changing, and what may seem like a distant concern today could become a pressing reality tomorrow. Regularly updating your knowledge base through credible news sources, scientific reports, and community insights can provide early warnings of emerging risks.

Equally important is the practice of scenario planning. This involves considering potential future events, no matter how unlikely they may seem, and considering how they could impact your preparedness strategy. By doing so, you can identify gaps in your current plan and adjust accordingly. This might mean diversifying your food storage, learning new skills, or strengthening your community ties.

Another critical aspect of staying prepared is the continuous review and rotation of your supplies. Over time, stored food can expire, equipment can become obsolete, and personal needs can change. Regularly auditing your supplies ensures that everything you have stored remains useful and accessible when needed. This also allows you to test your gear and practice your skills, ensuring that both remain sharp and effective.

In addition to physical preparations, mental resilience plays a critical role in navigating future uncertainties. Cultivating a mindset that embraces adaptability, problem-solving, and calmness under pressure can significantly improve one's ability to respond effectively to unexpected challenges. This can be achieved through mental exercises, stress management techniques, and learning from past experiences.

Lastly, building and nurturing a community of like-minded individuals offers a support network that can be invaluable during times of crisis. Sharing knowledge, resources, and skills not only strengthens individual preparedness but also enhances the collective resilience of the community. This sense of solidarity and mutual aid is a powerful asset in facing future uncertainties.

In conclusion, staying prepared for future uncertainties requires a dynamic and proactive approach. It involves not just a well-stocked pantry or a set of survival skills but a comprehensive strategy that includes staying informed, scenario planning, continuous learning, mental resilience, and community building. By embracing these principles, you can confidently navigate the path forward, ready to face whatever challenges the future may hold.

Inspiring Others to Prepare

In the journey toward self-reliance and preparedness, one of the most profound steps we can take is to inspire others to embark on this path with us. A community's resilience during times of crisis is not solely dependent on the preparedness of individuals but on the collective preparedness of its members. As we have navigated through the intricacies of preparing for a grid-down scenario, extending this knowledge beyond our immediate circle is imperative, fostering a culture of preparedness that can withstand the tests of unforeseen challenges.

Inspiring others to prepare is not about instilling fear but sharing knowledge and experiences that empower and motivate. It begins within our families, extends to friends, and eventually permeates the wider community. Sharing stories from those who have experienced natural disasters or other emergencies can be a powerful catalyst for change. These narratives and practical advice and demonstrations can transform apathy into action.

Education plays a crucial role in this endeavor. Organizing workshops or informational sessions on basic survival skills, such as water purification, food storage, and first aid, can demystify the process of preparedness for many. These sessions can be held in community centers, schools, or online platforms, making them accessible to a broader audience. The key is to present this information in a manner that is engaging, practical, and devoid of sensationalism.

Moreover, leveraging social media and other digital platforms can amplify our reach, allowing us to share resources, tips, and personal experiences with a global audience. Blogs, podcasts, and video tutorials are excellent mediums for disseminating information on preparedness strategies, gear reviews, and survival skills. By creating informative, relatable, and actionable content, we can inspire a wave of preparedness that transcends geographical boundaries.

However, it is crucial to approach these efforts with empathy and understanding. The journey toward preparedness is personal and unique for each individual. Some may be motivated by personal experiences with adversity, while others may be driven by a desire to protect their loved ones. Recognizing these motivations and addressing the barriers that prevent people from taking action is essential. This may involve debunking myths about preparedness, offering cost-effective solutions, or simply providing a supportive community for individuals to share their concerns and achievements.

Inspiring others to prepare cannot be overstated as we look to the future. In a world fraught with uncertainties, our communities' collective preparedness is our strongest asset. By sharing our knowledge, experiences, and resources, we not only enhance our own resilience but also contribute to a more prepared and resilient society. This is the path forward—a journey not walked alone but together, with a shared vision of preparedness that safeguards our collective future.

Concluding Thoughts

As we draw this guide to a close, we must reflect on our journey together. From understanding the basics of survival in a grid-down scenario to mastering the skills necessary for long-term resilience, we've covered a broad spectrum of knowledge and strategies. The importance of preparation cannot be overstated, and by now, you should feel more equipped to face the uncertainties of a world without the conveniences of modern infrastructure.

However, the path forward requires more than just individual readiness. It demands a collective effort and a shared commitment to survive and thrive in the face of adversity. A community's resilience can significantly amplify the efforts of the individual, creating a network of support that can withstand the toughest challenges. Therefore, as you continue to hone your skills and expand your knowledge, consider how you can contribute to your community's resilience. Whether through sharing resources, offering training, or simply fostering a spirit of cooperation, your efforts can inspire others to prepare and create a stronger, more resilient society.

Remember, the goal of this guide is not to instill fear but to empower you with the knowledge and skills to confidently navigate a grid-down scenario. The journey doesn't end here; it evolves with each new skill learned, every piece of knowledge shared, and through every challenge faced with courage and determination. As you move forward, remember that preparation is an ongoing, lifelong commitment to ensuring the safety and well-being of yourself and those around you.

In conclusion, the path forward is continuous learning, adaptation, and community engagement. It's about building a survival kit and a survival mindset that embraces the challenges of a grid-down world as opportunities to grow, learn, and strengthen the bonds that tie us together. As you close this guide, remember that the most powerful tool at your disposal is not the gear you've acquired or the supplies you've stockpiled but the knowledge you've gained and the community you've built. Together, there is no challenge too great to overcome.

Your Feedback Matters

Thank you for joining me on this journey. If the book inspired you, please share your thoughts by leaving a review on Amazon using the QR code below. Your feedback is invaluable and helps guide others. I'm grateful for your time and hope the insights you've gained enrich your quest for knowledge.

ABOUT THE AUTHOR

Anthony Bennett is a passionate advocate for sustainable living and self-sufficiency. With a background in environmental science and years of hands-on experience in homesteading, his practical advice and innovative solutions for living off the land have inspired many to pursue a more sustainable and independent lifestyle. Through his "Self-Sufficient Living" series, including "How to Build the Perfect Backyard Homestead" and "How to Survive When the Grid Goes Down," Anthony shares his wealth of knowledge on creating resilient and productive homesteads. When he's not writing, Anthony tends to his homestead.

www.ingramcontent.com/pod-product-compliance
Lightning Source LLC
Chambersburg PA
CBHW050223100526
44585CB00017BA/1778